DEFOE'S AMERICA

The Americas appear as an evocative setting in more than half of Daniel Defoe's novels and often offer a new beginning for his characters. In the first full-length study of Defoe and colonialism, Dennis Todd explores why the New World loomed so large in Defoe's imagination. By focusing on the historical contexts that informed Defoe's depiction of American Indians, African slaves, and white indentured servants, Dennis Todd investigates the colonial assumptions that shaped his novels and, at the same time, uncovers how Defoe used details of the American experience in complex, often figurative ways to explore the psychological bases of the profound conversions and transformations that his heroes and heroines undergo. And by examining what Defoe knew and did not know about America, what he falsely believed and what he knowingly falsified, *Defoe's America* probes the doubts, hesitancies, and contradictions he had about the colonial project he so fervently promoted.

DENNIS TODD is Associate Professor of English at Georgetown University. A specialist in eighteenth-century American and British literature and culture, he has written on Daniel Defoe, Alexander Pope, Jonathan Swift, William Hogarth, John Arbuthnot, and early science. He authored *Imagining Monsters: Miscreations of the Self in Eighteenth-Century Literature* (1995) and edited, with Cynthia Wall, *Eighteenth-Century Genre and Culture: Serious Reflections on Occasional Forms. Essays in Honor of J. Paul Hunter* (2001).

DEFOE'S AMERICA

DENNIS TODD

CAMBRIDGE
UNIVERSITY PRESS

CAMBRIDGE UNIVERSITY PRESS
Cambridge, New York, Melbourne, Madrid, Cape Town, Singapore,
São Paulo, Delhi, Dubai, Tokyo

Cambridge University Press
The Edinburgh Building, Cambridge CB2 8RU, UK

Published in the United States of America by Cambridge University Press, New York

www.cambridge.org
Information on this title: www.cambridge.org/9780521195812

First published 2010

Printed in the United Kingdom at the University Press, Cambridge

A catalogue record for this publication is available from the British Library

Library of Congress Cataloguing in Publication data
Todd, Dennis, 1944–
Defoe's America / Dennis Todd.
p.   cm.
Includes index.
ISBN 978-0-521-19581-2
1. Defoe, Daniel, 1661?–1731–Criticism and interpretation.   2. National characteristics,
American, in literature.   3. Imperialism in literature.   I. Title.
PR3407.T56 2010
823'.5–dc22   2010022106

ISBN 978-0-521-19581-2 (Hardback)

To Barbara and Sasha

Contents

Preface

Defoe was enthusiastic about the British colonization of the New World. He wrote extensively about colonization in his economic and journalistic works, colonial concerns infiltrated his religious conduct books, and England's colonial enterprise became the explicit subject of one of the last pieces he had his hand in, the massive *Atlas maritimus et commercialis.* Many of his novels have some sort of colonialist bent, and one of them, *A New Voyage round the World,* at times seems to have little more purpose than to promote one of Defoe's favorite projects, creating an English colony on the tip of South America. *Robinson Crusoe, Colonel Jack,* and *Moll Flanders,* too, have colonial American settings, all three taking place in what regional scholars call "the extended Caribbean" – the coastal region stretching from the eastern tip of Brazil north to the Chesapeake. This locale is the "America" of my title, and these three novels are my subject.

It is significant that these three novels take place here. The Caribbean of *Robinson Crusoe* and the Chesapeake of *Colonel Jack* and *Moll Flanders* were plantation monocultures, societies organized around the cultivation of sugar and tobacco. As a consequence, they were utterly dependent on bound labor. With historical hindsight, we understand how important African slaves were for the growth and success of these British possessions, something Defoe knew, too. "Our Collonies in America," he acknowledged, "could no more be maintained ... without the Supply of *Negro* Slaves than *London* could subsist without the River of *Thames.*" But, to his mind, more significant and certainly of greater interest was a second class of bound laborers, white indentured servants. Moll and Jack are indentured servants, and, in his own way, Crusoe is too.

It is the argument of this book that indentured servitude is central to these three novels and that Defoe uses indentured servitude, both as an institution and as a complex metaphor, to explore the spiritual, moral, and economic transformations that Crusoe, Jack, and Moll go through as they move from being slaves of powerful psychological and social forces to masters of themselves and their environments.

There is another significant aspect to the American setting. Readers are often vexed by the fact that Defoe seems to have many purposes in these novels, so many that it is sometimes difficult to know what exactly these novels are: vindications of colonialist ideology, fictional autobiographies of spiritual conversions, studies of the psychology of moral growth and degeneration, or celebrations of material success through individual initiative. To his contemporaries, the American setting would make Defoe's purposes appear less variegated and random than they seem to us. In the twenty years preceding the publication of these three novels, events in the American colonies had pushed several issues to the fore. Imperial realities had made the civilizing and Christianization of the American natives the linchpin of British colonialist policy, something that could be accomplished, it was thought, only by the conversion to civil behavior and Christian belief of the white colonists themselves; religious leaders in England had begun to agitate for the education and conversion of African slaves; changes in policies of criminal punishment – and especially the passage of the Transportation Act of 1718 – had given new urgency to the belief that America offered indentured servants and transported criminals extraordinary opportunities for personal transformation, moral renovation, and economic advancement. Given these contexts, colonial policy, spiritual conversion, moral reform, and economic advancement are more intimately related to one another than they otherwise might appear to be.

Chapter 1 recovers something of the colonial contexts of these three novels and makes the case for the importance of indentured servitude for Defoe. Defoe's thinking about indentured servitude is complex, even contradictory, and the uses to which he puts it in his novels suggest tensions and contradictions in his thinking about larger issues, particularly about the mastery and freedom Crusoe, Jack, and Moll pursue. Chapters 2 and 3 focus on *Robinson Crusoe* and *Colonel Jack* respectively. Both novels are about the conversions of their protagonists (a religious conversion in the case of Crusoe, a moral conversion in the case of Jack), conversions which are played off against the parallel conversions of savage Others (an Amerindian in *Robinson Crusoe*, African slaves in *Colonel Jack*). In these two chapters, I show how these transformations are modeled on indentured servitude, which, as a metaphor and a reality, charts both protagonists' freeing themselves from being slaves of their own irrational drives to become masters of themselves and their circumstances. Simultaneously, I delineate the assumptions Defoe held about human nature and psychology that could explain how such radical transformations were possible. Chapter 4 examines the function of indentured servitude in *Moll Flanders* in order to account for the disparities between the literary use to which Defoe puts servitude in his three novels and the reality of the institution as it was experienced by actual indentured servants. Defoe's misrepresentation of indentured servitude is symptomatic of larger tensions and contradictions in his thinking about colonial matters, tensions and contradictions I attempt to elucidate in the Conclusion by putting Defoe's novels alongside some other fictional and nonfiction writings of the period which were also set in Defoe's America.

The first draft of this book was written at the Villa le Balze in Fiesole, Italy, and I am indebted to Michael Collins for making it possible for me and my family to reside there and to the staff of the villa for creating such a pleasant and productive environment. As always, the often twisted path of my research was made straight by the able staff of Lauinger Library, and especially by Jill Hollingsworth and Jeffrey Popovich, both of whom sprang to my aid whenever I got myself into a jam. Georgetown University provided me with two research grants that allowed me to pursue my research, and the Virginia Graham Healey Fund and the Grace Jones Richardson Trust awarded me grants that allowed me to finish the manuscript.

   I could not have written this book without the friendship, support, and substantive contributions of my colleagues Lyndon Dominique, Leona Fisher, Jeanne Flood, John Pfordresher, Alvaro Ribeiro, Michael Ragussis, Jason Rosenblatt, Peter Steele, Penn Szittya, and Kathryn Temple. Until his untimely death, David Kadlec patiently listened to my interminable rethinking of almost every detail of this project. Lucy Maddox was unflagging in her encouragement from beginning to end.

   I am indebted to Linda Bree at Cambridge University Press for her patience and counsel and to two anonymous readers whose suggestions helped me make this, I hope, a better work.

   My fascination with Defoe goes back over forty years when, as an undergraduate at the University of California, I sat in a class on the eighteenth-century English novel taught by J. Paul Hunter. Anyone familiar with Paul's groundbreaking study of *Robinson Crusoe* will immediately see how thoroughly his thinking has influenced me. Literally, this book would have been impossible without his guidance and continuing friendship.

   My greatest debt is to my wife and daughter, and to them this book is dedicated – a skimpy return for their great gifts of love, patience, and faith.

Abbreviations

CJ   *The History and Remarkable Life of the Truly Honourable Col. Jacque,* edited by Maurice Hindle. Vol. VIII of *The Novels of Daniel Defoe,* edited by W. R. Owens and P. N. Furbank, London: Pickering & Chatto, 2009.

FA   *The Farther Adventures of Robinson Crusoe,* edited by W. R. Owens. Vol. II of *The Novels of Daniel Defoe,* edited by W. R. Owens and P. N. Furbank, London: Pickering & Chatto, 2008.

MF   *The Fortunes and Misfortunes of the Famous Moll Flanders,* edited by Liz Bellamy. Vol. VI of *The Novels of Daniel Defoe,* edited by W. R. Owens and P. N. Furbank, London: Pickering & Chatto, 2009.

NV   *A New Voyage round the World,* edited by John McVeagh. Vol. X of *The Novels of Daniel Defoe,* edited by W. R. Owens and P. N. Furbank, London: Pickering & Chatto, 2009.

RC   *The Life and Strange Surprizing Adventures of Robinson Crusoe,* edited by W. R. Owens. Vol. I of *The Novels of Daniel Defoe,* edited by W. R. Owens and P. N. Furbank, London: Pickering & Chatto, 2008.

SR   *Serious Reflections during the Life and Surprising Adventures of Robinson Crusoe,* edited by G. A. Starr. Vol. III of *The Novels of Daniel Defoe,* edited by W. R. Owens and P. N. Furbank, London: Pickering & Chatto, 2008.

CHAPTER I

Defoe's America

Near the end of Daniel Defoe's *Moll Flanders,* Moll returns to America with her new husband, Jemy. They disembark on the Virginia shore of the Potomac, as bad luck would have it, near her son's plantation where her former husband (who is also her brother) lives. Moll, desperate to keep her past and present lives from colliding, convinces Jemy that they should seek their fortunes elsewhere. They pitch on Carolina as a place to settle. "We began to make enquiry for Vessels going to *Carolina,* and in a very little while got information, that on the other side of the *Bay* ... in *Maryland* there was a Ship, which came from *Carolina,* loaden with Rice, and other Goods" (*MF,* p. 265).

They were, Moll says, "full a hundred Miles up *Potowmack River,* in a part which they call *Westmoreland* Country" (*MF,* p. 265). They sail five days down the Potomac and across the Chesapeake Bay to the Maryland Eastern Shore, a "full two hundred Mile" (*MF,* pp. 265–266). They land at "*Phillips's Point,*" where they had hoped to board the Carolina ship, but it has already departed.

We immediately went on Shore, but found no Conveniences just at that Place, either for our being on Shore, or preserving our Goods on Shore, but was directed by a very honest Quaker, who we found there to go to a Place, about sixty Miles East; that is to say, nearer the Mouth of the *Bay,* where he said he liv'd, and where we would be Accommodated, either to Plant, or to wait for any other Place to Plant in, that might be more Convenient. (*MF,* pp. 265–266)

So they abandon their plan to move on to Carolina and settle instead on the Eastern Shore of the Chesapeake.

This brief episode in *Moll Flanders* is fascinating for what it implies about Defoe's knowledge of America. And, at first glance, it implies that he does not know much, for the passage contains a number of geographical errors. First, Westmoreland County is not, as Moll says, "full a hundred Miles up *Potowmack River*"; at that time, its most distant border was only 50 miles from the mouth of the river. In fact, Moll overstates all the

I

distances. When she reaches the mouth of the Potomac, she says that the Bay is "near thirty Miles broad" (*MF,* p. 265). It is less than that, about 20 miles. A negligible mistake, to be sure, but not so her next one: from the farthest border of Westmoreland County to Phillips Point, it is only about 75 miles, not the "full two hundred Mile" Moll says it is. And when Moll says that she and Jemy bought land "sixty Miles … nearer the Mouth of the Bay" from Phillips Point, she puts their plantation well into the Atlantic. Most egregious is Moll's statement that this land is "about sixty Miles East" of Phillips Point "nearer the Mouth of the Bay." The mouth of the Chesapeake Bay is, of course, due south.

Such errors seem to confirm our suspicions about Defoe's writing habits. Defoe creates the illusion of a real world by piling up detail after quotidian detail, some drawn from lived experience, some snatched from books or picked up from conversations or lifted from maps or fabricated out of his imagination. But when he writes rapidly and offhandedly, as he often seems to, and the details of his fictional world fail to match the details of the factual world, the patchwork seams of his creations become embarrassingly obvious.

And what else could these errors be attributed to but a lack of knowledge or to carelessness? Although Defoe never visited the Chesapeake, he had available to him very accurate geographical information about the region. Augustine Herrman's 1673 map of Virginia and Maryland spelled out distances and directions with a good deal of precision, and Herrman's work was copied by or deeply influenced almost every map of the region published in England after his.[1] One gets the impression that Defoe wrote this passage with a map in hand – Westmoreland County and Phillips Point can be found on most eighteenth-century maps of the region – but that he wrote it quickly and inattentively, perhaps estimating distances by eye but certainly not measuring them off.

Still, I am not certain about how far or in what direction to press the case. Placing the mouth of the Chesapeake Bay east of Phillips Point rather than due south is so flagrantly wrong that it could easily be a meaningless slip of the pen. True, the fact that he gets all the distances wrong suggests that he was not intimately familiar with the region, but even here one should be careful not to infer a thoroughgoing ignorance. Defoe often *does* make mistakes, but making a mistake about something does not necessarily imply being unknowledgeable. For instance, a few pages earlier in *Moll Flanders,* he wrote that Jemy had "robb'd five Grasiers … going to *Burford* Fair in *Wiltshire* to buy Sheep" (*MF,* p. 243). Burford Fair is in Oxfordshire, not Wiltshire, but even though Defoe is wrong, it would be a mistake to conclude that he does not know the region – his *A Tour thro' the Whole Island of Great Britain* shows us otherwise.[2]

In fact, details about Moll's journey – particularly details about the three locations Defoe specifies, Westmoreland County, the Eastern Shore, and Phillips Point – suggest that he may have known more about the Chesapeake region than his errors might imply.

It is impossible to date precisely much of what happens in *Moll Flanders*, but we can be pretty certain about the dates of Moll's two periods of residence in the New World. Her first sojourn, when she came over as the wife of an established planter whom she later discovered to be her brother, occurred over a period of about eight years in the 1640s. Her second sojourn began in the early 1670s, when she landed near her son's plantation and then traveled to Phillips Point, and ended in the early 1680s, when she left her Eastern Shore plantation to return to England. The plantation of her first husband, where she goes in the 1640s, is on the York River. Her son's plantation, which she chances upon in the 1670s, is on the Potomac, in Westmoreland County (*MF*, pp. 85, 258).[3]

Westmoreland County is a particularly apposite place to find a new plantation in Virginia in the 1670s. The county was created in the 1650s, between Moll's first and second voyages. It immediately became the site of an intense speculative land rush, and between the 1650s and the 1670s almost all the land was snatched up by the colony's wealthiest, established planters – that is, by planters like Moll's former husband and their son. The heaviest immigration into the region came from York and Gloucester Counties, on either side of the York River, where Moll's husband had his original plantation. Although it is an improbable coincidence that Moll disembarks exactly where her son has his plantation, it is more than plausible that the captain chose to discharge Moll and Jemy there, for the Northern Neck, where Westmoreland County is located, was the area where most transported convicts were sold and where they settled.[4]

That Moll and Jemy should settle on the Eastern Shore is credible, too. Much of the Maryland Eastern Shore was just being settled when Moll and Jemy would have arrived in the early 1670s. Somerset County, where they made their plantation, was frontier then, and there was an abundance of cheap land, the perfect place for new planters such as they to settle.[5]

Most striking of all is Defoe's mention of Phillips Point. On maps of the period, Phillips Point was shown as the tip of a peninsula lying between the Nanticoke river and a river which, depending on which map you read, is named the Catherine, Rappahanock, or Transquaking. (On a modern map, the peninsula is bordered to the south by the Nanticoke river and to

the north by Fishing Bay; Phillips Point is now named Clay Island.)[6] Here
is what Defoe says happened to Moll and Jemy there: "We immediately
went on Shore, but found no Conveniences just at that Place, either for our
being on Shore, or preserving our Goods on Shore." Surprisingly, Defoe was
probably right about Phillips Point. At this time in Maryland, there were
few storehouses:[7] goods were loaded and unloaded directly at the docks of
individual plantations, and it is doubtful that any "Conveniences" were
ever built at Phillips Point. For Phillips Point was then (and still is today)
almost totally marshland. Except for a few sand hills – Phillips Point at
its tip and Elliott Island halfway up the Fishing Bay shore of the peninsula – the area is all tidal meadows, cut by numerous creeks and providing
little fast land to cultivate or to build on. The area surrounding Phillips
Point was sparsely populated. The headwaters of the Transquaking, which
feeds Fishing Bay, were occupied by the Choptanks and the Nanticoke
river above Phillips Point by the Nanticokes. This region of poorly drained
salt marsh was not fit for cultivation. It was the last part of the Eastern
Shore to be settled by Europeans. A census taken in 1704 gave the whole
of Dorchester County – men, women, children, servants, and slaves – as
only 2,312, and when Moll landed there in the 1670s, there were only 350
taxable inhabitants.[8]

   Perhaps when Defoe wrote of a place where Moll could find "no
Conveniences … either for our being on Shore, or preserving our Goods,"
he chose Phillips Point because he knew Phillips Point was situated in
the middle of a vast, uncultivated, and unsettled region, a region that
could not support the kind of amenities Moll and Jemy were looking for.
Or perhaps he knew nothing at all about Phillips Point. And yet, even
if he conjured up this scene entirely in his imagination while dreaming
over a name on a map, he still appears to have known enough about the
Chesapeake to make an informed guess about what such a place must
have been like. For in colonial Maryland, people did not cluster in settlements but lived on plantations scattered thinly along shores of inlets and
up bayside rivers and creeks. Trade was conducted by boats that went from
plantation to plantation. As a consequence, there were no towns and few
villages. This settlement pattern was a matter of concern to English colonial administrators and legislators and to the Board of Trade in London.
In 1683, the Assembly of Maryland tried to summon towns into existence
by restricting trade to "Ports & places where all Shipps & vessells … shall
unlade … all goods wares & Comoditys that shall bee imported into this
Province."[9] These "Ports & places" were not ports and places at all but, for
the most part, 100-acre plots of empty land the Assembly hoped would

become settled by virtue of legislative fiat. The legislation of 1683 was the first of such acts by the Assembly. But all these attempts to create towns and ports in places where there was no rational economic reason for them were doomed. "There are indeed several places allotted for towns," complained an observer in 1699, "but hitherto they are only titular ones."[10]

The problems of settlement patterns, of low population density, and of the lack of towns were conditions of business that any merchant who traded in the Chesapeake would know well, and they were serious enough to be mentioned in many of the tracts and books written about the region. In point of fact, there were few places where "Conveniences ... for being on Shore" were to be had, and so, even if Defoe knew nothing about Phillips Point, he appears to have known enough about the Chesapeake to know what was and what was not to be found there. After all, he did know enough to know that the Eastern Shore was a more than likely place to meet an "honest Quaker" such as Moll does. Quakers had begun to arrive on the Eastern Shore in the late 1650s and had flourished there, and Somerset County, where the "honest Quaker" has his plantation, had a substantial population of them.[11]

Finally, one more detail about Phillips Point is suggestive about how much Defoe knew about the Chesapeake. "We ... got information," says Moll, "that on the other side the *Bay* ... in *Maryland* there was a Ship, which came from *Carolina,* loaden with Rice, and other Goods." Moll is at Phillips Point sometime in the early 1670s; rice was not introduced to Carolina until the late 1670s at the earliest, more likely not until the 1680s, and it was not cultivated extensively enough for export until 1695. Defoe's reference to it as an item of export is anachronistic, and perhaps one could cite this as one more example of his ignorance, but in fact it is an error that tells us how much he did know about the region. Though he was not correct about the exact date Carolina began exporting rice, he knew that rice was an important export for Carolina, and he knew that Maryland, though it had recently become self-sufficient in producing food, produced no rice and would have to import it.[12]

About all of this – the land boom in Westmoreland County, the opening up of the Eastern Shore, the conditions at Phillips Point and the scarcity of settlements and amenities in the Chesapeake, the prevalence of Quakers in the region, the production of rice in Carolina – about all of this Defoe might have been right by chance, but it is more plausible that he knew of many of these as matters of fact, for all of them are related to his deep interest in religion, economics, geography, and trade. Such information was readily available to anyone willing to search it out, and

Defoe easily could have learned it from books or from conversations with acquaintances and merchants who lived and traded there. He had many ties to the New World through family, friends, neighbors, acquaintances, and business associates, all of whom were potential sources of information: his uncle, Henry Foe, whose business as a saddler was mostly with the colonies of America; his friends Charles Lodwick and Charles' half-brother, Matthew Clarkson, both of whom were prominent in New York during the 1680s and 1690s and acted as Defoe's factors there; Charles Morton, his teacher at the Newington Green Academy, who immigrated to New England in 1686. Defoe had other acquaintances who had lived in or traded with America: John Dunton, William Penn, Josiah Abbott, John Sharp, Joseph Beaton, Dalby Thomas, and the printers John Watts and Samuel Keimer. And he had a direct connection with Virginia and Maryland. In 1688, he was a partner in a trading venture on the *Batchelor of London,* which sailed to Boston and New York, delivering merchandise and passengers, and from there to the Chesapeake, where it offloaded servants (whose indentures Defoe had invested in) and took on tobacco.[13] On this voyage, Defoe's factor in the Chesapeake was Samuel Sandford. When Moll and Jemy established their plantation south of Phillips Point, they were settling near Sandford's plantation in Accomack County, on the Eastern Shore of Virginia.[14]

Defoe's references to America bear paying attention to for they suggest that his level of knowledge about the region, though imperfect, was more than superficial. About some extremely important, even obvious, matters he was quite misinformed, and the knowledge he did have was not comprehensive. His interests, though sometimes deep, were usually rather narrow. Still, he did know some things about America, and certain kinds of experiences in the New World interested him intensely, and he returned to them again and again in his novels. In many cases, we will probably never know for certain what he knew, but knowing for certain what he knew is less important than learning about his interests and preoccupations by taking his references to America more seriously than we have.

Defoe sets much of his fiction in the Americas. Captain Singleton begins his freebooting career in the Caribbean, and in *A New Voyage round the World,* the anonymous narrator and his crew traverse the lower tip of South America. Three other novels of his take place almost wholly in the Americas or have lengthy and significant episodes set there: *Robinson Crusoe,* on an island at the mouth of the Orinoco; *Moll Flanders,* in Virginia along the York and Potomac rivers and on the Eastern Shore of

Maryland; and *Colonel Jack,* on the Western Shore of Maryland, near the Potomac, and, in the final episodes, in Cuba and Mexico.

Judging from these novels, Defoe had a range of interests in the New World: piracy, trade, colonization, the Amerindians, African slaves. But in *Moll Flanders* and in *Colonel Jack,* he was especially fascinated by an institution peculiar to America, indentured servitude. Indentured servants made up the majority of emigrants from Britain up to Independence. They were the principal source of labor in America through the seventeenth century, and though increasingly replaced by African slaves, they remained a significant source of labor in the eighteenth century. Throughout the fictional time periods of *Moll Flanders* and *Colonel Jack* and during the time Defoe himself wrote, the mid-Atlantic colonies were the most important destination for servants, and this apparently is why he set these two novels in Virginia and Maryland. In the seventeenth century, about 130,000 British immigrants came to the Chesapeake, and probably at least four out of every five came as servants. Between 1700 and 1780, over half of the 270,000 British immigrants who came to the thirteen colonies came as indentured servants, and the majority of them came to the Chesapeake. Defoe wrote in 1724 that "within thirty years past above 200000 [have] gone away voluntarily to *Virginia,* and the neighboring Colonies, meerly to seek their Fortunes."[15] His numbers are inflated, but they testify to his sense that what was happening in the mid-Atlantic colonies was of great moment.

People came to the colonies as indentured servants for many reasons. At various times throughout the seventeenth and eighteenth centuries, beggars, Gypsies, prostitutes, the poor, the orphaned, "lewd and dangerous persons, rogues, vagrants, and other idle persons, who have no way of livelihood, and refuse to work" were swept off the streets and packed off to the colonies.[16] During the Civil War, royalist prisoners were sent to the Americas, as were Scottish rebels between 1678 and 1685, the Monmouth rebels in 1685, and the rebels who took part in the 1715 and 1745 Jacobite risings (some of the rebels of 1715 end up on Colonel Jack's plantation). A number of individuals – though probably many fewer than contemporary rumor claimed – were kidnapped and forced into servitude (which is how Jack comes to Maryland). Large numbers of Irish were transported by force, often under the pretense of their being vagabonds.[17]

But, by far, most British indentured servants were of two kinds: those who immigrated to the New World and entered into servitude freely and those who were sent to the New World and forced into servitude because they were felons.

Those who entered into servitude freely did so as a way of getting to the New World. They sold a term of their labor to pay for the cost of their transportation to America. Usually, the servant bound himself (or, much less frequently, herself) by contract to perform such-and-such work for such-and-such a period of time. The master, for his part, promised to provide food, clothing, and shelter for the duration of servitude, and he often awarded his servant so-called "freedom dues" at the end of the stipulated term of service. In the Chesapeake in the late seventeenth and early eighteenth centuries, a servant typically bound himself for four to five years, and the freedom dues were specified amounts of food, clothing, tools, and weapons. In Maryland, a right of land was included in the freedom dues until 1683.

Criminals made up the second class of indentured servants. Before 1718, the prescribed penalty for all felons was death. Since nearly 300 crimes were counted as felonies, the principal way of making discriminations and mitigating the harshness of the law was to grant royal pardons to felons whom judges thought worthy of mercy, freeing them from the sentence of death on the condition that they be transported out of the country. The 1718 Transportation Act changed this policy radically by declaring transportation a punishment for a large body of non-capital offenses, mostly crimes that came under the heading of grand larceny. The older system of using transportation as a pardon for more serious, capital felonies was retained. How many criminals were transported before 1718 is not known, but between 1718 and 1775 perhaps as many as 40,000 convicts were sent to the colonies, the vast majority to Maryland and Virginia.[18]

Defoe is fascinated with indentured servitude, and in *Moll Flanders* and *Colonel Jack* he rehearses, sometimes by dramatic incident, sometimes by lengthy exposition, the gamut of ways through which one became indentured in the New World and the fate of those who came as servants. Moll first comes to Virginia as the wife of a successful planter, but the episode itself says next to nothing about the typical life of a free immigrant, chronicling instead Moll's mother's career as an indentured servant, highlighting the opportunities the colony offers criminals and portraying the New World as a place where transported felons can be reformed by servitude. In her second journey to Virginia, Moll and Jemy are themselves transported felons. Colonel Jack is an indentured servant, too, though he does not come to the New World as a transported felon. He is kidnapped by a ruthless agent. Still, as in *Moll Flanders,* transportation permeates the novel, for Jack himself sees his kidnapping as a kind of symbolic transportation, a punishment for his being "born a Thief, and bred up a Pick-pocket" (*CJ*, p. 123). The life stories of felons who actually were transported to Maryland as servants are interspersed throughout the novel. When the number of immigrants to the Chesapeake fell sharply in the 1680s, the shortfall was made up by turning to groups other than the young English males who had made up the preponderance of inden-tured servants to that point, groups who "lived near the margin of British society: women, the Irish, convicts, homeless orphans, young children, the poor."[19] It is an interesting fact that, taken together, Moll, Jemy, and Colonel Jack are representative of almost every one of these classes.

The lives of Moll and Jack follow the pattern that writers of colonial promotional literature claimed was the pattern of the lives of indentured servants who came to the New World. America was a place where the poor, the idle, and the criminal began as servants and ended as masters, a transformation that was not only economic but also moral. Of course, Defoe plays significant variations on this pattern (Moll, though trans-ported, buys herself out of servitude; Jack, though a criminal and a ser-vant, is not transported), but these variations simply give complex nuances to the moral and psychological trajectory that was implicit in the move-ment from servant to master: the rehabilitation of a life given over to guilt, criminality, and idleness through the discipline of exile, punishment, and hard work. Moll and Jack end as the colonial promotional literature prom-ised all transported servants would end, richer and better people. Both prosper in the New World, and, though we might quibble about the depth and sincerity of their regeneration, both end at least morally reformed, if not spiritually renovated.

But the Defoe novel that plays out most fully the drama of moral rehabilitation that is brought to pass by indentured servitude is *Robinson Crusoe*. There are two reasons, I think, why this has never been seen very clearly before. First, the entire sequence – imprisonment, judgment, trans-portation, servitude, and the founding and improvement of the planta-tion – is acted out in *Robinson Crusoe* on a figurative level whose terms of reference are religious and psychological, not legal and economic. Second, the episodes that plot this American story of servitude are neither univocal (the island, for instance, is figured as Crusoe's prison *and* the place of his servitude *and* his plantation) nor do they unfold neatly in the sequence they did in reality. In reality, one was imprisoned and then transported and then set to work on a plantation; in *Robinson Crusoe*, Crusoe is set to work on his plantation simultaneously to his being imprisoned on his island, and he is transported before he is imprisoned. There is a reason for this. In *Robinson Crusoe*, the plot of American servitude takes place less on the level of the sequence of literal events than on the level of Crusoe's unfolding consciousness: on the level of plot sequence, Crusoe is "transported" to his island before he is "imprisoned" on it; but on the level of his awareness, he first is *conscious* of the island as a place of imprisonment, then he becomes *aware* that he has been judged, and then he *understands* that his condition is that of a transported indentured servant, and so on.

Ever since the work of J. Paul Hunter and George A. Starr, we have become aware of how much *Robinson Crusoe* dramatizes emblematically the protagonist's spiritual crime, punishment, and redemption.[20] What I want to call attention to is the fact that Defoe shapes this story of Crusoe's spiritual bondage and deliverance as a narrative of transportation, indentured servitude, and the establishment of the plantation. For the "ORIGINAL SIN" of his innate rebelliousness, Crusoe is confined on his island, made a "Prisoner lock'd up with the Eternal Bars and Bolts of the Ocean, in an uninhabited Wilderness" (*RC*, pp. 200, 140). As a prison, the island becomes the place where he is held for judgment (prisons in eighteenth-century England were rarely places of punishment; the accused were held in prison until they were brought to trial and, if found guilty, they were punished by death, whipping, transportation, branding, or fining). Here, Crusoe meditates on his crime, assesses his guilt, worries about the judgment that will be passed on him. Only when he begins to realize that "the Island was certainly a Prison to me, and that in the worse Sense of the Word," does he begin to recognize his culpability and to understand that he needs to be delivered not simply from this physical "Captivity" but from the "Load of Guilt" that comes from his "Sin" (*RC*, pp. 128–129).

Crusoe is judged guilty, and he acknowledges that the consequence of this "Judgment from Heaven" is his being "cast on this dreadful Place" in the Americas (*RC*, p. 123). In short, the judgment of God and the consequences of Crusoe's sin are figured as his being transported to the New World and forced to labor in the fields as if he were an indentured servant until he can redeem himself from his bondage.

In *Robinson Crusoe,* this punishment and servitude is portrayed very ambiguously, and the terms of this ambiguity are those which defined criminal transportation. Before 1718, transportation was not legally conceived of as punishment. The punishment for a felony was death, and transportation to the colonies was considered a pardon extended by the sovereign as a gracious act of mercy (thus, Moll Flanders speaks about how her mother "obtain'd the Favour of being Transported to the Plantations" [*MF*, p. 28]). Of course, this was a patent charade, for to be forced into exile and hard labor was a punishment, and those who suffered it thought of it as such (Moll's mother comments that those transported to America "to be sold as Servants … are more properly call'd *Slaves*" [*MF*, pp. 85–86]). Under the Transportation Act of 1718, transportation continued to be used to pardon capital felons, but the Act also created a new class of non-capital felons who could be *sentenced* to transportation, not as an act of mercy, but as a *punishment*. The Act thus articulated explicitly what was understood implicitly and experienced viscerally: transportation was both a punishment *and* an act of mercy.

Robinson Crusoe, Moll Flanders, and *Colonel Jack* were all written within five years of the Transportation Act, and I think that the Act's making explicit the twofold nature of transportation as both punishment and pardon affected the way Defoe used transportation and indentured servitude to organize these three novels. The "editor" of *Moll Flanders* forthrightly calls "the Misery of Transportation" a "Disaster," but then he immediately says that it "will go a great way to deliver us from [a low condition and] will in time raise the meanest Creature to appear again in the World, and give him a new Cast for his Life" (*MF*, p. 25). In *Colonel Jack,* transportation is all "Sorrow and Misery," and Jack believes that he "was brought into this miserable Condition of a Slave; by some strange directing Power, as a Punishment for the Wickedness of my younger Years" (*CJ*, pp. 156, 121). At the same time, he understands that his servitude is a "Mercy" (*CJ*, p. 156), and in the novel transportation and servitude are cast in the same religious language of divine retribution and deliverance we find in *Robinson Crusoe.* A reformed servant explains to Jack how transportation has "wrought in [his] Soul" a "blessed Change":

Do you think that when I receiv'd the Grant of Transportation, I cou'd be insensible what a Miracle of Divine Goodness such a thing must be, to one who had so many ways deserv'd to be Hang'd, and must infallibly have Died? … There began the first Motive of Repentance, for certainly the Goodness of our Great Creator in sparing us, when we forfeit our Lives to his Justice, and his Merciful bringing us out of the Miseries which we Plunge ourselves into, when we have no way to Extricate ourselves, his bringing those very Miseries to be the means of our Deliverance, and working Good to us out of Evil, when we are working the very Evil out of his Good: I say, these things are certainly the strongest Motives to Repentance that are in the World; and the sparing Theives from the Gallows, certainly makes more Penitents than the Gallows it self. (*CJ*, p. 156)

This double face of transportation as both mercy and punishment is at the center of Crusoe's experience of America. Driven toward the shores of his island, Crusoe and his mates see nothing before them but certain death, and, knowing they will "be inevitably drowned," they nevertheless row toward land, "like Men going to Execution" (*RC,* p. 89). Crusoe alone is "sav'd, as I may say, out of the very Grave" (*RC,* p. 90). He feels, he says, like "a Malefactor who has the Halter about his Neck … and just going to be turn'd off, and has a Reprieve brought to him" (*RC,* p. 90).

Crusoe comes to understand his exile on the island as "Punishment of my Sins," but he also feels that he has been reprieved, "singled out … to be spar'd from Death" (*RC,* p. 106). He realizes that he "ought not to complain, seeing I had not the due Punishment of my Sins; that I enjoy'd so many Mercies which I had no reason to have expected in that Place" (*RC,* p. 154). Thus, he sees his life in America as an "Affliction," "a Life of Sorrow, one way" but also "a Life of Mercy, another" (*RC,* p. 155). He feels at once "banish'd" and "miraculously sav'd … from Death" (*RC,* p. 106).

Having been transported to the New World for his crime, Crusoe finds himself in "Bondage," living "by the Labour of [his] Hands" (*RC,* p. 83), like an indentured servant, eating hard fare and working the land. His condition, the emblematic language of the novel with its pervasive rhetoric of master and slave repeatedly tells us, is that of a slave (indentured servants quite often referred to themselves and were referred to by others as "slaves"). But after Crusoe serves several years in this desperate condition, he begins to achieve the status which the promotional literature of America promised freed indentured servants. His life becomes less a "Captivity" and more a "Reign" (*RC,* p. 158). He becomes a master of a plantation, with Friday as his bound servant and the Spaniard his overseer. He is so successful that he parlays his original single holding into several "Plantations" (*RC,* p. 168). And he is successful in the way those who were indentured servants were reputed to be successful, building their new lives on the basis of hard work and their freedom dues, that stock of tools, clothing, seed, tobacco, and a parcel of land given to servants at the end of their terms. (In 1640, the Maryland Assembly specified that a servant would receive at the end of his indentures "one good cloth Suite of Keirsey or Broadcloth, shift of white linen, one pair of Stockins and Shoes, two hoes, one axe, 3 barrels of corne, and fifty acres of land whereof five at least be plantable.")[21] Crusoe finds his freedom dues in the wreckage of the ship.

Transportation and servitude could be mapped so cleanly onto religious retribution and redemption because at heart both were narratives of punishment and mercy. Both transportation and divine retribution were punishments because they chastened, but by chastening they encouraged the recognition of guilt and thus spurred the desire to reform. And since they opened up the possibility of reformation, both were merciful pardons because they offered the opportunity for a person to alter the conditions for which he was punished in the first place. Defoe's conflation of these two narratives was waiting to happen. Colonial promotional literature had long argued that servitude in the New World offered a chance for moral renovation. By becoming servants, immigrants could not only become economically successful but could erase the stigma of criminality or poverty because they were given the opportunity to reform those attitudes and habits that had driven them to crime or that had kept them poor. When Defoe said that Virginia and Maryland were places where even criminals "are effectually deliver'd from a Life of a flagrant Wickedness, and put in a perfectly new Condition" (*CJ*, p. 162), he was simply echoing promotional writers such as Hammond, who claimed that those "who in England have been lewd and idle ... not only grow ashamed of their former courses, but abhor to hear of them, and in small time wipe off those stains they have formerly been tainted with"; or such as Alsop, who said that "those whose Lives and Conversations have had no other gloss nor glory stampt on them in their own Country, but the stigmatization of baseness, were here brought to detest and loath their former actions."[22] Hugh Jones, writing contemporaneously with Defoe, promoted Virginia as a "new paradise" where a "favorable providence" offered a "blessed opportunity" for "both ... temporal and spiritual" regeneration.[23]

Yet, Defoe's protagonists' experiences of servitude are not merely spiritual allegories: the transportation Moll and Jemy are sentenced to is part of a legal and economic system they become caught up in as a consequence of their lives of crime; the indentured servitude Jack endures is (according to its defenders) an institution designed to open up economic and social opportunities the poor and disadvantaged otherwise would not have; the plantation Crusoe establishes he establishes in the teeth of a recalcitrant nature that yields to his desires only because of his hard work and his skills in wielding gunpowder, fire, and the ax.

Defoe was fascinated by the quotidian colonial realities and the social, legal, and economic circumstances of the New World, and in *Robinson Crusoe, Moll Flanders,* and *Colonel Jack,* he created characters who, for all their spiritual dimensions, seized on the sheer material promise of America which Defoe himself enthusiastically embraced.

In these three novels, Defoe has his protagonists extricate themselves from a variety of kinds of servitude (to straitened circumstances, to privation and distress, to economic need) by creating lives of independence and mastery, and in this, too, he echoes New World promotional tracts, whose central promise was that America was the place where men could free themselves from the "Vexation of Dependence."[24] In America, Defoe said, one can "begin the World upon a new Foundation" and "deliver" one self from a life that is "low," "despicable," and "empty of Prospect" (*MF,* pp. 246, 25). Moll Flanders' mother paints a picture of the Chesapeake as an economic utopia, where the poor and the criminal can better themselves by becoming indentured servants. "Many a *Newgate* Bird becomes a great Man," she concludes,

and we have … several Justices of the Peace, Officers of the Train Bands, and Magistrates of the Towns they live in, that have been burnt in the Hand … and they are not asham'd to own it; there's Major – – … he was an Eminent Pickpocket; there's Justice *Ba – – r* was a Shoplifter. (*MF,* p. 86)

In *Colonel Jack,* Defoe is equally optimistic. In the Chesapeake, entering into servitude is "beginning the World again" (*CJ,* p. 122). Twice in the novel, Jack delivers lengthy sales pitches for the region, touting the advantages of indentured servitude. "There is not the poorest, and most despicable Felon that ever went over," he claims enthusiastically, "but may after his time is serv'd, begin for himself, and may in time be sure of raising a good Plantation" (*CJ,* p. 146).

Every *Newgate* Wretch, every Desperate forlorn Creature; the most Despicable ruin'd Man in the World, has here a fair Opportunity put into his Hands to begin the World again, and that upon a Foot of certain Gain, and in a Method exactly Honest; with a Reputation, that nothing past will have any Effect upon; and innumerable People have thus rais'd themselves from the worst Circumstance in the World. (*CJ,* p. 147)

"In *Virginia,*" he concludes, "the meanest, and most despicable Creature after his time of Servitude is expir'd, if he will but apply himself with Diligence and Industry to the Business of the Country, is sure (Life and Health suppos'd) both of living Well and growing Rich" (*CJ,* p. 162).

These promises were the standard fare of colonial promotional literature.[25] The yoke of indentured servitude was easy, this literature proclaimed. "The Laws of *Virginia* take great care for the good Usage of Servants, as to Necessities, Diet and Clothes: And the labour of the Country … is so easy, that, as hard work as 'tis represented to be, the Day-Labourers in *England* are much the greater Slaves."[26] Servants "live well in the time of their Service, and … are made capable of living much better when they come to be free."[27] Indeed, many "live plentiously well."[28] In America, the poor can become great, provided, as Defoe himself always stressed, they were industrious and diligent: "It is knowne (such preferment hath this Country rewarded the industrious with) that some from being wool-hoppers and of as mean and meaner imployment in England have there grown great merchants, and attained to the most eminent advancements the Country afforded."[29] Above all, in the Chesapeake the poor can live a life of honest labor as opposed to a life of penury and immorality in England:

I cannot but admire, and indeed much pitty the dull stupidity of people necessitated in England, who rather then they will remove themselves, live here [in England] a base, slavish, penurious life; as if there were a necessity to live and to live so, choosing rather then they will forsake England to stuff New-Gate, Bridewell, and other Jayles with their carkessies, nay cleave to [T]yburne it selfe, and so bring confusion to their souls, horror and infamie to their kindred or posteritie.[30]

In contrast, those who came to America as servants,

being Industrious since they came out of their times with their Masters ... have gotten good Stocks of Cattle, and Servants of their own ... And many that went thither in that condition, are worth several Hundreds of Pounds, and live in a very plentiful condition, and their Estates still encreasing.[31]

In some promotional literature – such as in this piece by Durand, who was trying to persuade his countrymen to immigrate to Virginia – the prospects are little less than paradisal:

The land is so rich and so fertile that when a man has fifty acres of ground, two men servants, a maid & some cattle, neither he nor his wife do anything but visit among their neighbors. Most of them do not even take the trouble to oversee the work of their slaves, for there is no house, however modest, where there is not what is called a Lieutenant, generally a freedman, under whose command two servants are placed. This Lieutenant keeps himself, works & makes his two servants work ... & the master has only to take his share of the crops.[32]

Such promises inform that final picture we have of Jemy, who, being "bred a Gentleman," went "out into the Woods with his Gun" for pleasure shooting while his "new Plantation grew ... insensibly" (*MF*, pp. 264, 274) – or, on a more modest and plausible level, that thumbnail sketch of Colonel Jack's housekeeper, who, when "out of her Time ... was married and turn'd Planter" (*CJ*, p. 223).

And it is not simply that Defoe repeats the substance of the promoters' claims. One can often hear in his enthusiastic assurances echoes of the huckster's feverish rhetoric and hyperbole – echoes, say, of Alsop's extravagant promise, *"Dwell here, live plentifully and be rich."*[33] In the colonial lives of Moll and Colonel Jack, Defoe charts an untroubled trajectory in which they begin in "the worst Circumstance in the World" and end "in very considerable Circumstances," "grown very Rich" (*CJ,* p. 147; *MF,* pp. 274, 26). The New World allows them "to begin the World again, and that upon a Foot of certain Gain." *Certain Gain!* "No Diligent Man *ever* Miscarried," says Jack, and, when she promises Jemy that he can "begin the World upon a new Foundation," Moll adds, "and that such a one as he *cou'd not fail* of Success in" (*CJ,* p. 147; *MF,* p. 246; my italics).

How truthful were these claims that indentured servants "cou'd not fail of Success" in America and, if they were not entirely truthful, did Defoe knowingly misrepresent the facts or was he himself taken in by the colonial promoters?

The impression Moll's mother gives of the extraordinary opportunities open to immigrants to the Chesapeake in the mid-1600s, though overstated in some important particulars, is essentially accurate. The tobacco economy was robust. Advancement was the rule given the ready availability of servants and the easy access to credit and good land. Since most planters came from similar stock as the newly arriving immigrants, there was little prejudice about the immigrants' social roots or antagonism toward their upward mobility. William Reavis estimates that 82 percent of Maryland immigrants who achieved gentry status in Maryland did not have that status in England but were middling sorts who were able to take advantage of the abundant opportunities of the colony to move into the upper strata quickly.[34] Russell Menard discovered that, of indentured servants who came to Maryland before the end of 1642, more than 90 percent of those who lived for more than a decade in the colony as freedmen became landowners. They rose in social status, too, holding offices in Maryland government as justices of the peace, sheriffs, burgesses, and officers in the militia with a frequency that "testifies to the impressive status mobility they achieved in the mid-seventeenth century."[35] "Opportunity was abundant," Menard concludes.[36] "Almost any healthy man in Maryland in the 1640s and 1650s, if he worked hard, practiced thrift, avoided expensive lawsuits, and did not suffer from plain bad luck, could become a landowner in a short time."[37] Three-fifths of the ex-servants who settled Charles County, Maryland, by 1664, for instance, became not only landowners but landowners with substantial holdings.[38]

Upward mobility, especially for those among the lower ranks, was more restricted in Virginia than in Maryland, and freedmen probably had less opportunity for landholding or political participation. Still, opportunity did exist, largely because of the availability of relatively cheap land in the vast frontier regions, where social and financial advancement were relatively easy. Although the most powerful, lucrative, and prestigious positions in the colony were closed to all but the rich and well connected, local positions were open to all ranks, and even through the 1650s men who had come to Virginia as servants sat in the House of Burgesses. In 1665, a planter wrote from Virginia sounding as sanguine as Moll's mother: "Many of our Country men, living better then ever ther forfathers, and that from so mean a beginning as being sold slav[e]s here … are now herein great masters of many servants themselfs."[39]

But if Moll's mother's claim about a rosy future is essentially correct, it is correct only about the prospects for her own generation. The prospects for Moll's and Jack's generations were quite different. Someone like Moll, who came a second time to the region in the 1670s, faced tougher economic realities, and by the 1690s, when Jack began his career as a planter in the Chesapeake, the economy had worsened considerably.[40]

By the 1670s, the years during which Moll and Jemy "grew *Rich*" on their plantation (*MF,* title page), the golden era of the Chesapeake had passed. Prospects were not good, particularly for the low and middling sort, and for someone newly freed from servitude, opportunities had declined sharply.[41] Tobacco had become less profitable. Prices throughout the first half of the 1670s sagged to 1 pence per pound (they had averaged almost 3.6 pence for Moll's mother's generation), and they drifted lower and lower so that, by 1683, when Moll was in London living off the profits of her plantation, they had sunk to 0.8 pence. Governor Culpeper of Virginia wrote to the British authorities that such low prices could lead only to the "fatal and speedy ruin of this once noble Colony."[42]

Small landowners were unable to cultivate tobacco in sufficient quantities to survive in a depressed market. Labor was increasingly expensive, and credit, which would have allowed ex-servants or small landowners to purchase more land and servants, became more and more restricted. In this chronically stagnant economy, those who were just freed from their servitude slid into debt. Fewer freedmen were able to own land than previously, fewer could purchase bound labor, and fewer could raise themselves above small-planter status. Beverley recalled that "most of the poorer sort" were unable "to cloath their Wives and Children": "There was nothing to be got by Tobacco; neither could they turn any other manufacture to Advantage."[43] So many Virginians were so desperately poor, wrote Governor Berkeley in 1673, that "we may reasonably expect upon any small advantage [that they] would revolt … in hopes of bettering their Condition."[44]

And revolt they did. In 1676, precisely when Moll and Jemy "grew *Rich,*" these economic difficulties helped ignite Bacon's Rebellion. Though a small group of substantial planters who had been excluded by the ruling elite actually headed the revolt, Berkeley was correct when he described it as the rising up of the "Rabble" against "the better sort [of] people," for the rebellion was stoked by servants and freedmen who felt exploited by the established, wealthy planters and who were embittered by their diminishing prospects.[45] When the king's commissioners investigated the causes of the rebellion, they found that a significant proportion of the rebels had been "Free men that had but lately crept out of the condition of servants."[46]

The hardships that led to the rebellion continued after it was quelled. In 1681, Governor Culpeper wrote that conditions in the Chesapeake were "so fatal and desperate that there is no remedy; the market is overstocked and every crop overstocks it more. It is commonly said that there is tobacco enough in London now to last all England for five years."[47] The next year, plant-cutting riots broke out as desperate farmers sought ways to reduce the oversupply of tobacco that was glutting the market.

The situation in Maryland appears not to have been as critical as in Virginia, though it was bad enough. There were two attempted rebellions in the years immediately preceding the successful overthrow in 1689 of the proprietary government, and they seemed to be fueled in part by the poor and by ex-servants, who, because of higher taxes, constricted credit, and rising prices of English goods, felt their opportunities for economic advancement slipping away.[48]

The bare statistics of Charles County, Maryland (Jack's plantation was probably in either Charles County or its neighboring county, St. Mary's), reveal the difference between Defoe's fiction and the colonial reality.[49] In the mid-1600s, three-fifths of former indentured servants had acquired land in the county and the mean average of their holdings was over 1,000 acres; by 1705, fewer than 8 percent of the landowners in the county were ex-servants, and the mean average of their holdings had dropped to 248 acres.[50] And it was not just Charles County. The whole region of the Chesapeake came under serious economic pressure. Defoe implies that Jack's success was "certain," but the period from the early 1690s, when Jack begins his rise from servant to planter, through the first two decades of the eighteenth century, when his plantation prospers, was one of severely declining opportunities, especially for ex-servants. The tobacco economy collapsed, slipping into a thirty-year depression beginning in 1680 and lasting (with the exception of two brief spikes in the mid-1680s and at the turn of the century) until 1715. Continued overproduction and a flattening of demand drove the price of tobacco to the lowest levels of the entire colonial period, 0.7 pence per pound in 1689 and, by 1694, a disastrous 0.55 pence. Per-capita income began to decline in the 1680s, and, by the turn of the century, inventoried wealth had fallen sharply. Opportunities for economic mobility decreased markedly.[51]

Opportunity for status mobility decreased too. By the turn of the century, a native-born elite emerged and, with it, nascent dynasties based on marriage, blood relationships, and inherited land and labor. Economic levels began to diverge more and more, the gap between the rich and the poor not only widened but also solidified, and immigrants and freed servants were locked out of positions of power and prestige.[52]

In spite of bad times, money could still be made from tobacco, but only by those who had large tracts of land and a large number of servants, and during these hard times, large landowners were consolidating their wealth and moving from gain to gain. Because they could take advantage of depressed land values and because they could afford to purchase slaves and servants and profit from an economy of scale, they not only weathered bad economic times but thrived.[53]

While the rich, as the phrase has it, got richer, the small and middling planters fell further and further behind. As early as the 1650s in Virginia, wealthy speculators were grabbing up large parcels of land, and well before the turn of the century, newly freed servants who could afford to buy property could afford only inferior land abandoned by the wealthier planters or land at the frontiers.[54] By the turn of the century, such vast tracts of prime land had been granted away and so much of what remained had been engrossed by the wealthy that freed servants could not get land. Those who served their time found they had to become tenants or had to move to the distant frontier, "higher up than the Rivers are navigable, and out of the way of all business."[55] In Maryland, land prices more than doubled between 1660 and the turn of the century.[56]

Further, to advance in a tobacco economy, more important than the ability to acquire land was the ability to acquire labor. And by the 1680s the ability to acquire labor was increasingly restricted to the wealthy. A rise in real wages in England slowed immigration to America, and the supply of white servants dwindled.[57] Fewer servants meant that their price rose, and poor and middling planters were less and less able to purchase them. The alternative to white labor was out of their reach, for black slaves were two to almost three times as expensive as white servants. The ownership of black labor was concentrated in the hands of those who were already wealthy; fewer and fewer of those who were not wealthy owned either servants or slaves.[58]

Those just released from servitude simply did not have the wherewithal to gain a foothold in such a depressed economy. To establish a household, a newly freed servant needed capital – capital to purchase land, tools, seed, and livestock, capital to build a house, and, between the time the land was cleared and the first harvest sold, capital to tide him over. Even in the mid-century, when the economy was strong and credit was relatively easy to come by, the transition from servant to landowner was hard enough (upon gaining his freedom, a servant typically took seven and a half years to acquire land).[59] But when the economy began to stall in the 1660s, and then moved into a depression, it became more difficult for a freedman to better himself by dint of his labor alone, and the likelihood of his raising himself from a servant to an independent planter became smaller and smaller.

In mid-century Maryland, only about 10 percent of those who served out their indentures and lived in the colony for ten years failed to become landlords; just a few decades later, nearly 60 percent failed to acquire land. In Charles County, Maryland, in the last decades of the seventeenth century, the majority of servants who became freedmen never became landowners but made their living as laborers, sharecroppers, or tenants; over half never established their own households; fewer than a third ever bought land, and, of these, few ever rose above small-planter status.[60] It was the same story in Virginia. Only 17 percent of servants who arrived in Accomack County between 1664 and 1697 ever acquired land as freedmen. In Northampton County, only 9 percent were able to. In Lancaster County, only 10 percent of the servants freed between 1662 and 1678 are recorded as householders in the county in 1679. Elsewhere, prospects were worse: "it is safe to say that not more than five or six per cent of the indentured servants of this period succeeded in establishing themselves as independent planters."[61]

If the typical career of an indentured servant in the mid-century was to serve out his indentures, work for several years as a hired laborer, sharecropper, or tenant, accumulate enough capital to acquire land, and then become a planter, the typical career of a servant at the end of the seventeenth century and throughout the rest of the colonial period was quite different:

When they completed their terms they found themselves free men with no capital and little credit in a depressed economy that offered little chance of advancement. After a few years as hired hands or sharecroppers, or perhaps a brief attempt at tenant farming, they left the tobacco coast for more promising regions.[62]

By the 1690s, "outmigration reached epidemic proportions."[63] Perhaps as many as one-half to two-thirds of the servants in the tidewater left the region upon completing their terms. "Young English Natives and Servants when they are free," wrote Governor Nicholson to the Board of Trade in 1697, "leave these Colonies, and goe either Southward or Northward" – to the Carolinas, the Jerseys, and Pennsylvania. The Chesapeake, which had long been touted as the best poor man's country in the world, was now a place to avoid.[64]

It is instructive to compare Jack's fictional life to the life of an actual indentured servant, William Roberts. Roberts worked in Anne Arundel County, not far from where Jack himself was a servant, several decades after Jack served, but in an economic climate that was probably a bit less gloomy than that which Jack faced. Like Jack, Roberts came from London, but he came from better circumstances. Both of his parents were alive, though poor, but his two brothers were able to become tradesmen, and his uncle, John Broughton, was wealthy and felt enough responsibility to his family that he occasionally helped them financially. Even so, by his early twenties, Roberts was in such desperate economic straits that he decided to try his fate in the New World. He arrived in Maryland in June 1756, as an indentured servant. "Thank God," Roberts wrote, "I happen[ed] to meet with a Good master," one who, like Jack's master, gave him his freedom after three years of service, one year before it was due.[65]

But after he won his freedom, Roberts' life diverged radically from Jack's, for it was a life of penury and failure, a life, unlike Jack's, typical of the lives of indentured servants in the eighteenth-century Chesapeake.

Jack's rise in status is signaled by new clothes. When he is promoted to an overseer, he is sent into a warehouse to be suited with a new outfit. "Go in there a Slave," he is told, "and come out a Gentleman" (*CJ*, p. 127). Roberts slipped progressively downward, and his tale of failure is told by his clothes, too. Two years after leaving servitude, he was working wherever he could, mostly as a hired laborer. "As for my Clothes," he wrote to his parents,

they ware veary bad, I had but t[w]o Sharts for a year and as Courss as [the] apron as you ware When you Scower pewter ... I hope you Speek to my Uncle to send me some Cloths such as Check Shirts and a Suet of Cloths as he done veary Little for me yet.[66]

Six years later, Roberts' lot had not improved. Illness had put him out of work, and he continued to ask for help from his uncle – the clothes he had been sent earlier were hand-me-downs ("my Brothers coat fitt as well as if

I had been Measured for it, my Shirts did veary well all but a little to short in the sleves").[67] He began asking not for clothes but for the material to make them. "I should be Oblige to you for as much fustain as woud make me a coat and some Nankeen for a Jacket and Breeches ... Some Check or Stripe Holland for Shirts, Ozinbourg for Trowsers and what you think proper for a great Coat in Winter."[68] He asked for money, too, and a large stock of goods "as I intend to go to house keepin."[69]

But Roberts' efforts to set himself up independently failed. He simply could not get on his feet to deliver himself out of poverty, and his dream of establishing himself as a planter sputtered and stalled. In 1768, he became, like Jack, an "Overseer for over twenty Blackamoores."[70] He appears to have worked hard, and he was able to get a letter from "a Gentleman of a veary great account" to attest to his industry and honesty, which he used as a character reference to get something from his uncle.[71] "I hope by Gods Blessing to live an honest Life if it is a hard one. Thank God I have got an honnest Character as any young man that Ever crost the Seas."[72] He asked for more money or a stock of goods, but in fact he would settle for anything. "If you have aney more old Clothes I shud be ablige to you for them."[73]

In an attempt to pull himself up by his bootstraps, he became a tenant farmer with a partner. But tenancy had long ceased to be a way for an ex-servant to raise enough capital to acquire his own land, and apparently Roberts failed. His last extant letter is from 1769 – another letter to his uncle begging him to "sent me some Check of a Bout thirteen pence a yard I can dispose of it at half a Crown Current money for Shirts."[74] After that, we do not know what happened to him. The name William Roberts appears in official records, which show a man who married and had nine children but who acquired no land, no servants or slaves, and scarcely any personal property. Whether this is the same William Roberts is not certain – perhaps our William Roberts died or moved on looking for better opportunity – but it is certain that, given the economic realities of the time, our William Roberts could not have ended up much better than the poor William Roberts we do have records of, for his life was the life of a typical indentured servant.[75]

When Defoe used his novels set in the Chesapeake to suggest to his readers that they could succeed spectacularly in the Atlantic economy by becoming indentured servants, he was seriously misrepresenting the historical facts. The stories Moll's mother tells may have had some truth seventy or eighty years before Defoe wrote his novels – though even here he is gilding the lily – but they do not give an accurate picture of the prospects for Moll's and Jack's generations, and they certainly do not give an accurate appraisal of prospects for Defoe's own contemporaries. The actual conditions in the Chesapeake were so out of joint with Defoe's enthusiasm that there seems something dishonest about both *Moll Flanders* and *Colonel Jack*. Defoe promised that "the meanest, and most despicable Creature after his time of Servitude is expir'd, if he will but apply himself with Diligence and Industry to the Business of the Country, is sure (Life and Health suppos'd) both of living Well and growing Rich" (*CJ*, p. 162). But historians, after reviewing the deterioration of servants' economic conditions and the narrowing of their prospects for social mobility, have concluded otherwise:

A society which once promised indentured servants eventual integration into the community they served had become one that offered newly freed workers a choice between poverty and emigration. Over time, servitude in the Chesapeake colonies had become less like English apprenticeship, less a means of preparing for full membership in a New World community, and more a kind of short-term slavery.[76]

It is not clear how cognizant Defoe was of this precipitous decline of opportunity, but he knew enough to know that his enthusiastic endorsement of indentured servitude was not entirely grounded in reality. The lives of Moll and Jack are not at all typical of the lives of real indentured servants, and to give Defoe his due, he does not pretend that they are typical. Indeed, in dramatizing their successes in the Chesapeake, he gives them exactly what they need to be successful in the colonies and exactly what most freed servants lacked – capital, or the next best thing, credit. Moll and Jack "grow Rich" not because they are more industrious than other immigrants but because they begin their careers with a stock of riches they can bankroll into even greater riches. Jack has an uncommonly generous master who buys him "about 300 Acres of Land in a more convenient Place, than it would have otherwise been Allotted me" (*CJ*, p. 145) and then extends credit to stock it with cattle and slaves before Jack is even out of service. He is doing a lot more than setting Jack on his feet. A plantation this size was well above the median acreage held by landowners in Maryland at this time, and the "three Rooms, a Kitchin, an Out-House, and two large Sheds at a distance from the House, for Store-houses" (*CJ*, p. 146) that Jack's master builds for him are the kind of structures that would be owned by someone in the upper reaches of the middling third of planters in Maryland. Moll starts off in an even more advantageous position than Jack. She comes to the New World with £246, then has sent to her £150 more; her annual income from the plantation her mother deeded to her is £60, and she has shipped to her a cargo of goods valued at another £250. The plot of land she buys on the Eastern Shore is so large she immediately becomes among the top 10 percent of landowners in the region.[77]

Moll succeeds wonderfully in the New World, her plantation yielding "at least, 300*l*. Sterling a Year" (*MF*, p. 274), and Jack's plantations return "eight Hundred Pound, and one Year almost a Thousand," his workforce consisting of "upwards of three hundred" servants and slaves (*CJ*, pp. 220–221).[78] In the Chesapeake, successes such as these, though exceptional, are credible, but they are credible only because Moll and Jack had the economic wherewithal to start where they did.

Defoe knew exactly what was needed to succeed in the New World, and *Robinson Crusoe* confirms it. For all the novel's emphasis on his industry and diligence, Crusoe's plantation is successful only because he, like Moll, landed in America with capital, that stock of tools, clothing, raw material, and seed from the ship, without which, he acknowledges, "I should have liv'd, if I had not perish'd, like a meer Savage" (*RC*, p. 153).

So, even as Defoe puts forward his protagonists' stories as exemplary of the opportunities of the New World, tributes to the ability "to begin the World again, and that upon a Foot of certain Gain," he reveals an odd, even scrupulous regard for historical accuracy by intimating that their successes are not typical, as if he were unwilling to allow their stories to be thought of as exemplary at all. For all of the promotional inflections in Defoe's novels, they are filled with throwaway phrases that rub against the grain of his New World boosterism, brief, unguarded moments in which he shows himself to be conscious of another reality than the one he seems so intent on foregrounding, moments in which he seems to be aware that there is something tendentious in his enthusiasm. The "editor" of Moll's memoirs remarks that hers is "a Story fruitful of Instruction, to all the unfortunate Creatures who are oblig'd to seek their Re-establishment abroad; whether by the Misery of Transportation, or other Disaster" (*MF*, p. 25). Transportation, Moll acknowledges, is a "hard Condition," and those who are transported "wretch'd" (*MF*, p. 239). Jemy "could not think of [transportation] with any Temper, and thought he could much easier submit to be Hang'd" (*MF*, p. 244). Jack, too, for all his zealous championing of indentured servitude, admits that it is a "miserable Condition of a Slave": "we work'd Hard, lodg'd Hard, and far'd Hard," and he later thinks back on his lot as "the wretched State of a *Virginia* Sold Servant: I had Notion enough in my Mind, of the Hardships of the Servant, or Slave, because I had felt it, and Work'd thro' it; I remember'd it as a State of Labour and Servitude, Hardship and Suffering" (*CJ*, pp. 121, 149). Although his own master was kindly and generous, Jack concedes that his was a special case, and he explains the terror one of his own servants feels toward him now that he is a master as perfectly understandable, "*for Masters in* Virginia *are terrible things*" (*CJ*, p. 223). The man Jack appoints his overseer mentions that he himself "struggl'd with hard fare" and endured "hard Lodging" when he was a servant; "Naked and Hungry, Weary and Faint, oppress'd with Cold in one Season, and Heat in the other," he "labour'd till Nature sometimes was just sinking under the Load" (*CJ*, p. 157). The overseer rushes over these physical pains to dwell instead on the fact that transportation has "deliver'd [him] from the horrid Temptation of Sinning," and he concludes that the "bless'd Calm of Soul" he has achieved by virtue of his servitude would "make any Man be thankful for *Virginia*" – but he adds, "or a worse Place, if that can be" (*CJ*, p. 157).

There is a significant elision in both *Moll Flanders* and *Colonel Jack*. For works which speak so glowingly about indentured servitude, they seem anxious to avoid portraying it. Moll buys herself and Jemy out of service while still in England; Jack's servitude is passed over quickly, his experiences in the Chesapeake not dramatized in any detail until he becomes an overseer and is living the life more of a master than of a servant. The only Defoe novel that actually portrays in any detail the wretched emotional toll of servitude and its physical misery of hard fare, hard lodging, and hard work is *Robinson Crusoe*, but, of course, servitude is figurative here, hovering in the background as a pattern of Crusoe's experiences and as a metaphor for their significance, and the novel is not "about" the plantation experience in the way *Moll Flanders* and *Colonel Jack* are. So in this way *Robinson Crusoe*, too, elides the experience of servitude as Defoe knew it.

Defoe was enthusiastic about the colonization of the New World. He rejected the proposition put forward by many of his contemporaries that the colonies profited at a cost to the mother country. England and her colonies were interdependent. "The Wealth and Strength of our Colonies is our own Wealth and our own Strength": "they are part of ourselves, and their Wealth is really our Wealth; we are Great in their Greatness, and Rich in their Encrease."[79] "If they die, we decay; if we decay, they die; if we cannot support them, they fail; if they fail, we must in Proportion sink; their Blood runs thro' our Veins, *I speak in the Language of Commerce,* is formed, centers and circulates just with ours."[80] Thus, it was in England's self-interest to be always "adding to the Power, Trade, Riches, and Numbers of People in our Collonies."[81]

This is the Way to raise new Worlds of Commerce, to enlarge and extend new Funds of Trade, to open Doors for an Encrease of Shipping and Manufacture; the Places are so many and the Advantages so great for the making such Attempts; that I say nothing is more wonderful of its kind, than to see how backward we are to push on our own Advantages, and to plant in the most agreeable Climates in the World, in a manner so advantageous as never to be supplanted, and such as should make the *English* Possessions abroad five Times as Great, as Opulent and as Profitable to Old *England,* as they have been yet.[82]

It was specifically planting with which Defoe was enamored. Spain, he thought, had been wrongheaded to mine the New World for silver and gold and not realize that a greater benefit could be derived from planting. Spain reaped but a "little Share ... from the Returns of Gold and Silver," while the English, inspired by their "improving ... Genius," "by the meer Force of indefatigable Application, planted, inhabited, cultivated those inhospitable Climates" and "brought them to be the richest, most improved, and most flourishing Colonies in all that Part of the World."[83] The exploitation of minerals extracted wealth, but plantations generated wealth and, by expanding production, demand, and trade, created the conditions that continued to generate more wealth, invigorating the whole of the British economy: "An Encrease of Colonies encreases People, People encrease the Consumption of Manufactures, Manufactures Trade, Trade Navigation, Navigation Seamen, and altogether encrease the Wealth, Strength and Prosperity of *England.*"[84] As a result, "more real wealth is brought into *Great Britain* every year from those Colonies, than is brought from the *Spanish West Indies* to *Old Spain* ... notwithstanding the vast quantity of gold and silver which they bring from the mines of *Mexico* and the mountains of *Potosi.*"[85]

Plantations benefitted the British economy in one other way. Indentured servitude and criminal transportation provided an important pool of labor for the colonial planters, rid England of troublesome felons, and, most importantly, created opportunity for the poor, who, through industry and diligence, could "begin the World on a new Foundation."

Here you dispose of your encreasing Numbers of Poor; they go there poor, and come back rich; there they plant, trade, thrive, and encrease; even your transported Felons, sent to *Virginia* instead of *Tyburn;* Thousands of them, if we are not misinform'd, have, by turning their Hands to Industry and Improvement, and, which is best of all, to Honesty, become rich substantial Planters and Merchants, settled large Families, and been famous in the Country; nay, we have seen many of them made Magistrates, Officers of Militia, Captains of the good Ships, and Masters of good Estates.

This Way therefore, I say, we dispose of the growing Numbers of our Poor to an inexpressible Advantage, as well as a private Advantage ... The Consequence of the diligent labouring Man there, is always this, that from a meer Labourer he becomes a Planter, and settles his Family upon the Land he gains, and so grows rich of Course.[86]

Defoe's championing of the colonial enterprise in the Americas and his excitement about the prospects of the New World spill over into his journalism and economic writings. Much of it finds its way into his novels, most obviously, as we have seen, in those moments when Moll's mother or Jack tout the economic opportunities of the Chesapeake or in the last half of *A New Voyage round the World*, where Defoe argues openly for English colonization of Patagonia. Sometimes, he is less obvious. "Planting is the Life ... of [the English] Settlements," he argues, and so in *Robinson Crusoe, Moll Flanders*, and *Colonel Jack* he links upward mobility not simply to colonial activity but specifically to planting (even risking the wild improbability of making Moll and Jack, both quintessentially urban people, become successful by growing tobacco).[87] It is not surprising, then, that many critics have concluded that these novels "may be regarded ... as economic propaganda for the planting of new English colonies and the continued development of those already established in North America and the West Indies"; they are "colonialist fictions," "not just novels but argumentative fiction designed to serve an imperial idea."[88]

But why, then, does Defoe make exaggerated claims for servitude even while betraying the fact that he knows his claims are overstated and perhaps false? Why does he assert that indentured servants succeed because of their industry and self-discipline but simultaneously construct plots that dramatize his protagonists succeeding for different reasons entirely?

Defoe must have made such glowing proclamations about opportunities in the New World because, on some level, he believed them to be true. He was hardly the only one to think so. The promotional tracts traded in such assurances, of course, but less biased travelers slipped into the same hyperbolic language Defoe used. And Defoe's optimism about prospects in the Chesapeake was not entirely a fantasy. Starting in 1713, prices for tobacco slowly began to revive and the economy showed signs of a renewed prosperity; prices peaked in 1719, just when Defoe had begun to publish his novels set in America. Others, too, must have thought that the Chesapeake was once again becoming a place of opportunity, for there was a brief resurgence in the number of immigrants who were willing to take a gamble on the colonies by becoming indentured servants. The recovery never became robust enough in Defoe's lifetime to make good on its promise, but he probably genuinely thought that the recovery was substantial, and he certainly thought trade in the Chesapeake, both in tobacco and in provisions to the Caribbean, was thriving again.[89]

Nor was Defoe's optimism about social mobility in the New World entirely baseless. For all its dwindling opportunities, it continued to offer possibilities to the poor that the Old World did not. Chesapeake society did not replicate that of England. The gentry and aristocracy had no important presence in the region, and the social structure had been pared down to a much simpler form. Many of the status markers of the Old World had not migrated with the new inhabitants, and the determinants of social status and mobility were reduced to their fundamentals. The most fundamental determinant was wealth. Defoe appears to have idealized this aspect of the Chesapeake, seeing it as a place where people's lives were not circumscribed by their class or by their pasts, where their status and mobility depended to a great degree on their talents and willpower.[90] Thus the story line of his novels set in America: Crusoe, Jack, and Moll seize hold of their lives when they come to the New World and raise themselves by hard work and determination.

But the idyllic Chesapeake Defoe portrays in *Moll Flanders* and *Colonel Jack* – a world so economically fluid and socially open that most immigrants of modest means might become independent plantation owners and even criminals and the poor had a chance of bettering their social status – had disappeared well before Defoe wrote his novels. The accumulation of land and wealth by those who were already economically and socially established, and above all the shift to a slave-based economy, meant that the society of the Tobacco Coast became more dominated by the creole gentry, more ruled by networks of blood and inheritance and open only to those who came to the region with reserves of money or access to credit to bankroll their success. And, curiously, Defoe seems to have known this, too. Thus, the second story line in his American novels, the one that shadows the first: Crusoe, Jack, and Moll succeed in the New World because they come with (or are given) large stocks of material goods and money.

Both these story lines, as contradictory as they are, give voice to some of Defoe's deepest commitments. His fables of the poor bootstrapping themselves to extraordinary levels of economic success spring, for instance, from his ideological conception of England's colonial project, from his faith in the invigorating force of trade, from his perception that, for the poor, the New World did in fact offer opportunities denied in the Old World, and most especially from his moral commitment to the virtue and efficacy of an individual's industry and diligence. And what does that second story line speak to, that plot in which the success of the protagonist turns on his having a stock of wealth to jump-start his climb to success? In part, it springs from his perception that the realities of success in America were more complicated than he sometimes cared to admit. And it springs from something else, too. Consider the case of *Robinson Crusoe*. At the end of the novel, Crusoe finds himself "Master, all on a Sudden, of above 5000*l.* *Sterling* in Money, and ... an Estate ... in the *Brasils,* of above a thousand Pounds a Year" (*RC,* p. 269). And where does this estate come from? Well, first, from the £200 he left with the captain's widow, the wife of his "first Benefactor" (*RC,* p. 270). Next, from another "Benefactor," the "generous" Portuguese captain who rescues Crusoe, who gives him 220 pieces of eight (*RC,* p. 269). By means of this money, Crusoe acquires land, implements, slaves, and servants, and establishes his plantation in Brazil. And his plantation grows while he is absent on his island – due to the "Integrity" of his partner, the "just Dealings" of the Monastery of St. Augustine, and the "very fair honest" management of the trustees and their survivors (*RC,* pp. 271, 266). This plantation, provided and superintended by generous benefactors, is an "Estate that Providence had ... put into my Hands," and it is obviously analogous to that stock of goods from the ship which is given to Crusoe by "the Goodness of Providence" (*RC,* pp. 269, 153). Thus, the novel is cunningly constructed so that Crusoe's labor and his profit operate in parallel universes, as it were; while Crusoe works on his figurative plantation on the island, he reaps the reward of that labor on his real plantation in Brazil. As a consequence, his reward seems both to be and not to be the result of his work.

In *Robinson Crusoe,* then, the story of transportation, servitude, and planting dramatizes Crusoe's success through self-mastery, initiative, and willpower, and it also plots out a religious trajectory of sin, punishment, and salvation, a providential narrative in which Crusoe's success is a reward bestowed by unmerited grace. In this, Defoe is not naively contradicting himself, for it is precisely the conundrum of human free will coexisting with an overarching Providence that he seeks to explore in *Robinson Crusoe,* and he used the two story lines, both drawn from his knowledge of the colonial situation, to set the framework for this exploration.

The money and goods that Jack and Moll bring to the Chesapeake do not function, as they do in *Robinson Crusoe,* as part of a hidden providential design in their lives. The stocks of both protagonists, though crucial to their successful rise, have a completely different significance. Nevertheless, as I hope to show, what Jack and Moll bring to the New World allows Defoe to dramatize, once again, the same knotted problem of human freedom and the web of necessity he dramatized in *Robinson Crusoe,* but in these two novels, a web of necessity woven not by divine Providence but by large social forces, overwhelming economic pressures, crass circumstance, and psychological need.

In his fictional America, Defoe repeatedly plays out variations of this drama of freedom and necessity, and it is remarkable how few other colonial issues we know Defoe was interested in are broached in these novels, issues such as whether emigration might depopulate England to its economic detriment, whether colonial manufacturers would undermine the economy of the mother country, whether colonists would break away from England and declare their independence – all issues debated at the time and issues with which Defoe was passionately engaged. Even more surprisingly, with the exception of *A New Voyage round the World* and the last episode of *Colonel Jack,* questions of trade are quite muted, though Defoe knew the importance of trade for English colonization and wrote about it extensively.

What is noticeable about his use of America as a setting is how tightly focused Defoe is. He frames *Robinson Crusoe, Moll Flanders,* and *Colonel Jack* identically: all three are narratives of moral, material, and spiritual regeneration, a regeneration he dramatizes in his protagonists' relationship to indentured servitude, for indentured servitude neatly figured the trajectory of regeneration as he conceived it, from a life determined by necessity to a life of freedom, from a life enslaved to forces both inside and outside the self to a life in which the self is master. I believe this is why Africans play a significant role in *Colonel Jack* and Indian cannibals in *Robinson Crusoe.* They are important to Defoe's symbolic narrative because, as in so many narratives that grew out of the circum-Atlantic world, the freedom and mastery of Europeans were imagined against the savage Other, for savages were unfree and were meant to be mastered.[91]

In all three novels, the transformation from servant to master is a spiritual, moral, or psychological transformation as well as a social and material one. In *Moll Flanders* and *Colonel Jack,* Defoe exploits the genre of criminal biography, working against its simple-minded formulae and evasions in order to push the examination of criminality both further inward to more complex psychological and moral levels as well as further outward to a more comprehensive analysis of the social and economic causes and consequences of transgression.[92] I think that Defoe saw the same two possibilities in the colonial plot of transportation, servitude, and planting. In their figurative reaches, these colonial experiences gave readers access to the interiority of their novels' characters, revealing their conditions and plotting out their psychological progress. But transportation, servitude, and planting were material and economic actualities, and the way they worked, literally, was revelatory of broader, complex social and economic realities that determined human life, and perhaps liberated it. Because colonial experience could be pushed in both directions, as it were, inward and outward, I think that Defoe found in it a compelling language – a rhetoric, a system of symbols, a pattern of emblematic events – that would also speak to the complex interpenetration of man's spiritual and material condition.

Defoe's exploration of this complex reality inevitably becomes at times opaque and snarled. Often, his toggling back and forth between a literal, material world and a psychological, moral, and spiritual world is confusing, occasionally inept. These worlds follow quite different economies, and Defoe tries to make indentured servitude fulfill so many disparate roles and functions in his American novels that it is not surprising that fissures and contradictions appear. Sometimes, the language of transportation, servitude, and planting simply collapses under the burden of trying to signify so much.

It is precisely because of these difficulties that Defoe's America needs to be taken seriously. We have an opportunity to understand Defoe's America – that imagined world that he used to give shape to his ideas, anxieties, and aspirations – by playing it against the historical America. Defoe knew more than is commonly acknowledged about the colonies, and by being attentive to the historical details that make their way into his fiction, we can see the elements he drew on to construct his vision. Occasionally, he knowingly misrepresented what he knew about America, and there is a lot he did not know, but here, too, it is valuable to contrast his America to what we know about the historical condition of the real one, for that contrast clarifies the lineaments of Defoe's imagination. What I will do in the following chapters is examine the way Defoe represents Indians, Africans, and especially white indentured servants in the New World, and how he engaged the promise of America for freedom and mastery. I will set the New World experience next to Defoe's representation of it in an attempt to specify what he knew about America and what he did not know, what he falsely believed and what he knowingly falsified, what he made use of and what he suppressed – all as a way of illuminating his purpose in his American novels.

CHAPTER 2

Mastering the savage: conversion in
Robinson Crusoe

Robinson Crusoe is a colonial novel and a religious novel. It simultaneously traces the spiritual regeneration of its protagonist and reflects on England's colonial venture in the New World. In important respects, these two stories are parallel. Both are plotted out in terms of mastery – Crusoe's mastery of the wilderness of his island and his mastery of his own sinful nature, that wilderness within. In both of these stories, cannibals play a central role. In the story of Crusoe's religious awakening, they are the savage Other against whom his spiritual and psychological growth is measured. In the story of England's colonial project, they embody the wilderness England's settlers had to come to terms with. In both stories, they are disturbing presences.

Crusoe is "perfectly confounded and amaz'd" when he stumbles on evidence of cannibals on his island, "seeing the Shore spread with Skulls, Hands, Feet, and other Bones of humane Bodies" (*RC,* p. 178). He struggles to quiet his confusion and fear by fortifying his "Castle" and by daily climbing the hill above it to keep a constant watch (*RC,* p. 179). He indulges in fantasies of "a bloody putting twenty or thirty of them to the Sword" (*RC,* pp. 181–182). Gradually, he calms himself enough to entertain some tentative speculations about the cannibals.

As long as I kept up my daily Tour to the Hill, to look out; so long also I kept up the Vigour of my Design, and my Spirits seem'd to be all the while in a suitable Form, for so outragious an Execution as the killing twenty or thirty naked Savages, for an Offence which I had not at all entred into a Discussion of in my Thoughts, any farther than my Passions were at first fir'd by the Horror I conceiv'd at the unnatural Custom of that People of the Country, who it seems had been suffer'd by Providence in his wise Disposition of the World, to have no other Guide than that of their own abominable and vitiated Passions; and consequently were left, and perhaps had been so for some Ages, to act such horrid Things, and receieve such dreadful Customs, as nothing but Nature entirely abandon'd of Heaven, and acted by some hellish Degeneracy, could have run them into. (*RC,* p. 182)

This is something of a muddle. Cannibalism, Crusoe speculates, is a natural impulse (a "Passion" that springs from "nothing but Nature") and yet he also says that it is "unnatural." And then he implies that cannibalism is not a natural impulse at all but the product of acculturation, a "Custom" (he uses the word twice). And finally, as if to leave no inconsistency unarticulated, he offers a third explanation, and this, too, is contradictory. Although cannibalism proceeds from "nothing but Nature," it is "suffer'd by Providence in his wise Disposition of the World" and therefore must be implicated somehow in the supernatural.

Such a thicket of contradictions is understandable. After all, Crusoe is reeling in terror from the sight of the dismembered bodies scattered on the shore. But there is another possibility. Perhaps these contradictions are Defoe's, not Crusoe's, and perhaps they are less contradictory than they appear. Perhaps what seem to be contradictions are better understood as complex tensions and paradoxes by which Defoe (and others of his time) thought through ideas about human nature, civilization, and divine purpose that were deeply unsettled by the Europeans' experience of the New World.

Consider, for instance, the apparently contradictory statements that cannibalism springs from "nothing but Nature" and yet is "unnatural." If cannibalism is natural, why does Crusoe experience his disgust as an "Aversion which Nature gave me," and why does he vomit at the sight of "the horrid Spectacle" as if his abhorrence were so natural that it is, literally, visceral? "My Stomach grew sick, and I was just at the Point of Fainting, when Nature discharg'd the Disorder from my Stomach" (*RC*, pp. 178–179).

So which is natural, cannibalism or the aversion to cannibalism? Well, cannibalism must be natural, for Defoe says so in this passage, or more precisely, he says that it springs from "nothing but Nature ... acted by some hellish Degeneracy." "Nature," in this instance, must mean "Degeneracy" from some higher state. And since he says that the cannibals are driven not by their passions, but by their "vitiated Passions" – that is, by passions which, like "Nature," have degenerated – "nothing but Nature" must mean that cannibalism springs from energies, appetites, and passions native to human beings, but energies, appetites, and passions that are expressed in actions so base, so degenerate, that they are at degree zero of our humanity, the lowest point to which our natural passions can sink and still be within the boundaries of human nature. Cannibalism, Defoe says, is the ultimate "Degeneracy of Humane Nature" (*RC*, p. 178).

But how, then, can cannibalism be conceived of as "unnatural"? Nature, no matter what the degree of its "Degeneracy," is nature still, and passions, no matter how "vitiated," are still natural. The seeming contradiction must spring from Defoe's assumption that human beings have the capacity to understand what kind of behavior is appropriate, good, or simply useful and that they have the capacity to control and shape their appetites and passions to those ends. This capacity is inherent to human beings, every bit as natural as the passions themselves. If cannibalism is natural, so too is Crusoe's aversion to it.

Thus, cannibalism can be understood as being both natural and unnatural. The behavior of the cannibals is natural in the sense that it is driven by energies and passions that are inherent; the cannibals' allowing themselves to be governed by these appetites, however, is unnatural, for they have other faculties and powers, also inherent, also natural, whose function is to govern these appetites, and in failing to govern them, they fail to fulfill their natural potential.

This play of "natural" and "unnatural" is grounded in a traditional conception of human nature that sees us comprised of a lower stratum of energies, passions, and appetites and a higher stratum of faculties such as reason and conscience, faculties whose function it is to restrain and guide those passions and energies. Dynamically suspended between the two, human beings, as Defoe says, are "mixt up of a Nature convertible and pervertible, capable indeed of infinite Excellence ... but subject likewise to Corruption and Degeneracy."[1] Framing the matter this starkly, however, implies that degeneracy results when the higher faculties are eclipsed and the passions are set loose to follow their native trajectories. But degeneracy is *not* the result of passion liberated from any restraint. In the traditional moral psychology that was still widely credited in the early eighteenth century, the passions, even at their most degenerate, are always directed by the higher faculties.[2] It is the function of the higher faculties to determine the appropriate ends the passions should pursue and to articulate the shape they should take in pursuing those ends. If the faculties choose wisely, the passions are channeled into forms of behavior that are good and useful; if the higher faculties choose badly or if they are impaired in some way, the passions are channeled into forms that are not good or useful. But, whatever the case, it is always the higher faculties that shape the passions, never the passions that shape themselves. Like the fish in the Chinese proverb, human beings rot from the head downward.

Even in extreme instances such as cannibalism, the higher faculties, not the passions, cause degeneracy. The specific passion that drives cannibalism, according to Defoe, is "martial Rage" (*SR*, p. 137), that is to say, revenge.[3] Revenge, obviously, can be expressed in other ways than by devouring an enemy's body – by burning an enemy's town, say, or by decimating the enemy's troops. Although revenge is an inherent passion, then, like all passions it is formulated into specific habits of behavior by the higher faculties, and among the cannibals the particular habit of behavior the higher faculties have shaped this passion into is "the wretched inhuman Custom of … eating one another up" (*RC*, p. 179). And so, Defoe's assertion that cannibalism is a "Custom" does not at all contradict his assertion that cannibalism proceeds from "nothing but Nature." Cannibalism is natural in the sense that it arises from an inborn appetite, the desire for revenge, but this natural desire is given a specific shape and direction by the habits of an individual or by the customs and rituals instilled by society. In short, as a cultural formulation of an appetite, cannibalism is both a product of nature and a custom, a natural impulse and yet a "Ceremony" (*RC*, p. 181). This, I take it, is what Defoe's talk of "Degeneracy" and "vitiated Passions" means: it is the higher faculties that have degenerated and, having become corrupt, the behaviors they mold those passions into are depraved and corrupt, too.

Finally, the contradiction of the third assertion – that although cannibalism is natural, it has supernatural causes – is also more apparent than real and actually dovetails with Defoe's other explanations. Cannibalism proceeds from "nothing but Nature," but it is, Defoe says, a "Nature entirely abandon'd of Heaven." For, though cannibalism acts out natural appetites, its precipitating cause is supernatural: the withdrawal of God of His presence. God has "sentenc'd [the cannibals] to Absence from himself"; their "barbarous Customs [are] … a Token indeed of God's having left them … to such Stupidity, and to such inhumane Courses" (*RC*, pp. 212, 228). Now, cannibals have the "same Powers, the same Reason, the same Affections … [and] the same Passions" (*RC*, p. 212) as civilized Europeans. But when God abandons them, He withholds from them His enlightenment, which illuminates reason so that humans can act at the highest level of their capacity. Abandoned and unenlightened, the cannibals lose sight of the "best Uses to which their Faculties, and the Powers of their Souls are adapted" and can no longer conceive of the "right Uses" to which they should put their passions (*RC*, p. 212). Because of their "Stupidity" – the darkness caused by God's absence – they are incapable of formulating patterns of behavior, habits of action, or institutions that direct their appetites and energies to their best and highest ends. Unenlightened, they become morally and intellectually stupid, and they channel their natural passion of revenge into the "inhumane Custom" of cannibalism.

This is a remarkable and telling sentence in *Robinson Crusoe*. Its contradictions are more apparent than real, or, if it is contradictory, Defoe uses these contradictions to articulate a complex, coherent explanation of cannibalism. Cannibalism is natural because it is driven by energies and passions inherent in human nature; unnatural, because it transgresses the equally inherent capacity to regulate those energies and passions; customary, because those energies and passions are molded into their brutish and inhuman form by cultural practices and habits, and supernatural, because when God withdraws His presence, He no longer illuminates reason to help it construct cultural practices and habits that answer to the "right Uses" of their appetites and energies.

In the sentence I have been examining, Defoe dramatizes Crusoe's struggle to understand how the cannibals are different from civilized Europeans. But the same sentence reveals how, in some surprising ways, the European Crusoe is the same as the cannibals – as only makes sense since the cannibals share the same "convertible and pervertible" human nature that he does. And so, I would like to examine the sentence again, this time in the context of the entire paragraph of which it is a part.

As long as I kept up my daily Tour to the Hill, to look out; so long also I kept up the Vigour of my Design, and my Spirits seem'd to be all the while in a suitable Form, for so outragious an Execution as the killing twenty or thirty naked Savages, for an Offence which I had not at all entred into a Discussion of in my Thoughts, any farther than my Passions were at first fir'd by the Horror I conceiv'd at the unnatural Custom of that People of the Country, who it seems had been suffer'd by Providence in his wise Disposition of the World, to have no other Guide than that of their own abominable and vitiated Passions; and consequently were left, and perhaps had been so for some Ages, to act such horrid Things, and receive such dreadful Customs, as nothing but Nature entirely abandon'd of Heaven, and acted by some hellish Degeneracy, could have run them into: But now, when as I have said, I began to weary of the fruitless Excursion, which I had made so long, and so far, every Morning in vain, so my Opinion of the Action it self began to alter, and I began with cooler and calmer Thoughts to consider what I was going to engage in. What Authority, or Call I had, to pretend to be Judge and Executioner upon these Men as Criminals, whom Heaven had thought fit for so many Ages to suffer unpunish'd, to go on, and to be as it were, the Executioners of his Judgments one upon another. How far these People were Offenders against me, and what Right I had to engage in the Quarrel of that Blood, which they shed promiscuously one upon another, I debated this very often with my self thus; How do I know what God himself judges in this particular Case; it is certain these People either do not commit this as a Crime; it is not against their own Consciences reproving, or their Light reproaching them. They do not know it be an Offence, and then commit it in Defiance of Divine Justice, as we do in almost all the Sins we commit. They think it no more a Crime to kill a Captive taken in War, than we do to kill an Ox; nor to eat humane Flesh, than we do to eat Mutton. (*RC,* pp. 182–183)

In this paragraph, Crusoe swings between his lower energies and passions and his higher faculties, entangling himself in the very savagery he perceives in the cannibals and at the same time distinguishing himself from them as a civilized being.

From the moment of his landing on the island and long before he saw the cannibals, Crusoe has been struggling to order his passions, and he had achieved considerable composure by the time he saw the footprint. But when he sees evidence of the cannibals, he loses the self-possession he has painstakingly worked for. He begins to destroy the civilization he has constructed, proposing to himself "to throw down my Enclosures, and to turn all my tame Cattle wild into the Woods, that the Enemy might not find them" (*RC,* p. 174). He begins to degenerate into a savage. "Fir'd by the Horror" of what he has seen, debilitated by the "Confusion of [his] Thoughts" (*RC,* p. 175), gripped by fear, he abandons his reason, no longer using his higher faculties to consider the "right Uses" to which he should put his energies. Instead, he delivers himself over to his imagination, which shapes his "murthering Humour" (*RC,* p. 192) into irrational and immoral plans of action. To the cannibals' "bloody Doings," he responds with "bloody Schemes" of his own (*RC,* pp. 182, 184). And not only does he end up as bloodthirsty as the savages, but he ends up being driven by the very same "vitiated Passion" that has driven them to cannibalism: "my Mind," Crusoe acknowledges, "was ... fill'd with Thoughts of Revenge" (*RC,* p. 181).

Crusoe has had the savage in him from the beginning. Defoe's emphasizing Crusoe's "rambling" or "wandring Inclination" (*RC,* pp. 57, 58) can hardly have been accidental given the novel's New World setting, for Europeans thought that the Indians of America were savage precisely because they were "a shifting, wandering People."[4] To the English mind, the sign of the cultural primitiveness of the Amerindians was that they had no settlements, that, in the notorious assessment of Robert Cushman, they did but "run over the grass as do also the foxes and wild beasts."[5] This is Crusoe's unregenerate impulse, too, and the fact that Defoe calls it his "ORIGINAL SIN" is a reminder that Europeans by nature are the same as the cannibals. Everyone, Crusoe and cannibals alike, share a "native Propensity to rambling" that is "*bred in the Bone*" (*RC,* p. 200; *FA,* p. 5).

In the passage we are looking at, Crusoe's degeneration into savagery reaches its nadir. "Fill'd with Thoughts of Revenge," he considers "so outragious an Execution as the killing of twenty or Thirty naked savages." Yet, if Crusoe is similar to the cannibals in his bloody schemes for revenge, his very ability here to assess that impulse as "outragious" shows that he is beginning to distinguish himself from them. The cannibals are given over to their passions. Crusoe, though seized by his passions, is *also* acting out of the higher stratum of his nature when he judges his passions as "outragious." His self-condemnation springs from his knowledge of his own potential and of the "right Uses" of his energies. Those same higher faculties which "naturally" made Crusoe feel an "Aversion" to the cannibals make him censure his own impulses. Having judged his own passions as "outragious," Crusoe begins to control them, delivering himself from their power. He enters, as he says, into a "Discussion" with them until, "with cooler and calmer Thoughts," he begins "to consider what it was I was going to engage in."

This drama of Crusoe's descent into savagery and his recovery from it is played out in a second way. As the paragraph opens, Crusoe is governed by the passion of revenge, and it turns out that his passion has been conditioned, much like the cannibals' has. For Crusoe has formulated his passion as a "Design," has disciplined it into a "suitable Form." This is not an unstructured impulse but a custom, a piece of behavior routinized as a "daily Tour to the Hill." And, further, it is this habit that keeps the passion alive, not the passion that sustains the habit: "As long as I kept up my daily Tour to the Hill, to look out; so long also I kept up the Vigours of my Design" (*RC*, p. 182).

Like the cannibals, Crusoe is driven by an "unnatural Custom," but even here, when it seems that he has degenerated to the same level as the savages, Crusoe once again shows that he is capable of rising above them. For he breaks the tyranny of his own habit and thus loosens its hold over him: "When ... I began to be weary of the fruitless Excursion ... so my Opinion of the Action it self began to alter" (*RC*, pp. 182–183). Sensing how fruitless his habitual behavior is, he frees himself from it and consequently from the fears and schemes which that habit has shaped and enforced, and this allows him to examine the matter with "cooler and calmer Thoughts." He concludes that, in "laying ... bloody Schemes for the Destruction of innocent Creatures," he had been on the verge of committing "no less a Sin, than that of wilful Murthur" (*RC*, p. 184). And he attributes his success in elevating himself out of his own savagery to his liberating himself from his habit:

I never once went up the Hill to see whether there were any of them in Sight, or to know whether any of them had been on Shore there, or not, *that I might not be tempted to renew any of my Contrivances against them,* or be provok'd by any Advantage which might present it self, to fall upon them. (*RC,* p. 185; my italics)

In *Serious Reflections during the Life and Surprising Adventures of Robinson Crusoe,* Defoe proposes that the way to convert savages is to "unchain the Wills of Men, set their Inclinations free, that their Reason may be at Liberty to influence their Understandings, and that they may have the Faith of Christ preach'd to them" (*SR,* p. 210). The conversion of the savages should begin, significantly, with the suppression of their pagan customs. Here, in just a few phrases, is the logic of savagery, civilization, and conversion in *Robinson Crusoe.* The cannibals' inclinations are *not* free because they have been formulated as customs and habitual usages. Unenlightened, reason cannot argue against these powerful formulations, and, consequently, the will is chained, doomed to act out the passions in their degenerate form, again and again. But when a custom is broken, reason can consider other ways to meet the self's needs and to express its impulses, and the will is liberated to act out new behavior directed by reason. Defoe thought that savages could be converted by means of "inform'd Nature," a phrase which I understand to mean that their reason naturally has the capacity to see the truth once they have been liberated from their darkness and stupidity.[6] This is certainly true of that other savage, Crusoe. Once he frees himself from his customary "Tour of the Hill," he frees his reason to consider other ways of acting on his impulses; his understanding quickly grasps the "right Uses" of his powers, and he wills himself to act to realize them.

But in the end, is it reason alone that allows Crusoe to free himself from his custom? In the paragraphs that follow his resolution to rein in his savage passions, his actual thinking out of that decision is presented as if it were wholly the result of his reflecting on the matter soberly and rationally. I quote from the head of each paragraph that marks each turn of his reasoning:

"When I had consider'd this a little, it follow'd necessarily, that ..."
"In the next Place it occurr'd to me, that ..."
"These Considerations really put me to a Pause, and to a kind of Full-stop; and I began by little and little to be off of my Design, and to conclude ..."
"On the other hand, I argu'd with my self, That ..."
"Upon the whole I concluded, That ..." (*RC,* pp. 183–184)

After hearing him speak so insistently about how he reasoned through his decision, it comes as a real surprise that Crusoe attributes his success in raising himself above his savagery not to the powers of his own mind but to the intervention of supernatural forces:

Nothing was a greater Satisfaction to me, than that I had not been suffer'd to do a Thing which I now saw so much Reason to believe would have been no less a Sin, than that of wilful Murther, if I had committed it; and I gave most humble Thanks on my Knees to God, that had thus deliver'd me from Blood-Guiltiness. (*RC,* p. 184)

Crusoe has become as savage as the cannibals, but the one thing that distinguishes him from them is that he has not been abandoned by God. Cannibals and Christians may both share the same power of reason and the same capacities of doing good, but it is only the Christians, Crusoe says, who are "enlighten'd by the great Lamp of Instruction, the Spirit of God, and by the Knowledge of his Word, added to our Understanding" (*RC,* p. 212). It is true that earlier in his life Crusoe was as "Stupid" as the cannibals. When he takes ill soon after arriving at the island, he confesses "a certain Stupidity of Soul, without Desire of Good, or Conscience of Evil, had entirely overwhelm'd me," that he was "meerly thoughtless of a God, or a Providence; [and] acted like a meer Brute from the Principles of Nature" (*RC,* pp. 122–123). In that state of stupidity, his laughing off the fear of God "grew habitual to me," and these habits "harden'd" him and, in his "hardned Life," he became locked in unreasoned habitual behaviors, much like the savages (*RC,* p. 154). But God has never "sentenc'd" Crusoe, as He has the cannibals, "to Absence from himself." Crusoe can perceive his own stupidity precisely because God has made Himself present by means of a visionary dream, by providing him with a bible, by provoking him with twinges of conscience, by providentially shaping his life in legible patterns, and most of all by being present within the European Christian culture that Crusoe comes from. Thus illuminated by God, Crusoe becomes conscious of his own spiritual darkness and thinks himself out of it. So, too, his dealing with the fear of the cannibals. Although he does reason himself out of his bad passions and bad habits, he does so only within the context of divine Providence. The rational conclusion he reaches, he reaches naturally – that is to say, through the free exercise of his inherent intelligence – but he is able to exercise his higher faculties only because of a supernatural dispensation: "I had not been suffer'd to do a Thing which … would have been … a Sin." God providentially has kept the savages from the island to allow Crusoe a breathing space in which to exercise his natural reason, but a natural reason that is "inform'd" by the presence of God.

In the paragraph I have been examining, the sequence is *not* that Crusoe reasons about the morality of his impulse to kill the cannibals and *then* breaks the custom of his "daily Tour to the Hill," and *then* providentially is delivered from both the cannibals and his own sinful impulse. The sequence is exactly the opposite: Providence shapes events so that Crusoe sees that his custom is fruitless and abandons it; *this* frees him from the tyranny of his impulse; and *that* allows him enough self-composure to reason out his moral position and to reach a conclusion that is consonant with the will of Providence.

> But now, when … I began to weary of the fruitless Excursion, which I had made so long, and so far, every Morning in vain, so my Opinion of the Action it self began to alter, and I began with cooler and calmer Thoughts to consider what it was I was going to engage in.

What happens here is paradigmatic of Crusoe's whole island existence. The supernatural surrounds the natural, prompting or tolerating the impulses and potentials that are natural in human beings. The self, "mixed up of a Nature convertible and pervertible," acts freely (degenerating if it does not control its appetites or regenerating itself through its rational control of the passions) within the space given it by the sufferance of Providence.[7]

Implicit in the drama of Crusoe's coming to terms with the savage cannibals and with his own savagery is the assumption that savages and Europeans are both similar and different, and this assumption has a profound effect on Defoe's colonial thinking. Savages are different from Europeans because they are degenerate. But since all human beings share a common nature, since all are "capable … of infinite Excellence" as well as "subject … to … Degeneracy," savages are not simply different from Europeans, they are also the same.

When Defoe justifies the English colonial venture in *Robinson Crusoe,* he does so by appealing to this fluid dynamic of sameness and difference, and on the same foundation he will model a specific policy to govern relations between English colonists and New World natives.[8] All of this is an impressive achievement, but it is by no means original with him. Such thinking was at the heart of one strain of ideological argument from the outset of England's colonial activity, and Defoe engages this line of thinking as part of his own colonial argument.

Like Defoe, many English thinkers vindicated the colonial enterprise on the basis of the savages' similarity to the Europeans. Savages had "the same Maker" as Englishmen; they were of "the same matter, the same mould"; they shared "the same constitution."[9] And because "we all have *Adam* for our common parent," it followed that the savages of the New

World had the same intellectual capacities the Europeans had. They were reasonable, or at least they had the potential for reason: "One God created us, they have reasonable soules and intellectual faculties as well as wee."[10] Because they were essentially the same as Europeans, they were educable, convertible. They could be civilized and Christianized, for, though they were degenerate and under the influence of the Devil, "their souls are fit Materials which may be easily polish't."[11]

This similarity underwrote one of the strongest early justifications for colonial expansion. Colonialism would bring civility and true religion to the New World natives. "For to posterity no greater glory can be handed down," Hakluyt wrote, "than to conquer the barbarian, to recall the savage and the pagan to civility, to draw the ignorant within the orbit of reason, and to fill with reverence for divinity the godless and the ungodly."[12] Colonizing the New World would result in "the gaining and winning to Christ his fold, and the reducing unto a civill societie ... of so many thousands of those sillie, brutish, and ignorant soules, now fast bound with the claimes of error and ignorance, under the bondage and slavery of the Divell."[13] Indeed, since the Indians are the *"degenerate Part of our Race,"* "for the *Glory* of our Common MAKER," colonists have the duty to *"root out"* their vicious Habits, and to change their whole Way of Living."[14]

History, too, argued for the Indians' similarity to the Europeans and for the benefits of colonization. The English acknowledged that they themselves were "once as uncivil as they in Virginia."[15] "Were not *Caesars Britains* as brutish as Virginians?" William Strachey asked.[16] Did not the Britons once live "as naked, and as beastly as they ... rude and untutored, wandring in the woodes, dwelling in Caves, and hunting for our dynners, (as the wyld beasts in the forrests for their prey,) ... nay eating our own Children?"[17] And they would have remained "brutish, poore, and naked Britaines to this day, if *Iulius Caesar* with his Romane Legions ... had not laid the ground to make us tame and civil."[18]

Just as the English were civilized under the discipline of a superior culture – taught by the Romans "the powerfull discourse of divine Reason (which makes us only men, and distinguisheth us from beasts)" – so the Indians, equal in potential, would flower under the guidance of the English.[19] "It is not the nature of men," wrote Robert Gray, "but the education of men, which make[s] them barbarous and uncivill ... Chaunge the education of men, and you shall see that their nature will be greatly rectified and corrected."[20] John Eliot thought that the natives possessed "a great measure of natural ingenuity and ingeniousity" that had been "drowned out in their wild and rude manner of living," "but by culture, order, government, and religion they begin to be furbished up."[21] One of the conclusions Crusoe draws from observing Friday is that God has

bestow'd upon [the cannibals] the same Powers, the same Reason, the same Affections, the same Sentiments of Kindness and Obligation, the same Passions and Resentments of Wrongs; the same Sense of Gratitude, Sincerity, Fidelity, and all the Capacities of doing Good, and receiving Good, that he has given to us. (*RC,* p. 212)

Because of this sameness, Crusoe can school Friday in civility and Christianity.

Yet, for all their similarities, it is obvious that the savages are different from the Europeans – and inferior to them. They are not civilized. The generally accepted sign of the savages' uncivility was their failure to cultivate the land. Indians "inclose noe land," John Winthrop observed, "neither have any setled habytation, nor any tame Cattle to improve the land by."[22] In *Robinson Crusoe,* the cannibals' savagery is manifested by their peripatetic lives and their consumption of human flesh instead of the meat of tame cattle. Crusoe's relationship to the land is exactly the opposite. His obsession with fences, which we tend to see as symptoms of pathological fears, to Defoe are signs of his civility: his fences "inclose ... land" and thus become the basis of his "settled habytation" and the means by which he "tame[s] Cattle," all of which set him above the cannibals. For the English, constructing fences, both as a symbol and as a cultural practice, signified claiming land from the wilderness, improving it, and many English justified their seizing land in the New World on the grounds that it was waste land, unplowed, unfenced, and unsettled.[23]

Crusoe builds fences not because he is a superior person but because he comes from a superior culture. His desire to settle and enclose the land does not spring from a nature that is different from the cannibals' or from capacities the cannibals do not have. It is something he brought with him from England, like those tools he salvages from the wreck, which keep him from sinking into savagery on the island. Crusoe is different from the cannibals because God has not abandoned him or his culture. Enlightened by God and by the models of civility encoded in the customs and usages of his culture (many of them instituted, sanctioned, and sustained by God), Crusoe can look about himself intelligently and guide his conduct accordingly.

Yet, the savages are capable of the same achievements that make the Europeans superior. If the English in their difference are superior, they are justified in subjecting the savages – but they are justified in doing so because the savages are similar to them and therefore can be raised to the same level of religious enlightenment, civility, and moral development. The English raised themselves out of their own savagery by creating or adopting habits, customs, and institutions that shaped and controlled their impulses, and they can raise the natives from their savage condition by imposing forms of order and dominion on them. Colonizing the savages bestows on them the gifts of civilization and salvation which, because of their difference, they do not possess but which, because of their similarity, they are capable of possessing.

Because they are as reasonable as the English, natives can grasp quickly the advantages of adopting new beliefs and customs of an obviously superior culture. They are "apte to submytte them selves to good government" and "very ready to leave their old and blind idolatries and to learn of [the English] the right service and worship of the true God."[24] Because of their very sameness to the English, they would recognize their own cultural inferiority and could be "brought to our Civilitie … in short time."[25] They would convert, and they would convert eagerly. Though Friday is "a Cannibal in his Nature," he is taught by Crusoe to overcome his desire to eat human flesh, and he becomes "a good Christian" (*RC*, pp. 210, 220) so quickly and easily because he possesses the same reasoning capacities as Crusoe. Seeing the advantages of European civilization, he submits himself willingly to Crusoe in order to deliver himself from his own savagery. Philip Vincent, in a typical expression of colonial optimism, wrote about the natives that "Their correspondency of disposition with us, argueth all to be of the same constitution … Only Art and Grace have given us that perfection, which yet they want, but may perhaps be as capable thereof as wee."[26] Defoe shared Vincent's belief that it was only "Art and Grace" that separated the civilized from the savage. What Friday and the cannibals lack is the "Art" of Europe – those structures of beliefs and customs, those institutions that collectively define a civilized society. And they lack "Grace," God's withholding of which has put and kept them in their "Stupidity," that mental and spiritual darkness that has prevented them from constructing the beliefs, customs, and institutions that would raise them out of their savagery.

And yet, European culture was not uniformly superior. All human beings are "subject … to Corruption and Degeneracy," and Europeans, like savages, could degenerate. To the English, the colonial exemplars of this degeneration were the Spanish, who had expropriated Indian wealth by rape, murder, and plunder. When the English fashioned for themselves an image of their own colonial ventures, they distinguished their practices from the despotic and inhumane behavior of the Spanish. The English saw themselves not as conquerors or exploiters but as planters who brought with them the peaceful, profitable practices of a superior culture, practices the savages were eager to embrace and practices to which the English were eager to convert them. By 1700, as Anthony Pagden has shown, the "belief that theirs had been peaceful settlements mutually beneficent to both immigrant and native" had achieved widespread orthodoxy in England, as did the feeling "that they had, indeed, fulfilled some of their much acclaimed ambition to create a new, more virtuous social order in the New World."[27] The English, Defoe wrote, came to the New World as "Benefactors, rather than Conquerors" (*SR*, p. 218). Friday becomes a servant to Crusoe, but he becomes a servant freely, trading his freedom for the manifest advantages of a higher culture, and Crusoe repays Friday for his submission with gentle instruction in the arts of civilization and the truth of Christianity.

The ideological posture of the English, particularly in the initial phase of their colonization of the New World, was to advocate fair and humane treatment of the natives. Hakluyt argued that the best way to bring the savages "from the darknes[s] to light" was to eschew the cruelty of the Spaniards and instead to treat the natives with "all humanitie, curtesie, and freedome."[28] If the natives were dealt with fairly, they would "revolte cleane from the Spaniard" and "yelde themselves" to the English."[29] "A gentle course without crueltie and tyrannie best answereth the profession of a Christian, best planteth Christian religion; maketh our seating most void of blood, most profitable in trade of merchandise, most firme and stable, and least subject to remove by practice of enemies."[30] Hakluyt's position was echoed in the propaganda of the Virginia Company, who in their promotional literature portrayed the Indians sympathetically and the possibilities of the interaction between them and the English optimistically, and it became the official policy of the Puritans as they moved into New England.

But it was Sir Walter Ralegh who first acted out this policy concretely – and perhaps not coincidentally in the mouth of the Orinoco where Crusoe's island is. According to Ralegh, the Orinoco was a region of incalculable wealth, of "gold" and "abundance," of "rich and bewtifull cities," of "temples adorned with golden Images," and of "more sepulchers filled with treasure then either *Cortez* found in *Mexico,* or *Pazzarro* in *Peru*."[31] Ralegh presents the Orinoco as a region inviting exploitation to underscore his belief that English colonial policy needed to be founded on a resistance to the very temptations America offered in such profusion. "*Guiana,*" he said, "is a Country that hath yet her Maydenhead."[32] England's archenemy,

Spain, unable to resist the alluring virgin of the New World, had taken her by force and had enslaved the native people, "kept them in chains," "tooke from them both their wives, and daughters daily, and used them for the satisfying of their own lusts."[33] They ruled over them in "tyrannie" and "cruelty."[34] The wisest colonial policy was just the opposite of Spain's, and Ralegh presents himself as a model of such self-denial.

I am returned a begger, and withered, but that I might have bettred my poore estate … I could have laid hands and ransomed many of the kings & *Cassiqui* of the Country, & have had a reasonable proportion of gold for their redemption: But I have chosen rather to beare the burthen of poverty, then reproch.[35]

And he persuaded his men to follow his example:

I protest before the majestie of the living God, that I neither know nor beleeve, that any of our companie one or other, by violence or otherwise, ever knew any of their women, and yet we saw many hundreds, and had many in our power, and of those very yoong, and excellently favored which came among us without deceit, stark naked.

  Nothing got us more love among them then this usage, for I suffred not anie man to take from anie of the nations so much as a *Pina,* or a *Potato* roote, without giving them contentment, nor any man so much as to offer to touch any of their wives or daughters: which course, so contrarie to the Spaniards (who tyrannize over them in all things) drew them to admire his Majestie, whose commandement I told them it was, and also woonderfully to honour our nation.[36]

The policy, Ralegh insisted, should be followed everywhere: "many nations" will be "won to her Majesties love & obedience, & those Spanyards which have latest and longest labored about the conquest, beaten out, discouraged and disgraced."[37]

  Defoe took it for granted not only that English colonialism had the power to "quite change and alter the [native] people themselves," and he argued at some length in *Serious Reflections during the Life and Surprising Adventures of Robinson Crusoe* and *A Plan of the English Commerce,* among other works, that it was the obligation of England to instruct "barbarous Nations how to live," to "subdue whole Nations of Savages to a regular Life," and to teach them to "live under the regularity and Direction of a Civil Government."[38] But, in pursuit of these ends, he heartily subscribed to Ralegh's sentiments that the foundation of English colonial policy must be "just and generous Behavior to the Natives" (*SR,* p. 217). In *A New Voyage round the World,* he remarks of the South Sea islanders,

As the Natives of these Places were tractable and courteous, so they would be made easily subservient and assistant to any *European* Nation that would come to make Settlements among them; especially if those *European* Nations used them with Humanity and Courtesy; for I have made it a general Observation concerning the Natural dispositions of all the Savage Nations that ever I met with: That if they are once but really oblig'd, they will be always very faithful.

But it is our People, I mean the *Europeans,* breaking Faith with them, that first teaches them Ingratitude; and inures them to treat their new-Comers with Breach of Faith, and with Cruelty and Barbarity. If you once win them by Kindness, and doing them good … they will generally be honest, and be kind also, to the uttermost of their Power. (*NV,* p. 145)

Because the savages possessed the same human nature and the same powers of reason as Europeans, they would perceive the superiority of European culture quickly once their own habits of thinking and acting were broken. Therefore, conversion would proceed peacefully as long as Europeans treated the natives humanely and justly.

What have the People of *England* more to do, but to encrease the Colonies of their own Nation in all the remote Parts, where it is proper and practicable, and to civilize and instruct the Savages and natives of those Countries, wherever they plant, so as to bring them by the softest and gentlest Methods to fall into the Customs and Usage of their own Country, and incorporate among our People as one Nation.[39]

Merely engaging the natives with the "Customs and Usage" of civilization would be enough to civilize them, "quite chang[ing] and alter[ing] the people themselves": "the savage Part would soon be civiliz'd, and become so too."[40] The mysterious alchemy of cause and effect (savages would be pressed into civilized behavior – "be civilized" – and this would alter their nature – "and become so too"), though short on logic, betrays Defoe's faith in how deeply "Manners" and "Nature" are implicated in one another.[41] Though a mere change in manners and habits would not immediately result in a true spiritual conversion – "I say nothing of christianizing the Savages," Defoe confesses, "but I speak of an Incorporation of Customs and Usages, as may in Time bring them to live like Christians, whether they may turn Christians or no" – the introduction of European customs and manners would be a prelude to such a conversion.[42] For if the savages are given occasion to *act* civilized, they begin to *be* civilized. As with the cannibals in *Robinson Crusoe,* savages are unfree because their inclinations have been channeled into irrational customs that blind them to the truth, but once their benighted customs are broken, their understandings will be open to truth, and "inform'd Nature would soon direct [them] to civilize and govern themselves."[43] "Thus prejudices being removed, the Way to Instruction would be made the more plain" (*SR,* p. 217). For savages are different in that they govern themselves by customs and institutions formulated out of their stupidity, but since they are the same as Europeans in potential, they will become the same in actuality once they are freed from their savage customs and gently tutored in the truths of civilization and Christianity.

The role that conversion plays in colonial ideology in justifying the English venture in the New World helps explain its pervasiveness in the *Crusoe* books. In *The Life and Strange Surprizing Adventures of Robinson Crusoe,* Crusoe is converted and then converts Friday; in *The Farther Adventures of Robinson Crusoe,* Will Atkins and his native wife are made Christians and then the thirty-seven Caribs who had been captured during the cannibal raids are civilized; in *Serious Reflections during the Life and Surprising Adventures of Robinson Crusoe,* Defoe devotes many pages to promoting his grandiose project of a "bloodless Conquest" (*SR,* p. 208) of the entire non-Christian world through peaceful conversion.

And yet, at first glance, the centrality of conversion in all three *Crusoe* books is odd and anachronistic. The project of civilizing and Christianizing the savages, though eloquently advocated by some, was never among the leading motives that drove most Europeans to the New World, and what enthusiasm there was for the undertaking rapidly faded after the first years of colonization. Some Europeans came to the New World to practice their religious convictions freely and considerably more came to better their lives economically, and the American Indians were irrelevant to both these desires. Increasingly, they were seen as a positive detriment to achieving either. The New England colonists "did not consider the evangelization of the Indians to be a principal end of colonization, only an incidental one," and after the first years of contact, relations deteriorated so badly that most felt the Indians should be extirpated, not converted.[44] Whatever desire to civilize and convert the natives initially motivated some of the Jamestown colonists did not survive the depredations by the Powhatans or the massacre of 1622. The ferocity of the Caribbean natives and their putative cannibalism quickly blighted any wish to Christianize them. Although pronouncements about the value of converting the natives retained some toehold in metropolitan discourse, secular and commercial justifications steadily supplanted religious ones. Nicholas Canny concludes that, by the end of the seventeenth century, the "reforming ambition which had legitimized colonization in the first instance could be said to have been almost altogether abandoned."[45]

Yet, circumstances in the two decades preceding the *Crusoe* books conspired not only to resurrect the rhetoric of conversion that seemed to have played itself out but to make the conversion of the natives seem essential to the well-being of Britain's colonial empire. Perhaps the relationship of *Robinson Crusoe* to this turn of events has been obscured by the novel's setting in the Caribbean. Given the virtual disappearance of the Carib natives, relations between natives and colonists were irrelevant there. But just to the north, in the colonies along the Atlantic littoral, Anglo-Indian relations *were* crucial, and many colonial officials, both in North America and in London, felt that matters were rapidly developing toward a crisis point where the fate of empire was at stake. The urgency of this historical moment, I believe, shaped the image of the relationship between the colonist and the savage in *Robinson Crusoe* and made conversion one of the novel's central themes.

In the North American colonies, the Indians were too important and in many instances too powerful to be driven into the hinterlands. All colonies were vulnerable to Indian depredations, and it was vastly more sensible to cultivate good relations with the natives than to antagonize them. Maryland, Virginia, South Carolina, and the Bay Colony all used their "friendly" Indians as buffers against more distant, belligerent Indians. English colonists worked tirelessly, year after year, to appease and court the Five (later Six) Iroquois Nations. Because they were able to manage other, less friendly Indians, the Five Nations held the balance of power in North America, and because the English assiduously cultivated cooperative relations with them, from 1677 to 1755, the middle colonies lived in relative peace with the natives.

More importantly, good relations with the Iroquois had to be cultivated for reasons of imperial politics. It was becoming more and more obvious to the policymakers in London that they were the most important line of defense against the pretensions of New France. "The five Nations of Indians lying on the back of New York, between the French of Canada & settlements, are the only barrier between the ... French and their Indians & his Majesty's Plantations as far as Virginia & Maryland."[46] They were not only "highly serviceable to His Mat^{ys} Interests," but also "in a great measure [to] the balance of North America."[47] By 1715, the Board of Trade came to appreciate the point: "These Indians ... are capable ... of turning the European interest in those parts to which side soever they incline."[48]

In the decade preceding the publication of the *Crusoe* books, a succession of three wars – Queen Anne's, the Tuscarora, and the Yamasee – sharpened an emerging awareness in England of their new imperial identity and made obvious to them that the success of their colonial venture was dependent on good relations with the Indians. The English began to see the necessity of reanimating the policy of just and humane dealing with the natives that had been so compellingly articulated by the early promoters of English colonialism.

Fear of the threat of France had been percolating among colonial leaders and administrators for many years. As early as 1698, Francis Nicholson, then Governor of Maryland, catching scent of French designs to colonize the Gulf, warned that they would soon be able to "encompass all the English Dominions here," and "should [they] get all the Indians on their sides … they may be very troublesom to all our Frontier plantations on this Continent."[49] Defoe himself perceived the peril earlier than most of his countrymen. In the first decade of the century, he wrote about his fear that France would hobble English navigation in order to destroy trade with America and thus establish a trade monopoly for itself. But France posed a more direct danger to the colonies, and Defoe justified the War of the Spanish Succession (Queen Anne's War) in part on the basis of the threat. Because "the *French* are … Masters of the [St. Lawrence] River" and

lye just behind all our *English* Settlements, upon the Continent of America … they have … an opportunity, and very often improve it, of stirring up the *Indians* to make depredations, and Insult our Plantations … The increasing Power of the *French* in those Parts, makes our Colonies very uneasy, and in time may be more Fatal to them, than they yet apprehend.[50]

Should the King of France hold the throne of Spain, "our Collonies of *Virginia,* and *New-England,* would easily be destroy'd … What will the Virginia Collony be worth when the French come to be strong in the Lakes … and have a free Commerce from *Quebeck* to Mexico behind ye."[51] "It is a Maxim every man of Sense will own," he wrote at the end of the war,

that the Wealth and Strength of our Colonies is our own Wealth and our own Strength, but where is the Man that considers the Naked Condition of *New England, New York, Virginia,* &c. to the Land-side, and that the *French* in *Canada* grow Formidable to them, and will, in Time, Ruin and Remove them, if not provided against in Time?[52]

As France expanded in the interior of the continent, establishing a chain of forts and posts and settling Louisiana, colonial observers feared that the French were encircling the English colonies and, from their settlements near the mouth of the Mississippi, were poised to take the whole of the Caribbean, too, all in pursuit of France's "great schemes … for founding a universall power in America." Soon, France would "be in a condition to drive us down to the sea coast again and thence back to Old England."[53]

The threat was not from the French directly, of course – they did not have sufficient forces to mount successful attacks on English settlements – but from the powerful interior tribes with whom they had formed alliances. Soon, it was feared, the French would be able to monopolize trade with the western Indians and then use them as cats' paws to menace the English colonies.

Indian unrest along the western frontier of the English colonies began with the Tuscarora attacks on North Carolina in 1711, and then the devastating Yamasee War of 1715, a widespread revolt of southern Indians that nearly destroyed colonial South Carolina, galvanized colonial and London authorities to the dangers confronting the empire. "It is some years … that the Indians have been preparing … to seize the whole Continent and to kill us or chase us out of it," wrote a panicked inhabitant from South Carolina when the Yamasee first attacked.[54] From Virginia came word that there was "reason to apprehend, from the usual intercourse between the Southern and Northern Indians, that there is a general Combination between them to fall upon all the English plantations, wherein this Colony cannot hope to escape having its share in the Calamity."[55] In New England, which throughout the 1690s and the first decade of the eighteenth century had suffered withering attacks from the Wabanakis and allied tribes, often in collusion with the French, it was rumored that attacks would move northward and that "this war will be general."[56] The Board of Trade thought that even in the north there was "a general defection of the … Indians from the British interest on the Continent of America."[57] The Yamasee strike in South Carolina was the beginning; if the Indians succeeded there, wrote a group of planters and merchants to the Board of Trade, "all the other Colonies wou'd soon be involv'd in the same ruin, and ye whole English Empire, Religion and Name be extirpated in America."[58]

There was a sense of a looming catastrophe engineered by the French. "It is undoubtedly by the management of the [F]rench that the fire is kindled in Carolina," wrote Caleb Heathcote during the Yamasee War, "& they'le not be wanting in their endeavours to spread the flame through the whole coast." The plan of the French was "to angle us away, province by province, till at last all will be gon."[59] "Our danger [is] very great," he wrote four days later, "& his majestys subjects here [are] on the brinke of ruin, by wch meanes these vast Countreys, wch in time would become by much the most vallewable jewells belonging to the [B]rittish Crown abroad will be lost and destroed, & y^t the designes of France are very near being ripe for our ruin."[60] Governor Spotswood warned that the French, with their line of settlements "between Canada and Mississippi," created a noose that "surround[ed] all the British Plantations" and now "have it in their power ... to engross all the Trade of the Indian Nations" and "Either by themselves or with their Indians, fall upon and over-run w'ch of these Provinces they think fit."[61] The Board of Trade wrote to Secretary of State for the Southern Provinces, James Stanhope: "Numerous Nations of Indians ... at the instigation of [the French], seem to have entered into a general Confederacy against all our Plantations on the Continent, who have scarse strength sufficient to defend themselves, in case they shou'd be attack'd."[62]

Though it was the French who were threatening the existence of the British empire, it was the Indians the English had to actually deal with, and it was their past dealings with them, they thought, that were in large part responsible for the current crisis. At the height of the Yamasee War, Thomas Bannister laid the problems at the feet of the English and their failure to treat the Indians fairly and decently. The Indians now hate the English and have "conceiv'd an opinion that our design is wholly to exterminate and destroy them" because of "repeated injuries and provocations ... as divesting them of their land by force or fraud"; because of "our faithlessness in Treatys"; because the English have "butchered a number of them"; because of "our inhumanity to them whenever in time of peace they doe come among us." The only way to "beget trust and confidence and at last an intire friendship" with them is to "make due lawes and see them executed, to redress the wrongs and injuries of the Indians at least with as much care as they doe English ... to shew as little distrust and jealousy as possible ... and [to] take especial care the Indians are not cheated."[63]

Bannister's indictment is uncharacteristically blunt, but his view that the British had failed to behave honestly to the Indians was shared by other authorities in the colonies and in London. The Yamasee War, it was generally held, had erupted in large part because of British abuses. Up and down the Atlantic littoral, colonial authorities came to appreciate more keenly the importance of dealing with Indians fairly and justly, and in London, the Board of Trade took their warnings so seriously that they began to gather information and to canvass opinion in the colonies in order to put together a coherent imperial policy, "the first clearly formulated British program for challenging the progress of the French in the West."[64] In 1721, the Board delivered a finished report to the King. It was a document of considerable historical consequence. It pointed with alarm to the territorial ambitions and successes of the French in North America and, most importantly, it acknowledged that Britain's imperial ambitions were dependent on the Indians.

The Board made a number of recommendations, but at the heart of the report was a sense of urgency that the British must "lose no time ... in securing such Indian nations, as are not already in league" with the French.[65] In the end, the colonies could be secured only "BY CULTIVATING A GOOD UNDERSTANDING WITH THE NATIVE INDIANS," and such an understanding was to be cultivated by treating the Indians justly and decently.[66] In short, the Indians were to be won over, as Ralegh and early colonial thinkers had said over a century earlier, by fair and honest behavior.[67]

At the same time as English colonists and officials were rethinking their trade and political relationships with the North American natives, religious leaders in England were reformulating their ideas about converting the Indians and were instituting major changes in missionary policies and practices, in part because of the French threat in America. "Nor should it be forgotten," Thomas Secker reminded his listeners in a sermon urging the religious instruction of the Indians, "that every single *Indian,* whom we make a Christian, we make a Friend and Ally at the same time; both against the remaining Heathens, and a much more dangerous Neighbour, from whose Instigations almost all that we have suffered by them is allowed to have come."[68] Such great progress had been made by the French in converting the Indians that some feared "there will be in time become ten papists to one Protestant" in North America, and "the French will be as strong there in proportion to their neighbours as they are here in Europe."[69] Though their activities were deplored, the French missionaries themselves – their dedication, self-sacrifice, and probity – were admired and seen as models of behavior for English missionaries. Crusoe lavishly praises the French missionary in *Farther Adventures,* that "truly pious Papist" whose devotion to the conversion of the savages is a standing admonishment to English Protestants (*FA,* p. 101).

This emphasis on good character was not merely a response to the success of the French. From the beginning the English had founded the ideology of their colonial enterprise on the proposition that savages were best instructed in religion and civility by the example of the just and humane behavior of the colonists. Colonists were to be "patterns to the heathens"; the savages would be converted to civility and religion by "the example of our course of living."[70] "Draw the heathen by [y]our good example," the colonists were urged; behave "justly and courteously toward the Indians, thereby to draw them to affect our persons, and consequently our religion."[71] Defoe himself believed that Christianity was best taught by "just ... behavior," which "would in a little while bring [the natives] to embrace that Truth, which dictated such just Principles to those who espoused it" (*SR,* p. 217).

But the conviction that Indian conversion was best accomplished by example ran into a serious stumbling block. For the reputation of the colonists was dismal. In coming to the Americas, European immigrants had degenerated.[72] Given the conditions of settlement and the general lack of social and religious discipline in the New World, there was probably some basis in fact for this apprehension. The colonization of much of the New World had been carried out, after all, by adventurers and joint-stock companies, and neither made many provisions for religion. Outside of New England, there was little effort to supervise the moral and religious education of the tide of people who came to North America, and, as a consequence, wrote the Revd John Yeo in 1679, the colonies had become "a Sodom of uncleannesse, and a pest-house of iniquity."[73] The colonies were dominated by young, single men who, a bit like Crusoe on his island, lived "in a single and scattering way, remote from townships and neighbourhoods," isolated from the institutions of authority and public order that had structured life in the Old World and who were "degenerat[ing] into heathenish ignorance and barbarismc."[74] Colonel Heathcote called New York "the most rude and Heathenish Country I ever saw in my whole Life, which called themselves Christians, there being not so much as the least marks of Footsteps of Religion of any Sort."[75] Samuel Thomas wrote from South Carolina that the white settlers there were "in such a wilderness and so destitute of spiritual guides" that they "were making near approach to that heathenism which is to be found among negroes and Indians."[76] Those who lived away from settlements, William Hubbard thought, "were contented to live without, yea, desirous to shake off all Yoake of Government, both sacred and civil, and so transforming themselves as much as well they could into the Manners of the Indians they lived amongst."[77] George Berkeley opened his proposal for a seminary in Bermuda with what he considered a self-obvious truism: "It is ... acknowledged, that there is at this Day, but little Sense of Religion, and a most notorious Corruption of Manners, in the *English* Colonies settled on the Continent of *America,* and the Islands."[78]

The wave after wave of immigrants who came to the New World more for secular than religious reasons made for a population increasingly indifferent to religion, and, even in New England, church membership declined precipitously.[79] The colonists were quickly becoming "wicked, and dissolute, and brutal in every Respect," destined to "return in a few Generations to entire Barbarism."[80] "Many *English,* instead of gaining Converts, are themselves degenerated into Heathens … There can be therefore, in no Part of the Christian World, a greater Want of spiritual Things than in our Plantations."[81] In 1720, the Assembly of South Carolina petitioned the King, complaining that, because no religious education took place in the colony, the youth were "imbibing irreligion" and were in danger of becoming "as barbarous as the native savages."[82]

Since the colonists had become "as barbarous as the native savages," they had ceased to be good models for the natives. Most settlers were "worse than the heathen," wrote one missionary, and Indians refused to embrace Christianity because of the example of their "scandalous and immoral" lives.[83] A missionary in New York complained of

the *Indians* justifying their Infidelity by the Immoralities of the English. I have taken … some Pains to teach some of the Native *Indians,* but to no purpose. For they seem regardless of Instruction. And when I have told them of the evil Consequences of their hard Drinking, *&c.* they replied, that English Men did the same … They further say, they will not be Christians, nor do they see the necessity for being so; because we do not live according to the Precepts of our Religion.[84]

In 1724, the Bishop of London conducted a parochial survey, asking colonial rectors what steps they were taking to convert the heathens. One Virginian replied, "But all means used for their conversions … is like to prove ineffectual because of these obstacles which seems to impeded the conversion of infidels wherever Christianity is professed, i.e., – wicked lives of Christians."[85]

The belief that the colonists were not leading exemplary lives had a surprising consequence, one that can be seen most strikingly in the activities of the Society for the Propagation of the Gospel in Foreign Parts (SPG). The SPG was founded in 1701 to promote Christianity by sending missionaries, schoolmasters, and catechists to the colonies. Because of their missionary activities in the nineteenth century, I suppose, we tend to think that the principal activity of the SPG was the conversion of native populations. But because the colonists had become heathens, there came about what John Nelson has characterized as a "pervasive" logic "accepted not only by missionaries … but throughout the English community": the Indians could be converted only after the white colonists had been recivilized and re-Christianized and thus made proper exemplars for the savages.[86] This program was announced by Richard Willis, Dean of Lincoln, in the first anniversary sermon of the SPG:

The design is in the first place to settle the State of Religion as well as may be among our *own People* there, which by all accounts we have, very much wants their Pious care; and then to proceed in the best Methods they can towards the *Conversion* of the *Natives.*[87]

"To begin with the Indians is preposterous," wrote the Revd Thorogood Moore, a missionary in New York, "for it is from the behaviour of the Christians here that they have had, and still have, their notions of Christianity, which God knows, hath been generally such, that it hath made the Indians to hate our religion."[88] Moore himself gave up his evangelistic efforts among the Iroquois and took charge of a church for white colonists at Burlington, New Jersey.

If the goal of the SPG was to present the English in such a light that the Indians would imitate them out of love, they had first to convert the white colonists, "to train up a better Generation," as Bray exhorted the clergy in Maryland, "than the wretched one now in being."[89] The "main business" of the English Church was sending missionaries to English colonists, argued Joseph Wilcocks, for "there is little Hope in recommending our religion to the natives, till our own People in those Parts are brought to a better knowledge, and a stricter Observance of it."[90] "Our Designs upon Aliens and Infidels must begin in the Instructing and Reforming of our own People," Bishop Gilbert Burnet wrote in his 1704 SPG anniversary sermon.

If they were justly dealt with, and gently treated by our People; if they saw as much cause to esteem us for our Morals, as they do to admire us for our Ingeniousness; this might dispose them in time to think well both of us and of our religion. This might give them a desire to come under our Protection, and to become our Friends and Allies.[91]

George Berkeley thought that the colonists themselves were the greatest "Obstacle to propagating the Gospel."[92] "Mankind are more apt to copy Characters than to practice Precepts," he observed, and since the "ill manners and Irreligion" of the white colonists had done little but to "pollute" the reservoirs of religion, it was not surprising to see the persistence of the "Blindness and Barbarity of the Nations round them."[93] "The likeliest Step towards converting the Heathen," he concluded, "would be to begin with the *English* Planters."[94]

These developments in colonial policy and religious proselytizing, I believe, strongly affected Defoe's colonial thinking. All three *Crusoe* books are preoccupied with conversion, but conversion was not merely a religious matter but also part of a broader strategy of imperial politics. And in the *Crusoe* books, Defoe carefully fashions situations and incidents to speak to the crisis of Anglo-Indian relations that had developed in North America and focuses on conversion as a way of meeting this crisis.

The English colonies, constructed so painstakingly on the edge of the wilderness, suddenly were threatened by a massive irruption of savages, poised to descend on the frail settlements and destroy them. To deliver themselves from these savages, the English had to turn to other savages, the "friendly" Indians. These savages must be enlightened and converted and knotted into English ways so that they would become bulwarks and (like Friday) companions-in-arms to help protect civilization from destruction.

Friday, it should be noted, is not Christianized immediately. Defoe, like almost all other English colonial thinkers, thought it necessary first to civilize savages before making them Christians. The Indians were "incapable ... to be trusted" with admission into the church, argued John Eliot, for instance, "while they had so unfixed, confused, and ungoverned a life, unsubdued to labor and order."[95] Before they were Christianized, Defoe said, savages needed to be "subdue[d] ... to a regular Life," taught "the Art of Living": "clothing with Decency ... feeding with Humanity ... dwelling in Towns and Cities."[96] And so Crusoe first clothes Friday decently, then breaks him of his bad habit of feeding on human flesh, and then has him dwell within the boundaries of his fort. After, Friday is "subdue[d] ... to a regular Life" of "labor and order," working Crusoe's plantation by laboring in the fields, bringing in the harvest, making and repairing tools. Weaned from his "unfixed, confused, and ungoverned" ways, Friday is converted from living a marauding life to living a settled life – in English eyes, making the essential transition from being a savage to being a civilized human being. Acculturated to English ways, finally and most importantly, Friday defends civilization from the savages, fighting shoulder to shoulder with Crusoe when the cannibals descend on the island.

When Crusoe leaves his island for good, one of his last acts is to secure the safety of the colony by civilizing the thirty-seven cannibals who had been captured earlier. They had been living on an isolated "Nook of the Island," separate from the Europeans, "un-employ'd" and having "no manner of Business or Property to manage" (*FA,* p. 112). In order to enlist their help against further cannibal raids, Crusoe moves them within the pale of civilization, just as he had Friday earlier, settling them among the Europeans, "propos[ing] to them" to either "plant for themselves" or to become employed by "several Families as Servants to be maintain'd for their Labour" (*FA,* p. 112). This choice is not forced on the savages but "proposed" to them. The cannibals are civilized, not by coercion but by being treated justly and humanely – just as Crusoe had educated Friday in

English "Customs and Usage" by the "softest and gentlest Methods," just like the colonial authorities in North America were urging the colonists to act so that they could survive the depredations of the wild savages.

When Will Atkins and his cohorts bring the cannibals they have captured to the island, they are not as successful in civilizing them as Crusoe was, and, as a consequence, the natives do not provide the same degree of security to the settlement as Friday does.

> They made them Servants, and taught them to work for them; and as Slaves they did well enough; but they did not take their Measures with them as I did by my man *Friday,* (*viz.*) to begin with them upon the Principle of having sav'd their Lives, and then instruct them in the rational Principles of Life, much less Religion, civilizing and reducing them by kind Usage and affectionate Arguings; but as they gave them their Food every Day, so they gave them their Work, too, and kept them fully employ'd in Drudgery enough; but they fail'd in this, by it, that they never had them to assist them and fight for them, as I had my man *Friday,* who was as true to me as the very Flesh upon my Bones. (*FA,* p. 44)

Will Atkins only half-civilizes his savages because he is only half-civilized himself. To the degree that Crusoe is more successful than Atkins in civilizing and Christianizing the Indians and doing so humanely and justly, it is a result of his own civilizing and Christianizing of himself. Like the cannibals, he initially was a wandering marauder, as "Stupid" as the savages and having "no more Sense of God" than they had, "act[ing] like a meer Brute from the Principles of Nature" (*RC,* p. 123). Crusoe is able to convert Friday and numerous other savages to civilized behavior, and then some of them to Christianity, because he first has converted himself.

The plot of *Robinson Crusoe* is a double-conversion plot. This structure is predicated on the same assumptions that governed the political and religious policy in North America: the English colonists had to be converted first so that they became virtuous, humane, and just; by their example, they then could convert the Indians, and together they would prevail against the forces of unredeemed savagery.

Defoe presses this vision of Anglo-Indian policy with some urgency. This accounts, I believe, for the presence of the Spaniards in *Robinson Crusoe* and *Farther Adventures* and the surprising use to which Defoe puts them. From the time of Ralegh, the English had distinguished their colonial practices from those of the Spanish, whose "unexampled Cruelties," whose "Barbarities that almost exceeded belief," and whose "savage Treatment" of the Indians came to be known as the Black Legend.[97] Defoe subscribed to the Black Legend. He acknowledged that the Spanish were used by God to punish the idolatry and human sacrifice of the Mexican

Indians. But even though they were "Instruments in the Hand of Heaven, to execute the divine Justice, on Nations, whose Crimes … call'd for Vengeance," the Spanish were nevertheless "wicked in themselves" (*SR*, p. 206). "Cruel, inexorable, uncharitable, [and] voracious," in the end they alienated more Indians than they converted, and Defoe echoes Ralegh's assertion that the Indians so hated the Spanish that if England "would but come in and assist them … and support them in their Risings, they would soon rid their Hands of the whole Nation" (*NV*, pp. 117, 152).[98] Crusoe's initial reactions to the Indians – his "outragious" "bloody Schemes" of mass murder – recall the Spanish atrocities.

Yet, even though in the *Crusoe* books themselves Spaniards in general are condemned because of the "meer Butchery" they perpetrated on the New World natives, the "bloody and unnatural … Cruelty, unjustifi-able either to God or Man" that made them "a Race of Men … without Principles of Tenderness, or the common Bowels of Pity to the Miserable" (*RC*, pp. 183–184), the particular Spaniards on Crusoe's island are "univer-sally Modest, Temperate, Virtuous … and as to Cruelty, they had nothing of it in their very Nature, no Inhumanity, no Barbarity, no out-rageous Passions" (*FA*, p. 58). In contrast, it is the English who act out the role of cruel barbarians English colonial ideology had assigned to the Spanish. Will Atkins and his two companions – "the three *English* brutes," "the three Barbarians" – because of their "brutish and barbarous" behavior, bring the colony to the lip of disaster (*FA*, pp. 33, 29, 52). Driven by lust and power hunger, these "refractory, ungovern'd Villains" are so incap-able of disciplining themselves that they would have starved had they not been saved by the humane Spaniards (*FA*, p. 29). In repayment, the English concoct a "Design … to murther the *Spaniards* in cold Blood, and in their Sleep" (*FA*, p. 50). Governed by blind unreason, they uproot the fragile foundation of civilization on the island, nearly destroying it com-pletely. Like the Spanish of the Black Legend, they treat the Indians with "monstrous Cruelty" (*FA*, p. 50). They set out on an expedition to capture natives to make slaves of them. They come within an ace of killing one slave for no other reason than "because he did not, or perhaps could not, understand to do what he was directed" (*FA*, p. 50).

The systematic inversion of the Black Legend in the *Crusoe* books is intended to reprove an English audience. Responding to the threat of the loss of the colonies because of the crisis in Anglo-Indian relations in North America, Defoe wanted to return to the first principles of English colonial ideology, to reaffirm their importance, to admonish his countrymen for having fallen so far away from them, and to reinvigorate them as practical ideals: that the English are the bearers of civilization and religion; that to the degree that they had degenerated from these ideals they must be converted so that they conduct themselves with self-restraint and honesty; that in their relations with the natives, they must be just and humane; and that they must, whenever possible, civilize and Christianize the natives, for the fate of empire depended on it.

If I am correct that in his *Crusoe* books Defoe was giving voice to a colonial policy of conversion and of honest and fair dealing, we can understand some of the reasons why he would choose the Caribbean as a setting. Peter Hulme has characterized *Robinson Crusoe* as a "simplifying crucible in which complexities [of colonialism] can be reduced to their essential components": a "paradigmatic fable" about "the primary stuff of colonialist ideology," the "encounter between civilization and savagery."[99] As the representative of civilization, Crusoe possesses those traits of what one critic has called "colonial individualism"[100] – rationality, self-control, self-reliance, and self-assertion – that "improving … Genius" that allowed the English colonist to dominate and master alien lands and people.[101] And, contrariwise, the Caribs are embodiments of savagery pure and simple. Hence Defoe's choice of the Caribbean as a setting. For the Caribbean was synonymous with cannibalism, and cannibalism was the *non plus ultra* of savagery. By pitting Crusoe against the cannibals, Defoe makes this "encounter between civilization and savagery" as "paradigmatic" as possible, testing under the most extreme conditions a colonial policy of just treatment and conversion.

Although the Indian policy Defoe champions had its inception in North America, there was no need to set the *Crusoe* books there. It is clear from *Serious Reflections during the Life and Surprising Adventures of Robinson Crusoe, A Plan of the English Commerce,* and *A New Voyage round the World* that Defoe, responding to England's rapidly expanding trading empire, meant the policy to be pursued globally, and so potentially he could set the books anywhere and stock them with any of the world's savage people. And yet, although the Caribbean setting and the presence of the cannibals are useful in framing this "fable" as "paradigmatic," in other ways they are quite perplexing. By placing Crusoe's island in the Caribbean and making his savages cannibals, Defoe hobbles his ability to argue persuasively or even cogently for some of his most strongly held convictions about the English colonial venture.

For if Defoe wanted the *Crusoe* books to tout the English colonial project, to stock them with cannibals is unaccountable. One of the first lessons learned by the writers of colonial promotional literature was that portraying the American natives as barbarous had a negative effect on potential settlers.[102] When Defoe *does* propagandize colonization in *A New Voyage round the World,* he creates quite a different picture of the natives the English settlers will have to deal with – a "quiet, and inoffensive people," "honest and … harmless," not in the least "treacherous" or "perfidious": "Most of them were furnish'd with Fire-Arms, Powder, and Shot, and were very good Marks Men; but as to Violence against any Body, they entertained no Thoughts of that Kind" (*NV,* pp. 191, 199). Dramatizing colonists surrounded by huge forces of ferocious, aggressive, and implacably hostile cannibals is hardly calculated to make colonizing the New World an inviting prospect. It is also anachronistic. When Defoe wrote *Robinson Crusoe,* Caribs were no longer a serious threat to European settlers on the islands.[103]

And the Caribbean setting raises other problems. Defoe promoted colonies on the basis of the wealth they brought to Britain by increasing consumption, circulating goods more widely, and greatly expanding trade. "Without Commerce," he remarked, "of what use is a Colony?"[104] Yet, Crusoe's isolated Caribbean island is part of no economic network: no staple crop is shipped to the home country, no British goods are consumed, no trade takes place. In *A New Voyage round the World,* Defoe encouraged the colonization of the South Sea islands because the natives "wou'd … take off a great Quantity of *English* Woolen Manufactures, especially when Civiliz'd by our dwelling among them, and taught the Manner of Clothing themselves for their Ease and Convenience" (*NV,* p. 131), a point he returned to repeatedly in many of his other writings.[105] Friday's clothing has great symbolic weight in the novel, but Defoe does not even hint at its economic import. And he does not seem interested in creating the impression that the island ever would become a lively trading center, nor does he dramatize its economical potential. Sugar cane is mentioned once in passing. Tobacco grows there, but tobacco was not a competitive crop in the Caribbean. No drugs or medicinal herbs are alluded to, no spices, rare woods, or any other potential commodity, precious or staple. The one crop Crusoe develops on the island in abundance – barley – is precisely the kind of product that was *not* wanted from the colonies, for it would compete with home products.

In Defoe's other American novels, the settings are part of a larger argument about the economic advantages of establishing English colonies. The South American scenes of *A New Voyage round the World* are set in Chile and Patagonia because Defoe had long thought they were attractive places for English colonization. *Moll Flanders* and *Colonel Jack* are set in the Chesapeake because prospects for economic advancement were still alive in Virginia and Maryland – or at least Defoe thought they were. But if Defoe wanted to promote the benefits of colonization, the setting of *Robinson Crusoe* is not at all credible. The mainland around the Orinoco was hostile, and though some scholars have suggested that Defoe wanted Crusoe's island to be seen as a base from which the English could penetrate deeper into the South American interior, he makes no mention of it in the *Crusoe* books.[106]

Nor was the Caribbean a place where the English poor and middling could settle and substantially improve their lives, especially by becoming indentured servants, something Defoe promoted vigorously in much of his non-fiction writing and in *Colonel Jack* and *Moll Flanders*. In Defoe's time, the whole region, from Barbados to Jamaica, was dominated by the big sugar planters, and prospects for new settlers were dismal.[107] In Barbados, to become rich, one had to practice economies of scale that involved large investments in machinery and slaves. (In 1673, Richard Ligon estimated that a "competent stock" to begin a plantation could not be "less then 14000 £ Sterling.")[108] By the Restoration, with most of the productive land in the hands of a couple of hundred sugar magnates, there was little reason for servants to stay when they had completed the terms of their indentures and even less for servants to indenture themselves there. Perhaps as many as 30,000 whites who had not been able to leverage themselves into the planting society left Barbados between 1645 and 1700. The island was fiercely competitive – by mid-century it had become the most densely populated area in the English-speaking world except London – and with the introduction of slaves, there was little opportunity for a former white servant once he was out of his indentures. By 1695, the governor wrote,

there are hundreds of white servants in the Island who have been out of their time for many years, and who have never a bit of fresh meat bestowed on them for many years nor a dram of rum. They are domineered over and used like dogs, and this in time will undoubtedly drive away all the commonalty of the white people and leave the Island in a deplorable condition.[109]

In rapid succession, all the islands up the chain of the Leewards fell into the same pattern. As early as the 1650s, Barbados, St. Christopher, Nevis, Antigua, and Montserrat were so severely overcrowded that officials began to promote settlements in Surinam, Carolina, and Jamaica to relieve some of the pressure. When servants on these overdeveloped islands completed their terms, many fled to the colonies in North America, sold themselves back into servitude, or simply sank into an impoverished hand-to-mouth existence. A few tried their luck at buccaneering. Among the freedmen on the island, there was chronic unrest. By the 1670s, Nevis and Montserrat steadily began to lose their white population. Because of their small size and rapid development, St. Christopher and Antigua did not continue to offer enough economic opportunity to remain important magnets for indentured servants or middling immigrants. By 1708, the black population in all the Leeward Islands had more than trebled from where it was thirty years previously, and the white population shrank. In 1706, Daniel Parke observed that Nevis was "a rich little Island" but that it "was divided amongst a few rich men that had a vast number of slaves." It had "hardly any common people."[110]

Jamaica, the largest of the islands and the one settled last, would seem to offer the best prospects for ex-servants and small freeholders, but even by the end of the century small farmers there had few prospects. The island's economy developed slowly. The heavy death toll from tropical diseases, the presence of buccaneers, the difficulties of procuring black slaves, the predatory economic policies of the later Stuarts, the depredations year after year of war with the French, and finally the earthquake of 1692 – all these conspired to destroy the prospects for small planters and ex-servants. As elsewhere in the Caribbean, the best land was taken over by the large planters and absentee sugar-growers. "By the turn of the century," Dunn observes, "the servant population had … about disappeared."[111]

In pointing to some of the difficulties posed by his choosing to set *Robinson Crusoe* in the Caribbean and to make his savages Carib cannibals, I do not want to imply that Defoe set out to write a colonial novel and blundered terribly. To the contrary, I assume that he knew pretty much what he was doing. He wanted his savages to be cannibals, and therefore he set his novel in the Caribbean, and in doing so he chose *not* to explore certain aspects of colonialism – its economic potential, for instance, and particularly its promise to England's poor and middling. He would foreground these aspects of colonialism in his later American novels, and when he did so, he would choose settings – the Chesapeake, the tip of South America – that allowed him to dramatize these aspects realistically. The pertinent questions to ask about *Robinson Crusoe,* then, are these: *what* "primary stuff of colonialist ideology" did Defoe want to explore, and why are the Carib cannibals so crucial to this exploration that he was willing to turn away from so much he thought to be so important?

My speculation is this: the psychological, moral, and spiritual dimensions of conversion had a powerful and abiding hold on Defoe's imagination, and because of developments in North America, the conversion of both the English colonists and the savages had urgently been pushed to the center of colonialist thinking. Conversion, in all of these dimensions, is the central theme of the *Crusoe* books, and I think that Defoe found in cannibalism *a figure* that helped him dramatize the very process of conversion and that he was willing to follow his figurative argument in order to develop this theme even if it meant forgoing his exploration of other colonial concerns.

Crusoe is obsessed with cannibalism, and he sees it everywhere, from Africa, where he fears he and Xury will be "devour'd by … merciless Savages," to the Caribbean, where he is afraid less of being lost at sea than of "being devoured by Savages" (*RC,* pp. 73, 88). His fear is diffuse, and it possesses him from the opening of the novel, when during the storm he is paralyzed by his "Apprehensions of being swallow'd up by the Sea," to the end, when he is surrounded by ravenous wolves, who attack him like "three hundred Devils com[ing] … open mouth'd to devour us" (*RC,* pp. 9, 282). His fear is so recurrent and occasionally so chimerical – his encounters with friendly natives in Africa are faintly comic given his exaggerated apprehensions about their cannibalism – that one suspects that the cannibals must be expressive of some more extensive anxiety.

At its most generalized, cannibalism seems to stand for any force that threatens Crusoe, especially those forces within his own psyche.[112] If, as I have been arguing, Europeans and natives are the same in that they both possess a lower stratum of savage energies, and if the colonial narrative of *Robinson Crusoe* is a narrative of double-conversion – that is, of the mastery of this lower stratum of energies by European and native both – cannibalism in the novel is a way for Defoe to figure forth those savage appetites at the core of all humans.

Hunger for Defoe (I am speaking for the moment about mere hunger, not about cannibalism) can overwhelm all other needs and desires. The passengers Crusoe finds on the disabled ship in *Farther Adventures* are "so exceedingly hungry" that they "had no Command of themselves" (*FA,* p. 22). Hunger causes humans to abandon every obligation of morality, every tie of blood and affection, every bond of social affiliation. "Hunger knows no Friend, no Relation, no Justice, no Right, and therefore is remorseless, and capable of no Compassion" (*FA,* p. 25). Hunger *will* be satisfied.

You are an Honest Man, you say! Pray, Sir, was you ever Try'd? Have you seen your self, Wife, and dear Children, ready to Perish for Food, and having your Neighbours Loaf in your Cupboard … *I tell you, Sir,* you would not Eat your

Neighbours Bread only, but your Neighbour himself, rather than Starve, and your Honesty would all Shipwrack in the Storm of Necessity.[113]

Cannibalism signifies for Defoe a myriad of inborn energies and appetites which, like hunger, are aggressively self-satisfying ("Man ... devours his own Species, nay his own Flesh and Blood," for ends "such as Avarice, Envy, Revenge, and the like" [*SR*, pp. 130–131]). These self-seeking energies are implanted by nature, and they are ineradicable, a kind of original sin:

> Nature has left *this Tincture in the Blood,*
> That all Men *would be Tyrant* if they cou'd:
> If they forbear their Neighbours to devour,
> 'Tis not for want of *Will,* but want *of Power.*[114]

Driven by these energies, you will "not only rob your Neighbour, but if in distress, you will EAT your Neighbour, *ay,* and say Grace to your Meat too – Distress removes from the Soul, all Relation, Affection, Sense of Justice, and all the Obligations, either Moral or Religious, that secure one man against another."[115]

As a figure, cannibalism in *Robinson Crusoe* has two notable features: incorporation and dismemberment. These two features spell out precisely the nature of the threat the savage passions and appetites pose to Crusoe, those forces he must master if he is to be converted from a savage to a civilized Christian.

A cannibalized body is incorporated into another body, and the root fear provoked by this incorporation is suggested by several related images in *Robinson Crusoe.* When the earthquake threatens him, Crusoe is afraid "of being swallow'd up alive," "of being bury'd alive" (*RC,* p. 118). The fear here is not of death exactly, but of death-in-life, what Crusoe calls "this Death of a Life" (*RC,* p. 203) when he refers to his existence on the island (another instance of being swallowed up and confined in a larger entity). The horror lies in retaining awareness while being assimilated into an alien being: to be aware of the loss of one's customary self-will, the capacity to direct one's own life, and to feel that one is wholly subject to a larger force – the feeling Crusoe has, say, when he is "swallowed up in a Moment" by a wave, "buried ... deep in its own Body," then swept ashore in a "Confusion of Thought," "senseless, and indeed helpless, as to my own Deliverance" (*RC,* pp. 89–90).

These alien, devouring energies are outside the self – waves, earthquakes, cannibals, natural forces of all sorts, as well as the chains of circumstance all humans are subject to. But they are also inside. They are impulses which spring from so deep inside the self, from realms of the psyche so distant from our circle of consciousness, that they *seem* outside the self, Other to the "I." And, as much as waves and earthquakes, these energies can absorb the self and render it powerless.

The psychic energies that incorporate the conscious self are the energies of the appetites and passions, and to the degree that the appetites and passions govern the self, they produce a fragmented self. Hence the significance of the second feature of the fear of being cannibalized, the fear of being torn to pieces and scattered ("The Place was cover'd with humane Bones," Crusoe says when he sees the remains of the cannibal feast, "great Pieces of Flesh left here and there, half eaten ... I saw three Skulls, five Hands, and the Bones of three or four Legs and Feet, and abundance of other Parts of the Bodies" [*RC*, p. 210]). The appetites and passions scatter the self because they are various, incoherent, and changeable. Passions and appetites butt against Crusoe's reason and judgment; appetites and passions butt against other appetites and passions; they seize Crusoe and then peter out and leave him vulnerable to new, different appetites and passions. "To Day we love what to Morrow we hate; to Day we desire what to Morrow we shun; to Day we desire what to Morrow we fear" (*RC*, p. 172). Engulfed by these variegated energies, his self is torn asunder, tossed in different directions. It becomes incoherent. After speaking with his father, Crusoe says, "I resolv'd not to think of going abroad any more, but to settle at home according to my Father's Desire. But alas! a few Days wore it all off; and ... I resolv'd to run quite away from him" (*RC*, p. 59). His changeableness (underscored by new cycles of resolutions made and broken) continues, and his scatteredness is imaged by that traditional symbol of vicissitude, the sea. After his first experience with the storm, Crusoe makes many "Vows and Resolutions" and "resolv'd that I would ... go home to my Father" (*RC*, p. 61). "These wise and sober Thoughts continued all the while the Storm continued," but

as the Sea was returned to its Smoothness of Surface and settled Calmness by the Abatement of that Storm, so the Hurry of my Thoughts being over, my Fears and Apprehensions of being swallow'd up by the Sea being forgotten, and the Current of my former Desires return'd, I entirely forgot the Vows and Promises that I made in my Distress. (*RC*, p. 62)

The phrase "the Current of my former Desires return'd," collapsing as it does the movement of his mind with the object it is dwelling on, suggests a blurring of inside and outside, and in this way captures how the unregenerate Crusoe experiences passions as external forces that short-circuit his own will. Consider the moment he decides to go to sea:

I continued obstinately deaf to all Proposals of settling to Business, and frequently expostulating with my Father and Mother, about their being so positively determin'd against what they knew my Inclinations prompted me to. But being one Day at *Hull*, where I went casually, and without any Purpose of making an Elopement that time; but I say, being there, and one of my Companions being going by Sea to *London*, in his Father's Ship, and prompting me to go with them, with the common Allurement of Seafaring Men, *viz.* That it should cost me nothing for my Passage, I consulted neither Father or Mother … and in an ill Hour … I went on Board a Ship bound for *London*. (*RC*, p. 60)

Crusoe's over-protestation of "casually, and without any Purpose of making an Elopement that time," the absence of any real inducement, covered over by rationalization ("it should cost me nothing for my Passage"), and especially the verbal parallel between the two inducements (Crusoe's "Inclinations prompted" him to go to sea, one of his companions "prompting [him] to go with them") reveal that his life is propelled by hidden, dimly perceived drives. Although he later will admit that his own impulses are the cause of all of his problems ("I was … the wilful Agent of all my own Miseries," "born to be my own Destroyer" [*RC*, pp. 84, 86]), he experiences them as being outside ("one of my Companions … prompting me"). He does not desire; desires happen to him, and internal appetites and inclinations press on him as if they were external powers:

But my ill Fate push'd me on now with an Obstinacy that nothing could resist; and tho' I had several times loud Calls from my Reason and my more composed Judgment to go home, yet I had no Power to do it. I know not what to call this, nor will I urge, that it is a secret over-ruling Decree that hurries us on to be the Instruments of our own Destruction, even tho' it be before us, and that we rush upon it with our Eyes open. Certainly nothing but some such decreed unavoidable Misery attending, and which it was impossible for me to escape, could have push'd me forward against the calm Reasonings and Perswasions of my most retired Thoughts, and against two such visible Instructions as I had met with in my first Attempt…

That evil Influence which carry'd me first away from my Father's House, that hurried me into the wild and indigested Notion of rising my Fortune; and that imprest those Conceits so forcibly upon me, as to make me deaf to all good Advice, and to the Entreaties and even Command of my Father: I say the same Influence, whatever it was, presented the most unfortunate of all Enterprises to my View, and I went on board a Vessel bound to the Coast of *Africa*. (*RC*, pp. 66–68)

The "I" here is so stripped of its capacities that it seems little more than a helpless observer. It begins to fragment as desires and powers are hived off and projected outward so that they seem to flow in from the outside: they "push'd me forward," "push'd me on," "carry'd me," "hurried me." The

"I" neither protests nor judges these impulses and desires: reason and judgment issue "loud calls," as if the "I" exists remote from its own attributes, which are scattered far away, barely within hailing distance of one another. The "I" does not understand what is pushing it on ("I knew not what to call this"; "the same Influence, whatever it was") – perhaps they proceed from God ("secret over-ruling Decree"), from the Devil ("evil Influence"), or some implacable, impersonal destiny ("my ill Fate"). And the "I" has no power to stand its ground; the desires are "unavoidable," "impossible for me to escape." They drive the "I" to its death, "hurr[y] us on to … our own Destruction." Crusoe experiences all of this as he does the horror of cannibalism: it is experienced as a sort of life-in-death, for the "I" is hurried to its own destruction "with our Eyes open" – conscious that it is being incorporated into what is experienced as an alien body, the body of its own lower energies, but unable to act to protect itself since those energies seem to be those of an Other.

In such a state, the "I" is both actor and victim. Crusoe acknowledges that he is the "wilful Agent of my own Miseries," but he also feels "*born to be my own Destroyer.*" A slave to his own impulse, Crusoe "pursue[s] a rash and immoderate Desire of rising faster than the Nature of the Thing admitted; and thus I cast my self down again into the deepest Gulph of human Misery that ever Man fell into" (*RC*, p. 85). That contradiction – "I *cast* my self … *fell* into" – perfectly encapsulates the texture of Crusoe's mental state, a state which much later in his life he will capture in the oxymoronic phrase, "involuntary Agency":

There is an inconsiderate Temper which reigns in our Minds, that hurries us down the Stream of our Affections, by a kind of involuntary Agency, and makes us do a thousand things, *in the doing of which,* we propose nothing to our selves, but an immediate Subjection to our WILL, that is to say our Passion, even without the Concurrence of our Understandings, and of which we can give very little Account, *after 't is done.* (*SR*, p. 129)

The passions and appetites are blind, they will satisfy themselves no matter what the cost, and if they are not controlled by reason, they rule as alien energies that in the end swallow up and dismember the self.

To the degree Crusoe has allowed himself to be subject to his own energies and appetites, he is the same as the cannibals. But the story of *Robinson Crusoe* is the story of Crusoe's struggle, as he says, to "distinguish" himself from the cannibals by asserting control over this savage stratum of energies, keeping himself from being incorporated by his own desire by containing it, subduing his energies rather than allowing them to subdue him. In Defoe's lexicon, achieving such a condition is called "composure," a state in which one is possessed with "a steady Calm of Mind, a clear Head, and serene Thoughts always acting the Mastership upon him" (*SR,* p. 162). In this state, "a perfect calm possesses the Soul":

if Peace and Temper prevail, and the Mind feels no Tempests rising; if the Affections are regular and exalted to virtuous and sublime Objects, the Spirits cool, and the Mind sedate, the Man is in a general Rectitude of Mind; he may be truly said to be *his own Man*.[116]

Robinson Crusoe moves forward in pulses. Moments of agitation and disturbance caused by the irruption of the lower energies are followed by periods of self-possession and composure, periods when Crusoe imposes "Mastership" over these energies, thus becoming "*his own Man.*" The young Crusoe is shaken by a storm at sea but quickly establishes a "settled Calmness" when it passes; he suffers "terrible Agonies of Mind" when he is shipwrecked but soon manages to "master [his] Dispondency" and reduce his life to order (*RC,* pp. 62, 91, 106). He is thrown into emotional turmoil by the earthquake, by his illness, by his vision of the avenging angel, by the sight of the footprint, by the spectacle of the bones scattered on the beach, by the appearance of the ship with all souls lost, and so on. These shocks are almost always imaged as violent motion or shaking: the storms, the "terrible Earthquake" whose "Motion … made my Stomach sick like one that was toss'd at Sea" (*RC,* pp. 116–117), his illness, which begins as a "shivering" and ends with a hallucinatory vision of an avenging angel whose step made "the Earth tremble, just as it had done before in the Earthquake" (*RC,* pp. 121–122), and the footprint, at the sight of which Crusoe "shook with cold, like one in an Ague" and was possessed by "innumerable fluttering Thoughts, like a Man perfectly confus'd and out of my self … not feeling … the Ground I went on" (*RC,* pp. 174, 170). It is a shaking because in each of these moments, the "Ground [he] went on" is jerked out from underneath his feet: his previous assumptions and habits of thinking and behavior (that there is nothing sinful about his defiance of his father; that he is capable of surviving on the island without the assistance of God; that Providence has demanded that he acquiesce to the fact that he must live alone and never learn to reintegrate himself into the human community) are proven wrong, his life destabilized, and, in the panic that follows, his primitive fears and desires break out and seize hold of him. But these moments of discombobulation are moments of potential conversion. Crusoe's old self, bound in habits of "Stupidly" formulated passions, is briefly broken open, and he suddenly has the opportunity to "compose" himself anew, wresting himself from the tyranny of the lower energies and thus becoming "his own Man." Such was the moment he ceased his "daily Tour to the Hill," reined in his savage desire for vengeance, and refigured his stance toward the cannibals.

Crusoe's prototypical moment of self-composure is when he draws up his list of what is good and what is evil in his island existence.

I now began to consider seriously my Condition, and the Circumstance I was reduc'd to, and I drew up the State of my Affairs in Writing, not so much to leave them to any that were to come after me, for I was like to have but few Heirs, as to deliver my Thoughts from daily poring upon them, and afflicting my Mind; and as my Reason began now to master my Despondency, I began to comfort my self as well as I could, and to set the good against the Evil, that I might have something to distinguish my Case from worse. (*RC,* p. 106)

Crusoe writes out this list less to understand his new circumstances than to extricate himself from his own savage unreason ("to deliver my Thoughts from daily poring upon them"), and in this passage self-composure is literalized as an act of writing because, like writing, self-composure makes legible that which is obscure and orders the inarticulate once it is brought in to consciousness. Crusoe is hurried on by his cannibal impulses so easily in part because those impulses are unknown, dark energies "I know not what to call," but once he can call these impulses into consciousness and subject them to the rule of reason, he can order and master them, fixing them (again, like writing) in a new, more coherent and permanent form, a form in which the appetites and passions are now directed toward their "best Uses." Crusoe is able to "deliver" himself from his energies, is able to "master" them, because he has become an agent who articulates, orders, stabilizes, and shapes that which previously had controlled him.[117]

Crusoe's many acts of self-composure all follow the pattern of this one. Crusoe begins in self-fragmentation and powerlessness, swamped by his energies, but, by "conversing mutually with my own Thoughts" (*RC,* p. 157), he moves steadily toward a kind of self-consolidation, a psychic order and wholeness that leaves him more and more in command of himself and master of his circumstances. By converting himself, Crusoe becomes "his own Man," and this in two senses, both of which are the obverse of the psychological condition figured by cannibalism. Since mastering the self means subduing the appetites and passions and shaping the self in accordance with the higher powers of reason, Crusoe becomes "his *own* Man": he is no longer incorporated by his own appetites and energies, becoming *their* man. Second, he becomes "his own *Man*," for these higher powers, as we have seen, are the natural possessions of all human beings, and only by exercising these potentials does one become fully a "*Man*," for it is "the powerfull discourse of divine Reason" alone that "makes us ... men, and distinguisheth us from beasts."[118]

To be a cannibal is to be indistinguishable from an animal, to descend to "Brutality itself." And to be a victim of cannibalism is to be reduced to an animal, too. Crusoe is disgusted by the cannibals because they "would have seiz'd on me with the same View, as I did of a Goat, or a Turtle; and have thought it no more a Crime to kill and devour me, than I did of a Pidgeon, or a Curlieu" (*RC,* pp. 201–202). Crusoe is driven to become "his own Man" because he cannot abide the thought of being merely an animal, either as a savage himself or as the victim of a savage.

Now, throughout the novel, Defoe draws parallels between Crusoe and the various animals on his island – the parrot, the cats, and especially the goats. At the very moment Crusoe learns that he can tame the goats by penning them up, depriving them of food, and then feeding them, he himself is being domesticated by God, penned up on his island, made to fear for his survival, and then provided food by Providence. Like the goats, who have become "so loving, so gentle, and so fond" that they eat from his hand, Crusoe comes to live "mighty comfortably, my Mind being entirely composed by resigning to the Will of God, and throwing my self wholly upon the Disposal of his Providence" (*RC,* pp. 149, 157):

How mercifully can our great Creator treat his Creatures, even in those Conditions in which they seem'd to be overwhelm'd in Destruction. How can he sweeten the bitterest Providences, and give us Cause to praise him for Dungeons and Prisons. What a Table was spread for me in a Wilderness, where I saw nothing at first but to perish for Hunger. (*RC,* p. 166)

Yet, for all these obvious parallels, I believe the point of the analogy is to show that Crusoe is not an animal. Crusoe trained the goats in one week, but it took many years for Crusoe to become domesticated, and much of the novel is taken up with dramatizing Crusoe's intellectual and spiritual struggle, his backsliding, his ambivalence, and especially the complex reasoning he goes through to come to terms with his submission to God. Crusoe spreads a table in the wilderness for the goats, but God does not spread a table in the wilderness for Crusoe in quite the same way. God provides the stuff for eating – the seed and the right climatic conditions – but, as the long sequence detailing Crusoe's process of making bread demonstrates, it is Crusoe who does the work. Crusoe feeds the goats, and the goats respond mindlessly to him. But, as in the scene where Crusoe struggles to overcome his "outragious" impulse to kill the cannibals, so here too. God creates the circumstances for Crusoe's deliverance, but it is Crusoe who must exploit those circumstances by reasoning out his course of action.

Crusoe has a natural aversion to cannibalism because, as we have seen, the capacity to press one's passions to their highest human ends and "right Uses" is a capacity inherent in any man. And the capacity that drives Crusoe to become a "Man" by rising above his animal existence is, of course, the same capacity that allows Friday to transcend his own savagery. Indeed, English colonial policy was based on the belief that this capacity of conversion was shared by the English colonists and the Indians alike and that both could be brought to freely choose to master themselves and join together in the great project of civilization and Christianity.

And yet – and this is the crucial thing to understand about Defoe – the freedom and mastery that come with self-composure typically entail submission – submission to reason, submission to reality, submission to the will of God. This paradoxical notion of freedom and submission is the reason, I believe, why indentured servitude hovers so pervasively in the background of the novel (and why Defoe pushes it to the foreground in *Moll Flanders* and *Colonel Jack* as he continues to tussle with the problematic nature of freedom). If cannibalism is a symbol of decomposition, a figure for those lower energies a human being must free himself from to become "his own Man," indentured servitude is a figure for the composing of the self, for the trajectory he must follow in his bid for freedom and mastery. When Crusoe composes himself by itemizing what is good and what is evil about his situation, he draws up a list "to deliver my Thoughts from daily poring upon them, and afflicting my Mind" (*RC*, p. 106). "Deliver," of course, means "to free from bondage," and this is what Crusoe, enslaved to his passions, does here and elsewhere when he composes himself: enslaved to his own passions, he frees himself from them by mastering himself, and he masters himself by submitting himself to the rule of his higher faculties.[119] Indentured servitude plots out this evolution from servant to master, for as an institution it structurally embodies the very paradox that Defoe sees at the heart of freedom: *one becomes a master by voluntarily submitting himself to servitude.*

The transformation from slave to master characterizes Crusoe's development on every level. In the passage where he composes himself by drawing up a list, it points to his psychological act of freeing the self from his passions. Elsewhere, such as when he speaks of his "Deliverance from Affliction" (*RC*, p. 129), for instance, it maps out his triumph over the external world and his freeing himself from being a victim of natural forces by mastering the material circumstances of his environment. Most obviously, it charts his religious conversion, his "Deliverance from Sin" (*RC,* p. 129), to which he is a slave, and his attaining spiritual liberty.

But no matter whatever level on which it occurs, in this transformation from slave to master freedom is achieved through submission. "The true Greatness of Life," remarks Crusoe when he meets the Russian prince at the end of *Farther Adventures,* is "to be the Masters of our selves" (*FA,* p. 205). The prince agrees, touting his own self-mastery and his freedom, but he makes this claim when he is literally a prisoner, kept under house arrest by the Czar. And yet, he argues, this contradiction perfectly embodies the true meaning of spiritual liberty. He is a "happy Prisoner" because he is "now Master of his Soul's Liberty," for his "blessed Confinement" has "banish'd [him] from the Crimes of Life" and freed him from being "the miserable Slave of his own Senses" (*FA,* p. 210). Now that he has secured "the Liberty of [his] Reason," he explains, there is less threat that his "Passions and Affections [will] possess and overthrow me" (*FA,* p. 210). This paradox is reiterated by the tutor in *Colonel Jack* when he says that he has been "deliver'd from the wretched Life he had liv'd" in London as a sinner and a thief *because* he is now living "the Life of a Slave in *Virginia*" and thus has been "deliver'ed from the horrid Necessity of doing … ill things" (*CJ,* 153–154).

Defoe does not fully endorse either the prince's or the tutor's argument for a radical disengagement from the world and its temptations, as we shall see, but he certainly believes that the "Soul's Liberty" is thoroughly paradoxical. Such a paradoxical formulation was traditional, founded on the history of the Hebrews' enslavement in the Old Testament and the New Testament's conversion of this history into an allegory of Christ's redeeming humans from their bondage to sin, the flesh, and the law. The Hebrews freed themselves from slavery to the Egyptians by willingly becoming servants to God, and, in the Christian allegory, one gained spiritual liberty by submitting oneself to God's will. Crusoe himself becomes spiritually free, the "Master of his Soul's Liberty," only when he is put in the "Prison" of his island and, in this "Captivity," is made to understand his need for a "Deliverance from Sin" (*RC,* p. 128). Living a "Life of Slavery" and "Bondage" becomes for Crusoe, as it does for the Russian prince and the tutor, a "blessed Confinement." Crusoe frees himself by submitting himself, "resigning [myself] to the Will of God, and throwing my self wholly upon the Disposal of his Providence" (*RC,* pp. 58, 132, 157).

This same paradox informs Crusoe's dealings with nature. As John Richetti has shown, Crusoe's "masterful relationship to the environment" is "a formalization" of his relationship to God.[120] Just as Crusoe achieves spiritual freedom through his submission to God, so in the realm of nature, he "achieves freedom by perfect submission to ... circumstances."[121] Just as he learns to read the "Cautions, Warnings, and Instructions" of God's will in dreams and events, so he learns to read the signs of nature, and he is able to exploit nature by adapting himself to its forces (*SR*, p. 190). His freedom and mastery are founded on "observation and submission," "watching the unpredictable flow of events for an opening ... co-operating with events at the moment when they will serve."[122] True, Crusoe often indulges himself with illusions about the power of his own will, but when he coerces nature, such as when he builds a canoe too big for him to launch, he almost always fails. Typically, nature yields to him only after he has yielded first by regulating his desires and behavior in accordance with nature's patterns or the demands of reality. It is a lesson that is impressed on him at the beginning of his sojourn on the island when he grounds his raft in the creek and discovers "all ... I could do, was wait 'till the Tide was at highest, keeping the Raft with my Oar like an Anchor to hold the Side of it fast to the Shore" (*RC*, p. 96). It is an insight symbolically played out near the end of his solitary stay when, getting caught in the tides and currents off the coast of his island and almost being swept away to his death, he retreats to the hillside to observe the flux and reflux of the waters. Initially, he resigns himself to confinement on the island, but later, when he wants to visit the ship wrecked off the coast, he puts to use his knowledge of the tides and currents and yields to their forces until they sweep him to where he wants to go. Crusoe plants the grain saved from the shipwreck, and it fails to grow. After observing the cycles of dry and rainy weather, he plants again, and this time, the seed "yielded a very good Crop" (*RC*, p. 134). "By this Experiment I was made Master of my Business, and knew exactly when the proper Season was to sow" (*RC*, p. 135). Crusoe becomes a "Master of [his] Business" by submitting himself to the regimen of nature. Increasingly, he makes this his philosophy of action: "to wait to see what the Issue of Things might present," "to put my self upon the Watch ... and leave the rest to the Event, taking such Measures as the Opportunity should present, let be what would be" (*RC*, pp. 252, 204).

Spiritual freedom and freedom from the tyranny of circumstance are both predicated on another freedom – freedom from the bondage to one's own energies and appetites – and this freedom, too, is paradoxical. "Christian liberty" conventionally was defined as the "Freedom from the bondage of Sin and Satan, and from the Dominion of Men's Lusts and Passions and inordinate Desires."[123] Freedom resides not in indulging desire but in restraining it. Defoe argued that those who abuse "*Liberty* to indulge their Wickedness" and who think "that Liberty is a Freedom to Crime" or a "Freedom to do Wickedly" espouse "Notions of Liberty" that

are not only inconsistent with true Liberty, but destructive of it; for nothing is more certain, than that true Liberty consists in a freedom to do well, not giving Loose to the Passions, gratifying every vitious Gust, and taking off the Restraint of Laws, leaving every Man to do what is right in his own Eyes.[124]

He asserted elsewhere, more pointedly and paradoxically, "Liberty *to do* Evil is an abandon'd Slavery, the worst of *Bondage*; and Confinement *from doing Evil,* is the only *true Liberty.*"[125]

"I broke loose," Crusoe says, speaking of his father's injunctions as if they were physical bonds that kept him from his freedom, and yet his "breaking away" (*RC,* pp. 60, 85) precipitates him into servitude to the vicissitudes of his own passions and the bondage of circumstance ("the same Day that I broke away from my Father … the same Day afterwards I was taken by the *Sally* Man of War, and made a Slave" [*RC,* p. 155]). In pursuing what he misconceives of as his freedom, he simply abandons himself to his "wandering Inclination," that "fatal … Propension of Nature," and he finds that rather than acting in freedom he has "obey'd blindly the Dictates of my Fancy." He ends up, as his father had warned, "sold to the Life of Slavery" (*RC,* pp. 57–58, 86).[126]

To convert, to become "his own Man," Crusoe must achieve a "Composure of Soul," which is attained only when the "Soul [becomes] truly Master of it self," exercising its authority over the "Disorders of the Passions," "by bringing the Mind to be above the Power or Reach of the Allurement, and to an absolute Mastership over … wicked Desire" (*SR,* pp. 60–61). This sovereignty is achieved through submission. To cease to be "a Slave to his Passion," he voluntarily submits himself to "the Mastership of [his] Reason," which keeps his "Passions, Appetites and Affections in a constant due Subjection to [his] Understanding:"[127]

> The greatest Freedom Mankind e're obtain'd,
> Is to be *but from Doing ill* restrain'd;
> In vain Unbounded Liberties we boast,
> We're all but Slaves when just Confinement's lost.[128]

Like the indentured servant he is so often compared to, Crusoe becomes a master only after he has voluntarily submitted himself to servitude.

CHAPTER 3

Servitude and self-transformation in Colonel Jack

The paradoxical language of slavery and freedom was traditional in religious and ethical discourse, and its source was the Bible, whose rich body of figuration for the experience of sin and redemption was drawn from the ancient Hebrews' slavery in Egypt. Defoe and his English audience inherited this language, but, beyond the captivity narratives of New England or tales of enslavement by Barbary pirates, there was little in the world they experienced that could concretely body forth a narrative allegory or a system of symbols, emblems, and metaphors for the traditional sense of sin and deliverance. One exception was indentured servitude, a form of bondage endured by hundreds of thousands of British subjects.

The story of Crusoe's punishment and deliverance begins with a brief episode of Barbary captivity that proleptically identifies his experience on the island as a kind of slavery. Once Crusoe is on the island, however, Defoe uses the patterns of indentured servitude to plot out his protagonist's life, and he exploits the symbolic possibilities of New World servitude and mastery to give resonance to Crusoe's spiritual and psychological growth. Still, indentured servitude is a figure in the novel: Crusoe is *like* an indentured servant. After *Robinson Crusoe,* Defoe uses indentured servitude to shape the psychological, moral, and religious progress of his protagonists, but now literally. Moll and Jack come to the New World as actual indentured servants and end as masters of actual plantations.

In turning his attention to indentured servitude as an institution and not simply as a metaphor, Defoe expands his examination of servitude and freedom and moves into territory he did not explore in *Robinson Crusoe.* This chapter traces this new direction in his thinking in *Colonel Jack.*

Like Crusoe's, Jack's transformation and his transition from servant to master is played out against the background of the conversion of the Other – in Jack's case, the rebellious African slaves he oversees when he is an indentured servant in Maryland. Jack's is an extremely complex transformation, and I will analyze it in detail, but first I want to look at Defoe's indictment of the brutal treatment of slaves in *Colonel Jack,* for I believe this will help us pinpoint the new direction Defoe pursued when he wrote this novel.

As a brief against the inhumane conditions of slavery, *Colonel Jack* was part of a small but growing protest. Though the conditions of slavery, particularly in the Caribbean, had been reported on, if somewhat neutrally, long before Defoe's novel appeared, opposition to the institution itself was almost nonexistent.[1] But if slavery was seldom questioned and abolition rarely advocated, the barbarous treatment of slaves came under greater public scrutiny in the twenty years preceding the publication of *Colonel Jack,* largely because wholesale African slavery had spread to the Chesapeake, where the novel is set. Previously, the relatively few black slaves of the region worked alongside white servants and tended to be treated similarly, but with the Africanization of the labor force, African labor became more regimented and hours of work were extended. Ira Berlin has shown that in the decades immediately preceding the publication of *Colonel Jack,* violence against slaves increased dramatically in the Chesapeake. Slaves were driven harder, the frequency and intensity of the beatings and maimings increased, and new, more humiliating and painful punishments were invented. In response to these developments, critics (and especially the Society for the Propagation of the Gospel in Foreign Parts [SPG]) mounted a campaign to protest the abuses of slavery and to ameliorate the conditions of slaves in the colonies.[2]

Those who protested the treatment of the slaves had what are, to modern eyes, modest objectives: they argued for the religious education of slaves, for their conversion and baptism, and for humane treatment. The obstacles they faced in achieving even these limited goals were formidable. Above all, they ran up against unshakable notions of the Africans' inferiority. Francis Le Jau, an SPG missionary in South Carolina, wrote in despair that "Masters can't be persuaded that Negroes ... are otherwise than Beasts."[3] In 1699, the Virginia Assembly determined that the Africans were incapable of being educated or converted because of the "Gros[s] Barbarity and rudeness of their manners ... and the weakness and Shallowness of their minds."[4] After laboring in the vineyards of the New World, even some of the missionaries came to have doubts. One colonial clergyman feared that "few of [the slaves] are capable of being instructed" because "they are slow of apprehension, of a dull understanding, and soon forgetting what they have learned."[5]

The reformers denied that Africans were brutes. Slaves "are reasonable Creatures, as well as you," Richard Baxter told his English audience.

"Nature made them your equals. Remember that they have immortal souls, and are equally capable of salvation with your selves."[6] They "were made in [God's] Image, and endued with rational and immortal Souls," Thomas Tryon insisted; they had "the same Faculties, Understanding, Memory and Will" as Europeans.[7] Morgan Godwyn contemptuously dismissed the planters' belief that "the *Negro's* ... are ... *no Men*" as a "*Fiction hardly to be parall'd throughout the fables of the Poets.*"[8]

Since African slaves possessed reason, they were educable; since they had souls, they should be educated in the truths of religion and then baptized; since they were fully human, they should be treated humanely. In an influential sermon preached before the SPG, William Fleetwood took English colonists to task for their treatment of the slaves. Africans, he said, are "equally the Workmanship of God" as the slaveowners themselves,

endued with the same Faculties, and intellectual Powers; Bodies of the same Flesh and Blood, and Souls as certainly immortal: These People were made to be as Happy as themselves, and are as capable of being so; and however hard their Condition be in this World, with respect to their Captivity and Subjection, they were to be as Just and Honest, as Chast and Virtuous, as Godly and Religious as themselves: They were ... purchased with the same Blood of Christ, their common Saviour and Redeemer; and in order to all this, they were to have the Means of Salvation put into their Hands, they were to be instructed in the Faith of *Christ.*[9]

"They are the Creatures of God, and of the Race of Mankind for whom Christ died," Bishop Butler remarked, "and it is inexcusable to keep them in Ignorance of the End for which they were made; and the Means, whereby they may become Partakers of the General Redemption."[10]

Many colonists were not pleased by such talk. Recognizing the equality of the souls of African slaves was tantamount to acknowledging their personhood. The legal implications were disquieting. If slaves were baptized, slaveowners might well have to set them free. So anxious were the colonists that, between 1664 and 1706, Maryland, Virginia, the Carolinas, New York, and New Jersey passed legislation explicitly stating that baptism would not lead to manumission. Further, colonists feared that if their slaves were made Christians slaveholders would not be able to discipline them rigorously enough to make them profitable. Worse, education would give slaves expectations that would make them bridle at their condition. It was a "common prejudice," James Blair noted about his fellow Virginians, that Christianizing slaves "makes them prouder, and inspires them with thoughts of freedom."[11]

In the face of such resistance, reformers trod warily. Some, because they accepted the existing social order and respected property rights, saw nothing repugnant in the institution of slavery. Dr. Bray, one of the most active promoters of the conversion of African slaves in this period, thought slavery acceptable, and when in 1710 the SPG itself became the holder of nearly 300 slaves by virtue of a bequest from the Codrington estates in Barbados, they did not free them. Others had too realistic an understanding of where power lay to press for changes they felt had no chance of happening.[12]

And so, those who sought to ameliorate the condition of the slaves stated their positions and aims carefully. They explicitly acknowledged the legality of slavery and assured the colonists that, in ministering to the spiritual needs of slaves and in advocating more humane treatment, they were not arguing for the manumission of converted slaves or for the abolition of slavery. Thomas Secker insisted that their conversion to Christianity did not imply that slaves should be given freedom: "For as human Authority hath granted them none, so the Scripture, far from making any Alteration in Civil Rights, expressly directs, that *every Man abide in the Condition wherein he is called,* with great Indifference of Mind concerning outward Circumstances."[13] Edmund Gibson, Bishop of London, declared that the freedom promised by Christianity was the freedom from sin, "but as to [the slaves'] *outward* Condition, whatever that was before, whether bond or free, their being baptiz'd, and becoming Christians, makes no manner of Change in it."[14] In 1711, the position of the reformers was enunciated by Fleetwood, thousands of copies of whose sermon were distributed in the North American colonies and the West Indies to assuage the anxiety of slaveowners about the Society's missionary work. Slaveowners, said Fleetwood,

are neither prohibited by the Laws of *God,* nor those of the *Land,* from keeping *Christian Slaves;* their Slaves are no more at Liberty after they are Baptized, than they were before. There were People in St. *Paul's* time, that imagin'd they were freed from all former Engagements by becoming *Christians;* but St. *Paul* tells them, this was not the meaning of *Christian Liberty;* the Liberty wherewith *Christ* had made them Free, was freedom from their Sins, Freedom from the Fears of Death, and everlasting Misery, and not from any State of Life, in which they had either voluntarily engaged themselves, or were fallen into through their Misfortune. *Let every Man* (says He, 1 Cor. 7.20.) *abide in the same Calling, wherein he was called.* Let every Man know, that his being called to the Faith of Christ, does not exempt him from continuing in the same State of Life he was before; it makes no alteration in his Condition in the World; the Liberty of Christianity is entirely Spiritual.[15]

George Berkeley was outraged that the planters took no "Care ... to convert the Negroes of our Plantations, who, to the Infamy of *England,* the Scandal of the World, continue Heathen under Christian Masters, and in Christian Countries." But he, too, thought that "Gospel Liberty consists with temporal Servitude." His estate of Rhode Island was cultivated by slave labor.[16]

But, though they either agreed with or acquiesced to the planters' view on the legitimacy of slaveowning, reformers were less compromising about the slaveowners' fear that Christianizing slaves and treating them kindly would give "them better Notions of themselves than is consistent with their state of Slavery and their duty to their Masters."[17] When slaveowners claimed that humane treatment fostered pride in their slaves and made them impossible to control, reformers countered that kind treatment made them better slaves. Baptized slaves, one missionary pointed out, "behave themselves very well, and do better for their Masters profit than formerly, for they are taught to serve out of Christian Love & Duty."[18] Tryon contended that if the "Master deal justly" and treated his slaves "with tenderness," they would *all in general* become more tractable, obedient and diligent" and would "perform [their] Labour much better" – indeed, "twenty of [them] would dispatch as much Work and Business as thirty do."[19] Godwyn argued that humane treatment and a Christian education would not, as the planters claimed, "make them less governable" and more prone to "*mutiny* and *rebel,*" nor would it "strike *deep at their Profit,* and quite ruine their *Estates.*" To the contrary, it would encourage "*absolute* and entire *obedience.*"[20] The missionary Elias Neau concluded sanguinely that slave masters "will come to recognize that ... the Christian religion inspires in their slaves love and obedience to their masters and mistresses."[21]

In *Colonel Jack,* Defoe takes (with one important exception) the same position as other humanitarian reformers. Whether at bottom he questioned the morality of slavery is difficult to ascertain, but slavery was economically beneficial, and Defoe consistently subordinated whatever ethical objections he may have had to mercantile considerations. Slavery had become essential to the colonies, and with the acquisition of the Asiento rights in 1713, the slave trade provided an "infinite Advantage" to England's economic well-being. Both had to remain "uninterrupted."[22] Slavery simply had become so thoroughly interwoven in the economy that to pick out the thread would unravel the whole fabric and result in "a ruined Nation."[23] Defoe's rhetoric takes on a catastrophic edge when he speaks of these matters: "*No African* Trade, *no* Negroes; *no* Negroes, *no* Sugars, Ginger, Indicos, &c.; *no* Sugars, &c., *no* Islands; *no* Islands, *no* Continent; *no* Continent, *no* Trade; that is to say, farewell all your *American* Trade."[24] If "the Supply of *Negroes* [were] to stop one Year," he claimed, "the Colonies ... would bleed to Death." "Our Colonies in *America* ... could no more be maintained ... without the Supply of *Negro Slaves* ... Than *London* could subsist without the River of *Thames.*"[25]

Early in his career, Crusoe buys and sells "*Negroes* ... in great Numbers" (*RC,* p. 85). He works his plantation in Brazil with slaves, he sells Xury to the Portuguese captain, and in the voyage that ends in his shipwreck, he is on his way to the Guinea coast for a cargo of slaves. Moll and Jack work their plantations with slaves, and the unnamed narrator of *A New Voyage round the World* repays the generosity of his Spanish host by giving him "three Negroe-men, which I had bought ... for my own Use, but knew I could supply myself again ... at a moderate Price" (*NV,* p. 188). There is no indication that Defoe, who himself had invested in the Royal African Company, disapproved of any of this.

But many humanitarian reformers who protested the cruel treatment of slaves either supported or acquiesced to the institution of slavery itself. Like these reformers, Defoe insists that Africans are not brutes but human beings who possess the "Faculties of reasonable Creatures" as well as "some Sense of Kindness, [and] some Principles of natural Generosity" (*CJ,* p. 136), certainly enough to make it a moral imperative that they be treated as fellow creatures.[26] Humane treatment, he says, echoing the reformers, will not lead to "refractoriness, and sullenness," as plantation owners feared, but will make slaves better, more efficient laborers (*CJ,* p. 144). "Your Business shall be better discharg'd," says Jack to his master, "and your Plantations better order'd, and more Work done by the *Negroes,* who shall be engaged by Mercy and Lenity, than by those, who are driven, and dragg'd by the Whips, and the Chains of a merciless Tormentor" (*CJ,* p. 141). When slaves are "use[d] ... with Humanity," they "do their Work faithfully, and chearfully" – indeed, they will "delight in such Service" (*CJ,* pp. 145, 136).

Given the fact that in *Colonel Jack* Defoe reiterates the central points made by the other reformers, what is really remarkable is the one thing he does *not* talk about. He does not broach the issue of Christianizing the slaves by means of education and baptism – the very issue that was at the heart of the program of the reformers. In his portrayal of slavery, Defoe avoids any reference to religion at all.

It is a surprising omission. Defoe was adamant about the conversion of the slaves. In *Religious Courtship,* he draws a pathetic picture of a black slave who thirsts for religious knowledge but hides his reading of the Bible because he "was afraid his Master would think, if he turn'd Christian, he would be baptiz'd, and so think himself free."[27] In *The Family Instructor,* Defoe excoriates any master who has "neither Concern for [the] Soul" of his slave nor "for his Future State."[28] He indicts the white slaveowners in the colonies as "very wicked" and "very cruel Men" because they refuse to give their slaves religious instruction, more fearful that they "should be Christians, and get their Liberty," he concludes mordantly, "than they are afraid they should be Infidels, and go to the Devil."[29] He does not even qualify his call for the religious instruction of slaves with the typical feint of saying that they will remain slaves after baptism. He presents the spiritual salvation of the slaves unconditionally – they are to be instructed in the knowledge of God ("'tis our Duty to give Instruction to every one") and to be baptized no matter what the consequences – even implying that it is better they "run away" than "go to Hell."[30] Defoe intends no irony when he has Crusoe sell Xury with the condition that he be set free in ten years "if he turn'd Christian" (*RC,* p. 81).

Defoe's decision not to raise the issue of the religious conversion of the African slaves in *Colonel Jack* is even more perplexing given that in all three *Crusoe* books he argues vigorously for the worldwide conversion of the heathens. And, like *Crusoe, Colonel Jack* has all the appearance of being structured like another double-conversion novel, with Jack's transformation, like Crusoe's, played off against the conversion of the savage Other. Jack begins as a thief and ends an honest and successful planter, and he comes "at last to look with shame and blushes, upon such a Course of Wickedness, as I had gone through in the World" (*CJ,* p. 264). Jack's "conversion" of the slaves is instrumental in *his* being raised from a servant to a master, and given the religious resonances the figures of master and servant had in *Robinson Crusoe,* one would think that the conversions of the Africans as well as Jack himself are in some way religious conversions.

But they are not. The slaves convert from savagery to civility, not from heathenism to Christianity, and Jack does not betray the slightest interest in teaching them religion. And although Jack becomes a better and more successful man, he does not become a more religious one. In fact, the religious dimensions of his conversion – if that is how we are to understand his transformation from servant to master – are continually displaced or delayed in the novel. Twice Jack meets indentured servants who have led lives of crime like he has and who see their servitude as punishment the "very Miseries" become "the means of [their] Deliverance," a "Miracle of Divine Goodness" that has moved them to repent their past sins and that has given them the "Power to live an honest Life" (*CJ,* pp. 156, 122). Jack is so "exceedingly mov'd" by the example of both these men that he begins to speak of his own experience of indentured servitude in the same language of redemption and deliverance that we saw in *Robinson Crusoe*:

It was an inexpressible Joy to me, that I was now like to be, not only a Man, but an Honest Man; and it yielded me a greater Pleasure, that I was Ransom'd from being a Vagabond, a Thief, and a Criminal, as I had been from a Child, than that I was deliver'd from Slavery, and the wretched State of a *Virginia* Sold Servant. (*CJ*, pp. 122, 149)

And yet, Jack's religious stirrings peter out.

I cannot say my Thoughts were yet Ripen'd ... I liv'd now ... a very regular Sober Life ... but as to commencing Penitent ... I cannot say, I had any Convictions upon me, sufficient to bring it on ... So it wore off again Gradually. (*CJ*, p. 161)

Jack eventually does come to a religious conversion, but he does so, literally, in the last two pages of the novel, twenty-four years after he has completed his rise from servant to master.

Servitude and mastery as figures do not run on all fours in *Colonel Jack* the way they did in *Robinson Crusoe*. Unlike Crusoe's rise from slave to master, Jack's rise marks no spiritual progress. Nor does his servitude and mastery reflect the divine machinery of God's justice and mercy. Crusoe's slavery on the island is just punishment for his "original sin," but Jack had given up his life of crime long before he became an indentured servant. Even on a literal level, he is not made an indentured servant because of a crime he committed. He is kidnapped. His indentured servitude is a gross injustice. He is an innocent victim.[31]

This is not to say that Jack's rise from servant to master is emblematic of nothing. Jack *does* experience a real conversion on his way to becoming a wealthy planter. He becomes "not only a Man, but an Honest Man," a man who "liv'd ... a very regular Sober Life, always taken up in my Business, and running into no Excess" (*CJ*, pp. 149, 161). But this is not a religious transformation. Jack's is a perfectly *secular* conversion.

And that is precisely the nature of the Africans' conversion, too. Defoe dramatizes their transformation from savage to civil behavior, their maturation and growth as social and ethical creatures, but he studiously avoids any reference to their spiritual conversion. I think that Defoe resisted his own convictions and purposely chose not to broach the issue of their religious conversion because his focus is elsewhere. As in *Robinson Crusoe,* the conversion of Jack and the savage Other follow parallel paths, but in *Colonel Jack,* the focus of that transformation is very much on this world. There is no religious epiphany in *Colonel Jack,*

nor are there any egregious providential interventions. The new direction Defoe takes in this novel is to chart a transformation that is almost
wholly psychological and moral, a transformation that takes place in a
world whose determinants, unlike those of *Robinson Crusoe,* are largely
material and social.

In shifting his focus in *Colonel Jack* to secular transformation, Defoe
engages a different order of causality and freedom than he did in *Robinson
Crusoe.* Jack's transformation takes place entirely within social space. The
choices open to Jack and the parameters of his freedom are quite different
from what we observed in Crusoe. Most significantly, the very processes
of Jack's growth and change are different. Crusoe is guided by the supernatural, and the story of his becoming the master of his soul is plotted out
under the figure of indentured servitude, a figure whose tenor is largely
religious. Jack's transformation is also plotted out by indentured servitude,
but his growth is economic and social. The mechanism of this economic
and social growth is, appropriately, a concrete economic and social institution. Jack's indentured servitude is literal.

This shift from the figurative to the literal raises a crucial question that
Defoe would have to answer in *Colonel Jack.* How, exactly, *did* indentured
servitude transform individuals? Colonial promoters entertained two
explanations, but thoughtful observers considered both of them insufficient, and Defoe appears to have thought so too.

The first and most common explanation is offered by Jack himself. "Poor
young people … that go voluntarily to [America], and … freely bind themselves there," he claims, are certain to succeed because "they are sure to be
immediately provided for, and after the expiration of their time, to be put
into a Condition to provide for themselves" (*CJ,* pp. 162–163). And how
were they put "into a Condition to provide for themselves"? When "he had
serv'd his time out faithfully," a servant has "50 Acres of Land allotted him,
for Planting"; "Some have a Horse, a Cow, and three Hogs … lent them as
a Stock for the Land"; "Custom has made it a Trade, to give Credit to such
Beginners as these, for Tools, Cloths, Nails, Iron-Work, and other things
necessary for their Planting; and which the Persons so giving Credit to
them, are to be paid for out of the Crop of *Tobacco* which they shall Plant"
(*CJ,* pp. 146–147). The servant becomes a master because he is "immediately provided for" during his indentures and then is given land on which
to grow tobacco and is lent everything to make tobacco grow; he repays
the loan with the tobacco grown on the land he has been given from seed
he has been provided with, cultivated with tools he has been lent. In short,

men become servants and are "immediately provided for" and upon completion of their terms are "put into a Condition to provide for themselves" by ... being provided for.

Indentured servitude is bound to succeed, according to this logic, because the servant is given everything within a closed circuit of nurture. The promise of indentured servitude, it turns out, is underwritten by that most persistent myth of the New World, the myth of its natural abundance. The abundance of America, William Byrd enthused, made the transition from slavery to freedom inevitable:

> Did the miserable inhabitants of countrys that lived under the oppression of despotick government know how charming a part of the world this is, how fruitful the soil, how wholesome and how pleasant the clymate, and upon how easy terms they might take up land, they would abandon their calamitys and flock over like swallows in the spring towards affluence and a warm sun. Here they would exchange slavery for freedome, want for plenty[,] barren mountains for fruitful plains, and when they labour it would be for themselves and their familys.[32]

But such an explanation was not completely satisfactory, and in his less buoyant moments Byrd thought that material abundance was more a curse than a blessing. From the founding of Virginia, he observed, its reputation as a "Paradise" encouraged immigrants to think "they might live without work."[33] As a consequence, they became "Indolent Wretches" who took "no thought for the Morrow" and who had "a thorough Aversion to labour."[34] "Idleness is [their] general Character": "Plenty and a Warm Sun confirm them in their Disposition to laziness for their whole Lives"; "The Air is so mild, and the Soil so fruitful, that very little Labour is requir'd to fill their Bellies."[35] Robert Beverley wrote that the inhabitants of Virginia were sunk into a "slothful Indolence" because they depended "altogether on the Liberality of Nature without endeavouring to improve its Gifts by Art or Industry. They spunge upon the Blessings of a warm Sun and a fruitful Soil, and almost grutch the Pains of gathering in the Bounties of the Earth."[36] Benjamin Martyn worried that immigrants to Georgia, people who "have never been used to look forward, [who] live but to the present Day, and are unwilling to labour for any Thing but an immediate Subsistence," would not reform at all if their needs were immediately provided for by the natural abundance of the New World.[37] "Many of the poor who have been useless in England," the Trustees of the Georgia project glumly concluded, "were inclined to be useless likewise in *Georgia,*" and they forbad slave-holding in Georgia not because they had any moral objection to slavery but because they thought it would encourage immigrants to persist in their idleness.[38]

Even enthusiastic colonial propagandists admitted that material abundance alone was insufficient to make a master out of a servant.

Poor labouring Men, so secur'd of a fix'd future Settlement; will be thereby induc'd to go thither more willingly; and act, when there, with double Diligence, and Duty; And when their Time expires, possessing just Land enough to pass their Lives at Ease, and bring their Children up honestly.

Transported criminals will succeed, too, though again there are conditions:

These if they forsake their roguery ... when they are free, may work at day-labour, or else rent a small plantation for a trifle almost; or else turn overseers, if they are expert, industrious, and careful, or follow their trade ... The plenty of the country, and the good wages given to work-folks occasion very few poor.[39]

The New World will provide abundantly, but the gift must be labored for. The servant must pursue his ends with "Diligence," must discipline himself to "Duty"; criminals must "forsake their roguery," must be "industrious." In spite of Jack's excitement about the promise of the abundance of America, his optimism is tempered elsewhere in the novel. His master promises his servants that they will "be encourag'd" by the favorable material conditions of the New World, but they will succeed only if they will "be diligent, and sober"(*CJ*, p. 122). "Diligence" echoes through all Defoe's comments on indentured servants: "diligent Servant[s]" will succeed in the New World, but only if they exercise "their own Diligence in the time of Service," for conditions are so favorable there that "no Diligent Man ever Miscarried" – all he need do is "but apply himself with Diligence and Industry to the Business of the Country," and then he "is sure ... both of living Well and growing Rich" (*CJ*, pp. 146–147, 162).

And therein lay the problem. Many people – and certainly many indentured servants – had ended up in the New World precisely because they lacked the diligence and industry that would have led to success in the Old World or more often because they had had diligence and industry beaten out of them by circumstance. In Scotland, Defoe discovered that indentured servants went to the colonies "upon better Terms than the *English*,"

without the scandalous Art of Kidnapping, making Drunk, Wheedling, Betraying, and the like; the Poor People offering themselves fast enough, and thinking it their Advantage to go; as indeed it is, to those who go with sober Resolutions, namely, to serve out their Times, and then become diligent Planters for themselves; and this would be a much wiser Course in *England* than to turn Thieves, and worse, and then be sent over by Force.[40]

Faced with hard circumstances, the English do not, like the Scots, make "sober Resolutions" to work diligently to better their lives, and lacking sobriety and diligence, how could they possibly succeed? Having all things "immediately provided for" would not magically instill these virtues but simply would confirm the poor, the idle, and the criminal in their poverty, idleness, and criminality.

If material abundance could not explain how individuals could be transformed in the New World, the second most common explanation was just as inadequate. To be sure, America was a land of plenty and a warm sun, this explanation went, but it was abundant in necessities alone; in other respects, it was a land of scarcity, a land like Crusoe's island, so primitive that life was reduced to essentials, so devoid of temptations that it offered few opportunities for misconduct. Here, indentured servants "will have no room for Luxury, or any of its attendant Vices."[41] Thomas Rundle thought that life in America was regenerative because "Tis removing out of temptation those who might probably have had no means for a livelihood but rapine, violence and disorder."[42] "The Idle, the Sloathful, and the Vagabonds of England, Scotland, and Ireland," said one colonial promoter, had "a fair prospect … of living very Plentifully and Happily" because they had no "Temptation" to act immorally.[43] James Oglethorpe thought that once "Offenders" became indentured servants their "Manners and Habits … would meliorate in a Country not populous enough to encourage a profligate Course of Life."[44] Spotswood saw Virginia as a place where a sort of moral purity had been recovered. "I have observed here less Swearing and Prophaneness, less Drunkenness and Debauchery, less uncharitable feuds and animositys, and less knaverys and Villanys than in any part of the world where my Lot has been." "The natural Cause of this blessing," he thought, was "the people's living under less worldly Temptations."[45]

Defoe was deeply skeptical of such arguments. That "happy Prisoner," the exiled Russian prince in *Farther Adventures,* claims that his life of physical confinement leads to a higher freedom.

Here I am free from the Temptation of returning to my former miserable Greatness … Dear Sir, let me remain in this blessed Confinement, banish'd from the Crimes of Life, rather than purchase a Shew of Freedom, at the Expense of the Liberty of my Reason, and at the Expence of the future Happiness which now I have in my View, but shall then, I fear, quickly loose Sight of; for I am but Flesh, a Man, a meer Man, have Passions and Affections as likely to possess and overthrow as any Man. (*FA,* p. 210)

But to Defoe, such "blessed Confinement" smacks of a cloistered virtue. It is really a sign of weakness, "an Acknowledgment of … our Incapacity to bind our selves to needful Restraints" (*SR*, p. 60). Almost immediately after Crusoe extols the blessing of his being "remov'd from all the Wickedness of the World" (*RC*, p. 152), God reproves him with the sign of a footprint, reminding him that he must prepare himself to re-enter the world. In *Serious Reflections during the Life and Surprising Adventures of Robinson Crusoe,* Defoe criticizes those who have "Recourse to … Solitudes" as a way of "delivering themselves from the Temptations which Society exposed them to": "a vicious Inclination remov'd from the Object, is still a vicious Inclination" (*SR*, pp. 65, 61). To be in "blessed Confinement" – whether one is an exiled prince, an island castaway, or an indentured servant – does not make a genuinely renovated man. "Retreat from the World," Defoe said, was "both irreligious in it self, and inconsistent with a Christian Life" (*SR*, p. 63). Temptations were to be met head on, wrestled with, and subdued, not to be avoided by secluding oneself from the world.

> There is no need of a Wilderness, … no Necessity of a Cell on top of a Mountain, or a desolate Island in the Sea … If the Mind be confined, if the Soul be truly Master of itself, all is safe; for it is certainly and effectually Master of the Body, and what signifies Retreats? (*SR*, p. 60)

To seclude oneself is "a meer Cheat" – simply a change in circumstances, when what was needed was "a Change in the Soul, by bringing the Mind to be above the Power or Reach of the Allurement, and to an absolute Mastership over the wicked Desire; otherwise the vicious Desire remains as the Force remains in the Gunpowder, and will exert itself when ever toucht with the Fire" (*SR*, p. 61).[46]

Because the usual explanations for how an individual was transformed in America were so obviously deficient, it is easy to understand why many were skeptical of the promise of the New World. Real transformation was predicated on a reformation of attitudes and values, an amendment of the will. If changes in character were brought about by changes in material circumstances, the transformation was probably not much of a transformation. In *The Widdow-Ranter,* Behn exposes the low origins of those indentured servants who, in the changed circumstances of Virginia, have risen to positions of power and prominence. One leader of the colony was originally "a broken excise-man, who spent the king's money to buy [his] wife fine petticoats, and at last not worth a groat, [he] came over a poor servant, though now a Justice of the Peace, and of the Honourable Council."[47] But all these changes in title, profession, and station are illusory: Behn's colonists remain exactly the same cowards, drunks, and cheats they were in England. "The generality of the Men look as if they had just knock'd off their Fetters," Ward remarks about the newly transported felons to the

New World, "and by an unexpected Providence, escap'd the danger of a near Mis-fortune; the dread of which, hath imprinted that in their *Looks,* which they can no more alter than an *Etheopian* can his *Colour.*"[48]

Although Defoe was as wary of the explanations as these satirists were, he did not share their skepticism about the possibility of transformation. In recounting Jack's career in the Chesapeake, Defoe dramatizes evenhandedly and with considerably greater shading what others swept aside with dismissive sarcasm. While the satirists portrayed the lower-class upstart thrusting himself forward in America with unalloyed contempt, Defoe treats Jack's struggle to raise his social status sympathetically. And to those skeptics who claimed that there were no real new beginnings in the New World, Defoe responds not just with the tale of Jack's successful rise from indentured servant to plantation owner but with the story of how in that rise Jack becomes a morally renovated man. On the basis of his experience as an indentured servant, Jack creates a "new Life" as "an Honest Man" (*CJ*, pp. 149–150). There is no suggestion that this moral transformation is false. Indeed, the "new Life" he constructs for himself is symbolically severed from his immoral and criminal past when the goods he bought with the money he acquired dishonestly in London are lost at sea.

I had such an abhorrence of the wicked Life I had led, that I was secretly easie, and had a kind of Pleasure in the Dissaster that was upon me about the Ship, and that tho' it was a loss I could not but be glad, that those ill gotten Goods were gone, and that I had lost what I had stolen; for I look'd upon it as none of mine, and that it would be fire in my Flax if I should mingle it with what I had now, which was come honestly by, and was as it were sent from Heaven, to lay the Foundation of my prosperity, which the other would be only as a Moth to consume. (*CJ*, p. 150)

The New World changes Jack as much as it changes Crusoe, and it changes them both deeply, no matter how imperfectly.

The Russian prince justifies his confinement by saying, "I am but Flesh, a Man, a meer Man, have Passions and Affections as likely to possess and overthrow me as any Man" (*FA*, p. 210). Of course man is flesh, trammeled by necessity and pressured by his needs. However, the prince implies here that he is merely flesh, incapable of transcending his passions and becoming his own master. But man is more than flesh. For Crusoe, cannibalism raised the specter that he was just flesh, no more capable of controlling himself than beasts were, possessing no more autonomy than a goat, subject to the ebb and flow of every external provocation and internal impulse, and he could not accept living like mere flesh. Nor can Jack. The transformation that Jack undergoes while serving as an indentured servant is a transformation from being "not only a Man, but an Honest Man" (*CJ*, p. 149). And "Honesty," Defoe insisted, is "tried in Affliction," and it is proved only "when Exigencies and Distresses pinch a Man" and when "Occasion … presses upon his Integrity" (*SR*, pp. 82, 79).

"While he was a servant," Jack knows, he "would have no Opportunity to be dishonest" (*CJ*, p. 123). But having no opportunity to be dishonest is not the same thing as being an "Honest Man," for since honesty is "tried in Affliction," Jack can become honest only after he has "arriv'd to an Independant State" and can "live by my own Endeavours" (*CJ*, p. 149).

Indentured servitude, then, is a temporary protective cocoon. Jack was "*form'd by Necessity to be a Thief*," and because his necessities are "immediately provided for" in his servitude, for a time he is "deliver'd from the horrid necessity of doing … ill Things" (*CJ*, pp. 31, 153). But his term as a servant is a privileged moment, much like Crusoe's time on the island. God had confined Crusoe on the island, fencing him off from temptation and providing for his needs, so he could have a period of time in which to reform himself, to establish a "Mastership over … Desire," and then to re-enter the world. Similarly, Jack does not luxuriate in his privileged moment of "blessed Confinement." Like Crusoe, he seizes it as an opportunity to cultivate "a Change in the Soul" so that it becomes "truly Master of it self," and then he eagerly returns to the world to prove himself as a man capable of standing up to affliction and temptation.

Colonel Jack dramatizes Jack's growth, but Defoe emphasizes the sheer puzzle of Jack's transformation into an "Honest Man." The novel presents itself as emphatically secular, so Defoe does not have recourse to those divine promptings that played such a prominent role in Crusoe's conversion. He rejects the simplistic explanations of the determinative influence of material and environmental conditions to which some of his contemporaries appealed. Jack's father thinks that "the very hint" that he was a gentleman "would inspire me with Thoughts suitable to my Birth, and that I would certainly act like a Gentleman, if I believed myself to be so," but the "editor" of *Colonel Jack* does not think this is "all the Education" he needs: "*If he had come into the World with the Advantage of an Education … what a Man might he not have been*" (*CJ*, pp. 33, 31). Jack's lack of education leaves him without the wherewithal to fashion himself into something better than he is. He may think himself a gentleman all he wants, but because he is ignorant, he cannot parlay his aspirations into behavior that is moral, socially appropriate, or even governed by enlightened self-interest.

Jack begins socially, psychologically, and morally at degree zero, his deficiencies so profound that it is difficult to understand how his life can be mended by a short stint as an indentured servant.

Nothing is more certain, than that hitherto being partly from the gross Ignorance of my untaught Childhood, ... partly from the hardness, and wickedness of the Company I kept, and add to these, that it was the Business I might be said to be brought up to, I had, *I say*, all the way hitherto, no manner of thoughts about the Good or Evil of what I was embark'd in; consequently, I had no sense of Conscience, no Reproaches upon my Mind for having done amiss. (*CJ*, p. 76)

Why would someone who has lived a life of deprivation like Jack want to pursue the rigors of an honest life when offered the immediate satisfactions of plenty and a warm sun? What could possibly pressure him into a life of diligence, industry, and honesty when he grew up with "no sense of Conscience, no Reproaches upon [his] Mind for having done amiss"? Born in ignorance and schooled in wrongdoing, how would he know how to go about being honest? And, above all, having "no manner of thoughts about ... Good or Evil," *why* would he want to become honest? "I had no Foundation lay'd in me by Education; and being early led by my fate into Evil, I had the less Sense of its being Evil left upon my Mind" (*CJ*, p. 77). Jack's lack of education has left him so ignorant that he is unaware of what he is or why it is better to live otherwise. He possesses nothing to drive him to reform himself, and he has no conception of what he should drive himself to become.

And yet, transform himself he does, as an indentured servant in Maryland.

"I knew no Good, and had tasted no Evil" (*CJ*, p. 62), says Jack. In spite of the biblical echo, his is less a prelapsarian innocence than a mere "State of Ignorance." Benighted and stupid, he begins the world not like Adam but like the cannibals in *Robinson Crusoe,* whose innocence is also a consequence of their stupidity. Because they are morally unenlightened, their evil behavior "is not against their own Consciences reproving"; "They do not know it to be an Offence" (*RC*, p. 183). Having "no sense of Conscience," it is the same with Jack. He "set out into the World so early, that when he began to do Evil, he understood nothing of the Wickedness of it" (*CJ*, p. 36).

There are no cannibals in *Colonel Jack,* but there are Africans, an equally benighted people in Defoe's eyes, and they live just as stupidly as the cannibals in *Robinson Crusoe.* And I think the Africans perform the same function in *Colonel Jack* that the cannibals did in *Robinson Crusoe.* Crusoe's conversion was dramatized by the way he dealt with the cannibals, a people to whom he is initially quite similar but from whom he progressively distinguishes himself as he transforms himself. So, too, Jack's secular transformation. For, in the beginning, Jack is like the Africans. Covered with the ash from the Glass House, he is one of the "black Crew," one of the "black Wretches," one of the "nak'd black Guard Boys"; kidnapped from his own country and whipped by English authorities, he is made a "miserable Slave in *Virginia*" (*CJ*, pp. 48, 77, 146). But progressively he becomes less like them.

Jack transforms himself from servant to master by learning how to manage these savages without beating them, and in many ways his transformation parallels theirs. Initially, Jack believes that, because of their "Brutallity" and "obstinate Temper," the slaves "must be rul'd with a Rod of Iron" (*CJ*, p. 128). But over time he comes to understand that, like the cannibals of *Robinson Crusoe,* they are degenerate but educable, for they possess the same capacities – "some Sense of Kindness, some Principles of natural Generosity" and "all the other Faculties of reasonable Creatures" – that Europeans possess (*CJ*, p. 134). "Nature is the same," he concludes, "and Reason Governs in just Proportions in all Creatures" (*CJ*, p. 140). And, because "the *Negroes* were to be reason'd into things as well as other People," the best course to take with them is to threaten them only if they disobey but otherwise to treat them mercifully and then "Work upon their Reason" by "explain[ing] the meaning of Gratitude to them, and the Nature of an Obligation" (*CJ*, pp. 144, 140). (All of this echoes the way in which Crusoe "tamed" Friday and the thirty-seven captured cannibals, first instilling a sense of gratitude by "begin[ning] with them on the Principle of having sav'd their Lives" and then going on to "instruct them in the rational Principles of Life ... by kind Usage and affectionate Arguings" [*FA*, p. 44].)

Defoe appears to have drawn these ideas of slave management from the forms of subordination with which he was familiar in London, not from actual attitudes and practices in the colonies. Rather than seeing chattel slavery as being fundamentally different, Defoe understands it as just one more relationship in the general order of authority and subordination that structures society – subjects to kings, wives to husbands, children to parents, servants to masters. Since Africans, for all their otherness, are essentially the same as Europeans, they are to be managed the way all European subordinates are to be managed, and Defoe's theories of managing the slaves in *Colonel Jack* mirror his more general thinking on managing subordinates which he explored in his own conduct books. Indeed, in *A New Voyage round the World,* the narrator controls his fractious white crew by using the same strategies Jack uses to govern the black slaves (*NV*, pp. 57–67).

Defoe thought that there had been a "strange Alteration" in relations between superiors and inferiors in English society.[49] In the past, relations between the two had been all "Softness and Tenderness."[50] Inferiors had "serv'd upon Principles of Love and Loyalty," superiors had ruled with a "kind, mild, and affable Temper."[51] Now, however, inferiors were insubordinate and superiors were "rigid, surly, cruel, tyrannick, and outrageous."[52]

This "Softness and Tenderness" did not disappear because superiors ceased to be soft and tender. Just the opposite. "The first Rise of the Insolence of Servants," Defoe says, was caused by "the unseasonable Lenity, Kindness, and Tenderness" shown to them by their betters, for "*easy Masters* make *sawcy Servants*,"; "while Masters act without the Authority of Masters, Servants will never shew the Submission and Obedience of their Place."[53] To restore harmonious relations, superiors must act in a way that will re-establish the authority they have ceded. "'Tis for you, to be Masters and Mistresses, and then you will have Servants be Servants again."[54]

To restore a sense of hierarchy, the master may well have to resort to physical coercion, including beating. But the crucial point is that once a proper hierarchy has been re-established, masters should bind themselves and their subordinates together by affection and strictly avoid all severe discipline whatsoever. For threats and beatings induce fear and terror, and in an atmosphere of fear and terror, a subordinate is neither able to learn nor eager to obey. In *The Family Instructor*, Defoe illustrates this with a fictional drama of a family badly governed because the father uses violent threats and coercion. These "estrange[d] rather than engage[d]" his children.[55] For a child is best instructed by "Affection," not by "Blows and Stripes."[56] "Once a Child is convinc'd that his Father loves him," a father's kind "Words," his "Perswasions" and "Arguments" do more "than meer Blows with Passion and Heat of Anger can ever do."[57] And so, the "intemperate Conduct" of the father in Defoe's story, "far from winning upon the Judgment of his Children, … rather stupifyd their Understandings, and made them incapable of getting Good by [his] Instructions."[58]

Defoe's views on the treatment of subordinates were very similar to Locke's theories of education, and it is worth looking at Locke briefly to see the ideas that underpin Defoe's assumptions. Locke, too, believed physical coercion counterproductive. "*Beating* is the worst, and therefore the last Means to be used," he thought, but like Defoe he made an exception for "one, and but one Fault": "*Obstinacy* or *Rebellion*."[59] (Jack, it should be remembered, resorted to beating because of the "terrible Obstinacy of the

Negroes" and their "Insolence and Rebellion" [*CJ*, p. 132].) "*Stubborness, and obstinate Disobedience,*" Locke insisted, "must be master'd with Force and Blows: For this there is no other remedy. Whatever particular Action you bid him do, or forbear, you must be sure to see your self obey'd; no Quarter in this case, no resistance."[60] "Parents and Governors" must resort to "blows" and even to "Terror and Affrightment" in order to "settle and establish their Authority by an Awe over the Minds of those, and Rule them by that."[61] But once having "establish'd … Authority" and having "imprinted on his Mind that Awe, which is necessary," the parent should make the child sensible of his

Care and Love of him, by Indulgence and Tenderness, especially, Caressing him on all Occasions wherein he does any thing well, and being kind to him … When … by the Ways of Tenderness, and Affection … you have … planted in him a particular Affection for you, he is then in the State you could desire, and you have formed in his Mind that true *Reverence,* which is always afterwards carefully to be continued … as the great Principle, whereby you will always have hold upon him, to turn his Mind to the Ways of Vertue, and Honour.[62]

Jack's management of the slaves follows this program to a tittle. Initially, out of compassion, Jack refuses to put the slaves "under the Authority of the … Lash" (*CJ*, p. 128). But as Defoe warned, "unseasonable Lenity, Kindness, and Tenderness" undermines authority and leads to the "Rise of … Insolence," and Jack discovers that for "the Compassion I shew'd them," the slaves returned "Ingratitude" (*CJ*, p. 128). "I had soon so much Contempt upon my Authority, that we were all in Disorder" (*CJ*, p. 128). All discipline having collapsed, Jack knows he has no choice but to re-establish order by means of physical and psychological coercion, even though it goes against his stomach. One disobedient slave he "ty'd … by the Thumbs for Correction," and then he told him "he should be Whipped and Pickl'd in a dreadful manner"; and after "he was strip'd and ty'd up, he had two Lashes given him, that were indeed very cruel" (*CJ*, pp. 133–134). Jack frankly acknowledges that "the *Negroes* are kept in Awe" by "Terror" (*CJ*, pp. 134, 132).

But once he has re-established the lines of subordination and authority, Jack implements the "happy Secret" he has discovered of managing the slaves "by gentle Means" (*CJ*, p. 132). To quote Locke again: "when … by the Ways of Tenderness, and Affection … you have … planted in him a particular Affection for you … and you have formed in his Mind that true *Reverence* … you will always have hold upon him, to turn his Mind to the Ways of Vertue." Thus, after Jack has threatened the slaves, he pardons them so that they will "Taste what Mercy is" (*CJ*, p. 140). The slaves develop a deep affection toward Jack and an appreciation of the "Principles of Gratitude" (*CJ*, p. 139). When they were simply beaten, "they had no Passion, no Affection to Act upon, but that of Fear, which necessarily brought Hatred with it"; but now that "they [are] used with Compassion, they ... Serve with Affection" and "act from a Principle of Love" (*CJ*, pp. 139–140).

There is no sentimental agenda behind Jack's forging a bond of affection between master and slaves. Of course, he does make use of the "sense of Kindness" and "natural Generosity" Africans share with Europeans in order to construct a "Foundation of Gratitude" (*CJ*, p. 134). But his goal is not to make the slave *feel* gratitude. He wants them to *understand* it. His purpose is less to provoke a sense of gratitude in the slaves than to "*explain the Meaning* of Gratitude to them" (*CJ*, p. 140; my italics). Jack criticizes colonial masters because they "take no pains with [their slaves] to imprint Principles of Gratitude on their Minds, to tell them what Kindness is shown them, and what they are Indebted for it, and what they might Gain in the End by it" (*CJ*, p. 133). Even when slaves are treated kindly and spared a beating, he notes disapprovingly, "they are not told what the Case is" (*CJ*, p. 133). Jack does just the opposite: he explains everything. He threatens a slave with a severe beating and then forgives him "after Talking to him in my way about his Offence, and raising in his Mind a Sense of the value of the Pardon" (*CJ*, p. 132). "*Negroes* were to be reason'd into things as well as other People," he discovers, and by "managing their Reason," he hopes to manage the slaves without resorting to beatings (*CJ*, p. 144). And so, Jack sets about to "argue with them, and Work upon their Reason, to make the Mercy that was shew'd them sink deep into their Minds, and give lasting Impressions; explain the Meaning of Gratitude to them, and the Nature of an Obligation" (*CJ*, p. 140).

The goal of Jack's treatment of African slaves, in short, is not obedience, but deference, and in a society like England, "deference is expected to be spontaneously exhibited" because it should proceed from the inferior's understanding that the hierarchical structure of society is "part of the nature of things," an order in which he "freely accepts an inferior ... role" to ensure the smooth functioning of the whole.[63] Jack's "happy Secret" is not to discipline the slaves but to educate them, and by education he, as well as Locke before him, meant moral education, the purpose of which was to manage subordinates by making them obedient to their own reason: they are taught to become masters of themselves, cultivating in themselves virtue and good behavior without the continual intervention of an overseer to restrain and direct them. "The great Principle and

Foundation of all Vertue and Worth, is placed in this," said Locke, "That a man is able to *deny himself* his own Desires, cross his own Inclinations, and purely follow what Reason directs as best, tho' the appetite lean the other way."[64] Beating is a *"slavish Discipline"* that "makes a *slavish Temper."*[65] It "contribute[s] not at all to the mastery" of ourselves because it "reaches not the Mind."[66] One "submits, and dissembles Obedience," but once "the Rod … is removed … he gives the greater scope to his natural Inclination."[67] To teach someone to "get a Mastery over his Inclinations, and *submit his Appetite to Reason,"* a master must treat his subordinates "as Rational Creatures."[68]

When I say … that they must be *treated as Rational Creatures,* I mean, that you should make them sensible by the Mildness of your Carriage, and the Composure even in your Correction of them, that what you do is reasonable in you, and useful and necessary for them … and there is no Vertue they should be excited to, nor Fault they should be kept from, which I do not think they may be convinced of.[69]

By introjecting the masters' values, subordinates become self-governing. "Let the Awe he has got upon their Minds be so tempered with the constant Marks of tenderness and good Will, that Affection may spur them to their Duty, and make them find a Pleasure in complying with his Dictates."[70] "Such a management," Locke concludes, "will make them in love with the hand that directs them, and the Vertue they are directed to."[71]

"The Rage and Fury with which Men correct Slaves," observed Defoe, merely "aims at breaking the Spirit" and works no better than treating any subordinate "as if he had no Capacity of receiving Instruction; that he had no Sense but that of Feeling; or Passion, but of Fear; and so you expect to reform him as you break a Horse."[72] Jack succeeds because he addresses the human potential of the Africans, making them rationally self-governing people who embrace their subordinate position in society and act accordingly.

Defoe's belief that the Africans would enthusiastically embrace their servitude is one of the most egregious failures of his imagination, but his assumption that slavery is just one more form of subordination within the English hierarchical system is telling.[73] For it is important to *Colonel Jack* that these slaves not be a special case. Their transformation is meant to mirror Jack's, just as Friday's mirrors Crusoe's. The Africans are "reason'd into" self-government by Jack's "working upon their Passions" of "Kindness" and "Generosity," instructing them how to direct their energies to their "right Uses" by rationally explaining to them "the meaning of

Gratitude" (*CJ*, pp. 144, 134, 140). By "thus managing their Reason," Jack teaches them to master themselves (*CJ*, p. 144). Correspondingly, in order to manage the slaves he oversees properly, Jack must bring his own feelings of kindness and generosity under rational management so he can direct these energies to the very end he teaches the Africans to direct theirs, putting into practice "the meaning of Gratitude."

When Jack becomes an overseer, he resists treating the slaves cruelly. Because he himself has been beaten, kidnapped, and put in bondage, he cannot bring himself to beat the slaves. The thought of whipping them, he remarks,

turn'd the very blood within my Veins, and I could not think of it with any tem- per; that I, who was but Yesterday a Servant or Slave like them, and under the Authority of the same Lash, should lift up my Hand to the Cruel Work, which was my Terror but the Day before ... Every Blow I struck them, hurt my self. (*CJ*, pp. 127–128)

Jack refuses to beat the slaves, and consequently he undermines his own power to command. The practical result of Jack's indulging his feelings of his kindness and generosity is that the "Plantation was not duly manag'd, and ... all things were in Disorder" (*CJ*, p. 129).

Hence the infolding and thickening of parallels at the very center of Jack's rise from servant to master. Jack has treated the slaves kindly, but he has been repaid with "Ingratitude ... for the Compassion I shew'd them" (*CJ*, p. 128). Their ingratitude, in turn, puts Jack in much the same position vis-à-vis his own master: for Jack, too, has been put under an "Obligation" to his master because he "has been so generous" to him by making him an overseer, but now Jack is in danger of ingratitude himself by being "careless of [his master's] Business" because the "Plantation is not well look'd after" (*CJ*, p. 131). "Your Conduct is complain'd of, since I set you over this Plantation," the master accuses Jack; "I thought your Sence of the Obligation I had laid on you, would have secur'd your Diligence, and Faithfulness to me" (*CJ*, p. 131). And the source of Jack's failure is his own undisciplined impulse of kindness and generosity, the two passions that form the "Foundation of Gratitude" in the African slaves and the two passions he works on in them to transform them (*CJ*, p. 134).

For all the tears, generous sentiments, and tender consciences in *Colonel Jack,* the goal of Jack's management of himself as well as the slaves is the restoration of patriarchal order and economic productivity, not the establishment of a paternalistic community bound together by feelings of gratitude, loyalty, and love. Jack's first obligation is the maintenance of the good order of the plantation. And yet, generous sentiments are not to be gainsaid, nor is the wish for society bound together by gratitude and loyalty, and Jack's desire for the slaves to serve with the "Obedience of Love" (*CJ*, p. 141), not the anxieties of fear, is a moral desideratum. The success of Jack's self-transformation lies in his ability to achieve these goals by disciplining his own passions of kindness and generosity, just as he has disciplined those same passions in the Africans – not extinguishing or suppressing them, but using his reason to find a form in which these passions can be expressed but directed to their "right Uses." Jack's "happy Secret" is a particularly elegant solution to the knotty dilemma in which he finds himself. He satisfies at once his obligation to his master and his own desire to deal humanely and generously with his subordinates. It is an act that is possible only after he masters both himself and others. For this he is promoted from servant to master.

But why did Defoe focus on these passions in particular? Crusoe, too, transformed himself by mastering his passions, though in his case the passions he had to discipline were the Hobbesian ones of fear, individualistic self-assertion, and a savage and rapacious egocentricity. Why is Jack's drama of self-transformation played out by his disciplining his impulses of kindness and generosity?

As I said, in *Colonel Jack,* Defoe faced the challenge of explaining how Jack transforms himself from a "meer Man" to an "Honest Man" (*CJ*, p. 149). It is a transformation so profound and so thoroughgoing that it cannot be accounted for by a change in material circumstances, and since the novel is secular, there can be no appeal to supernatural proddings. Jack changes under the pressure of his own passions. Jack, of course, is driven by many passions, including an ambition every bit as aggressively self-seeking as Crusoe's, but his determinative passions, the ones that play the leading role in his life as well as in his self-transformation, are his impulses toward kindness and generosity. For Jack grows from being an amoral outsider into an "honest" member of society, and so the passions that drive his transformation must be fundamentally sociable.

I suspect that my assertion that Jack is transformed by a "natural Generosity" and an innate "sense of Kindness" will be met with some skepticism (*CJ*, p. 134). Defoe is ordinarily thought to be something of a Hobbesian. Human nature is individualistic and self-assertive, and *Robinson Crusoe* is usually seen as a fable that dramatizes our savage, egocentric essence: at base, like Conrad's Kurtz, all of us are cannibals who want to eat up the world. Though Crusoe learns the value of social existence, it is something he learns only under the most extreme conditions.

Reason bullies him into being sociable. The novel shows us, it is generally accepted, that people affiliate with one another only under the formal pressure of contracts and oaths, which are a kind of violence against one's natural self-seeking inclinations. As Crusoe says, "Gratitude is no inherent Virtue in the Nature of Man" (*RC*, p. 237).

But the conviction that we are merely cannibals incapable of gratitude is Crusoe's, not Defoe's, and it is a projection of Crusoe's own obsessional energies. It is Crusoe who is the Hobbesian young man. Driven by his individualistic impulses, he throws over not only his obligations to society but even his own desire for fellowship and social ties. He sees the world as cannibalistic because what is driving *him* is cannibalistic. As it turns out, his view of the world is wrong much of the time. The African natives he thinks are cannibals turn out to be sociable, and even the Carib cannibals themselves – at least in the person of Friday – are deeply generous. The world that surrounds Crusoe is made up of people who act on principles and impulses entirely different from his, people who act out of "honesty" – generosity, kindness, and gratitude. When his ship founders in a storm, he is saved "after great Labour and Hazard" by sailors from another ship "venturing their Lives to save ours" (*RC*, p. 64); the captain who rescues Crusoe on his first voyage to Africa is a man of "Integrity and Honesty" who transports him "at no Expense" (*RC*, p. 68); the captain's widow, with whom Crusoe left his £200 for safe keeping, was not only "very just," but "out of her own Pocket" sent the captain who rescues Crusoe "a very handsome Present for his Humanity and Charity" to Crusoe (*RC*, pp. 69, 84); the "honest" Portuguese captain who rescues Crusoe and Xury and offers to carry Crusoe to Brazil "*in Charity*" and who is notable for "the Humanity of his Behavior" sets Crusoe up in his new country (*RC*, pp. 81, 83); a "good honest Man" teaches Crusoe how to build a sugar plantation in Brazil (*RC*, p. 82); the "Steward of the Monastery" which received a portion of the profits of Crusoe's plantation "gave every Year a faithful Account of the Produce" (*RC*, p. 265); Crusoe regains possession of his plantation with the help of the survivors of his trustees, "very fair honest People" (*RC*, p. 266); the Portuguese captain whom Crusoe meets again after thirty years proves to be such a "sincere ... Friend" and deals with him so "generously" that Crusoe was "too much mov'd with the Honesty and Kindness of the poor man, to be able to bear [it]" (*RC*, p. 267); even the owners of the ship Crusoe saved from the mutineers reward him – "one Piece of Gratitude ... which I did not expect" (*RC*, p. 264); and throughout, of course, Friday demonstrates himself again and again as an "honest grateful Creature" (*RC*, p. 222). As an old man, Crusoe retraces the "particular Steps by which I arrived [at] ... my Prosperity" and concludes, "much of it all depended ... upon the Principle of *Honesty,* which I met with, in almost all the People whom it was my Lot to be concern'd with in my private and particular Affairs" (*SR,* p. 67).

In this context, Crusoe may appear to be monstrously depraved. But his cannibal nature – that overweening egocentricity that thrusts itself forward against the pull of human fellowship and acts as if the world is his and his alone – is an aspect of human nature shared universally, and his island, as he himself comes to understand, is that existential "Solitude," that self-enclosure of "our Dear-self," where "Every Thing revolves in our Minds by innumerable circular Motions, all centring in our selves" (*SR,* pp. 57–58). But the fact that he is surrounded by this company of honest men and women who treat him with such kindness and generosity suggests that that Hobbesian energy that drives us to lead our solitary, ego-centric existences is only *one* of the energies inherent in human nature. In *Farther Adventures,* Defoe teases us with the possibility that at bottom we are nothing but cannibals when he has the starving young maid confess, "I question, whether if I had been a Mother, and had had a little Child with me, its Life would have been safe or not" (*FA,* p. 116). There is enough evidence of cannibalism in the novel to suspect that she would eat her own child, but in fact on the very same ship we see a woman who really is a mother and who, in the extremity of her starvation, "gave the last bit of Bread she had left to her Child" and "fed him at the Price of her own Life" (*FA,* p. 118).

The mother's gesture, springing from the same lower stratum of passionate energies that Crusoe's individualistic drives spring from, reminds us that human nature is comprised of numerous innate energies. If the solitariness of the island is a symbol of Crusoe's savage egocentricity, solitude is *also* "a Rape upon human Nature," as Defoe remarked (*SR,* p. 60). "Man is a Creature so form'd for Society, that it may not only be said that it is not good for him to be alone, but 'tis really impossible he should be alone" (*SR,* p. 64). Solitude, then, characterizes some of Crusoe's energies, but it is also a punishment for that self-sufficiency his Hobbesian energy presumes and a providential way of forcing him to acknowledge that there are other native impulses, impulses that drive us to other human beings, capacities of sympathy, of kindness, of generosity, impulses of sociability.

Human nature is both cannibalistic *and* affiliative (and many other things as well). By nature, humans are possessed by the energies of self-assertion, the will to thrust themselves forward no matter what the cost, no matter how much havoc is visited on other human beings or how much they seal themselves up in their own solitariness. But by nature they are also possessed by impulses of kindness and generosity, which drive them out of themselves into a sympathetic participation in the lives of their fellow humans. *Robinson Crusoe* tells the story of a man whose ruling passions are cannibalistic and who transforms himself by awakening (or being forced to awaken) another, more generous side of his nature and by controlling his self-assertiveness rationally so that it is directed to his best interests. *Colonel Jack* is just the opposite. Though, like Crusoe, Jack has drives that are nakedly self-assertive (to the degree that we understand it as sheer self-promotion, his desire to become a gentleman is the most obvious of these), his ruling passions are empathetic and affiliative. But, just as Crusoe's self-assertion is self-destructive, so too are Jack's affiliative impulses; in order to mature, like Crusoe Jack must learn to control these passions rationally and to negotiate the demands of all sides of his nature.

It is important to recognize that the affiliative passions are the engine of Jack's transformation into an "Honest Man." For "Honesty" has a very particular meaning in Defoe's lexicon. Honesty does not mean simply possessing a rectitude of mind or an integrity of purpose. Specifically, it means acting out of kindness, generosity, and gratitude. "To do Good to all Mankind," Defoe says, "is the *Chancery* Law of Honesty" (*SR*, p. 68).

Honesty not only leads to discharge every Debt and every Trust to our Neighbour ... but an honest Man acknowledges himself Debtor to all Mankind, for so much Good to be done for them, whether for Soul or Body, as Providence puts an Opportunity into his Hands to do: In Order to discharge this Debt, he studies continually for Opportunity to do all the Acts of Kindness and Beneficience, that is possible for him to do ... a Man is not a compleatly honest Man that does not do this.

Upon this Consideration; I question much, whether a covetous, narrow, stingy Man, as we call him, one who gives himself up to himself, as born for himself only, and who declines the Advantages and Opportunities of doing Good ... I say, I much question, whether such a Man can be *an honest Man*. (*SR*, p. 68)

The language of debt and repayment here is the language Defoe returns to repeatedly, as when, for instance, he defines "honesty" as "the Debt of Charity and Beneficence, which [we] owe to all mankind" in gratitude to God or the "Quit-Rent" we owe God which must be "paid in a constant Discharge of all good Offices, friendly, kind, and generous Actions" to "the rest of Mankind" (*SR*, pp. 68–69). Honesty is a repaid debt because, for Defoe, "Gratitude is a Branch of *Honesty;* and it is very hard to say, or even to think a man can be Honest that is not Grateful."[74] Thus, gratitude is "no more or less, than paying a Debt," either the debt one owes another for a kindness or, more generally, the debt one owes God for His mercy, a debt that is repaid by acting generously to God's creatures.[75] An "*honest Man*" is one who "pay[s] the common Debt of Mankind to one another," and the "highest and most compleat Act of Honesty" is "laying hold of an Opportunity to do Good to an Object offer'd by the Providence of Heaven, and thereby acknowledging the Debt he had to pay to his Maker, in the Persons of his most distress'd Creatures" (*SR*, pp. 69–70).

Jack's disciplining the impulses of kindness and generosity in both himself and the slaves by channeling these feelings into behavior that puts into practice "the meaning of Gratitude" marks a decisive step in his social maturation. But it also makes a larger point about the web of our social existence. To the degree that society is held together, Defoe suggests, it is held together by bonds of debt, obligation, and gratitude. Jack acknowledges his obligation to the King after he is pardoned ("I became sincerely given in to the Interest of King GEORGE; and this from a Principle of Gratitude, and a Sense of my Obligation to his Majesty for my Life" [*CJ*, p. 240]), and he becomes a faithful subject. These acts form "chains of gratitude" that run in both directions up and down the social hierarchy and that draw society together by acts of reciprocity and mutual support.[76] When Crusoe returns to civilization, he repays his own obligations, first by dismissing the debt the captain has accrued and bestowing a gift of money on him and his son, then by giving gifts of money to the widow, the monastery, and the poor of Brazil. The same reciprocal chains of gratitude bind together the society of *Colonel Jack*. Jack creates a system of slave management to act out his gratitude to his master, and the "Master own'd the Satisfaction … [and] shew'd the Principle of Gratitude to those that serv'd him" by setting Jack up as a master of his own plantation (*CJ*, p. 145). Jack forgives his first wife for betraying him, and she is grateful ("Let me be your Slave or Servant … as long as I live" [*CJ*, p. 224]). Jack's gracious act is repaid several pages later when, now as a faithful wife, she helps him escape from Maryland.

"Every Blow I struck them, hurt my self," says Jack when he becomes overseer to the slaves; whipping them

> turn'd the very blood within my Veins, and I could not think of it with any temper; that I, who was but Yesterday a Servant or Slave like them, and under the Authority of the same Lash, should lift up my hand to the Cruel Work, which was my Terror but the Day before. (*CJ*, pp. 127–128)

Here is sympathy in its fundamental sense, and Jack has this capacity for fellow feeling from the beginning. Throughout his criminal career, he is dogged by what he calls "a strange kind of uninstructed Conscience," for though he "made no scruple of getting any thing" by robbery, "yet I could not bear destroying their Bills, and Papers, which were things that would do them a great deal of hurt, and do me no good ... I was so Tormented about it, that I could not rest Night or Day" (*CJ*, p. 73). When he robs the poor woman, "an abhorance ... fill'd my Mind at the Cruelty of that Act" (*CJ*, p. 81).

Still, even though Jack becomes an "Honest Man" because of his innate impulses of kindness and generosity, these impulses are not in themselves moral impulses or evidence of some sort of "natural goodness." When he steals the bills in his first robbery, he cannot rest comfortably with his actions. "It came into my Head, as young as I was, that it was a sad thing indeed to take a Man's Bills away" (*CJ*, p. 53). A "sad thing," not a "bad thing." Although Jack calls these feelings an "uninstructed Conscience," and although the "editor" of *Colonel Jack* labels them *generous Principles*, they are not, properly speaking, principles at all, but simply feelings arising from his ability to inhabit another's skin (*CJ*, pp. 73, 31). They certainly cannot be construed as even a rudimentary code of values, for Jack, we need to remember, "had no sense of Conscience, no reproaches upon my Mind for having done amiss" (*CJ*, p. 76). Of course, this capacity for sympathetic feeling *can* be nursed into a moral code and worked up into "a solid Principle of Justice and Honesty," but the impulses toward kindness and generosity themselves seem to originate in some ethically neutral reservoir of highly generalized and undifferentiated feeling (*CJ*, p. 149).[77]

Notwithstanding all the Disadvantages of a most wretched Education, yet Now when I began ... to foresee, that I might be something Considerable in time, ... I found differing Sentiments of things taking Place in my Mind; and first, I had a solid Principle of Justice and Honesty, and a secret Horror at things pass'd, when I look'd back upon my former Life: That Original Something, I knew not what, that used formerly to Check me in the first meannesses of Youth, and us'd to Dictate to me when I was but a Child, that I was to be a Gentleman, continued to Operate upon me Now, in a manner I cannot Describe; and I continually remember'd the Words of the ancient *Glass-maker,* to the Gentleman, that he reprov'd for Swearing, that to be a Gentleman, was to be an *Honest Man,* that without Honesty, Human Nature was Sunk and Degenerated; the Gentleman lost all Dignity of his Birth, and plac'd himself, even below an Honest Beggar. (*CJ*, p. 149)

The impulse that finally eventuates in "a solid Principle of ... Honesty" and keeps Jack from becoming "Degenerated" is "a strange original Notion" (*CJ*, p. 76) – "strange" because it exists so far beneath the floor of consciousness that it cannot be identified beyond a "Something, I knew not what." It is experienced as an indecipherable pressure, an amorphous energy that exerts itself in the dark. It "Operate[s] on me ... in a Manner I cannot Describe"; "I had something in me, by what secret Influence I knew not, kept me from ... the general Wickednes of the rest of my Companions"; "I did not understand it very well, yet it lay upon my Mind" (*CJ*, pp. 76, 53).

Jack's "Original Something" without which "Human Nature was ... Degenerated" is a capacity analogous to Crusoe's capacity to be shocked at the degeneracy of the cannibals and his determination not to become degenerate himself. That shock springs from a facet of his nature, a higher potential he innately possesses, but *what* that potential is and how it is to be realized are things to be discovered by reason or illuminated by God and then molded by will and discipline into specific behaviors and habits. Similarly, Jack's "Original Something" is an unelaborated impulse that must be shaped and schooled into moral behavior. Just as the African slaves' kindness and natural generosity does not ripen into a principle of gratitude until Jack "work[s] upon their Reason" (*CJ*, p. 140), so Jack's inchoate natural sympathies need to be articulated by his reason into some specific ethical formulation for him to become an "Honest Man."

Jack shapes his amorphous energies in an ethical direction by casting himself into roles and by imitating social models and then testing their viability and validity by reason and experience. Throughout the novel, Jack tries out new roles, and these moments, as has often been noticed, are marked by his donning and doffing clothing. The first money he gets by stealing he lays out on shoes and stockings, less because he needs them than because it "call[ed] to mind my being a Gentleman," and dressing himself like one, he "began to live like" one, at least in his own mind (*CJ*, p. 42). Next he buys breeches because they speak to his sense of his growing success ("I thought my self a Man now I had a Pocket to put my Money in" [*CJ*, p. 52]). When he gives his money to an honest stockbroker, he reserves enough "to buy me some Cloaths" that answer to his new sense of himself (*CJ*, p. 61). When he begins to rise in his thieving career, he buys himself a new suit of clothing. It is no different for the most crucial moment of his life, the moment when he moves from servant to master. When Jack is told that he will be overseer, he says, 'Alas ... an Overseer! I am in no Condition for it, I have no Cloaths to put on, no Linnen, nothing to help myself" (*CJ*, p. 127).

The Ware-house Keeper ... gave me three good Shirts, two Pair of Shoes, Stockings and Gloves, a Hat, six Neckcloths ... and when he had look'd every thing out, and fitted them, he let me into a little Room by it self; here *says he,* go in there a Slave, and come out a Gentleman. (*CJ*, p. 127)

Clothes, as Jack says, can be a great "help": they make one's role visible, declaring one's position and signaling how one relates to others and they to him.

And yet the role of a gentleman Jack assumes here is not an arbitrary social guise, an artificial form of external behavior that Jack simply costumes himself with, as the metaphor of clothing may suggest. When the warehouse-keeper dresses Jack in clothes to reflect his new station, he conducts him "into a vast great Ware-house, or rather Set of Ware-houses, one within another" and then "into a little Room by it self; here *says he,* go in there a Slave, and come out a Gentleman" (*CJ*, p. 127). This warehouse – with its "little Room" by itself in an "Inner Ware-house" which is itself in a "set of Ware-houses," all "one within another" (*CJ*, p. 127) – is a remarkable and powerfully symbolic setting: if putting on clothing stresses the sheer exteriority, even superficiality, of playing roles, putting them on in a room within a room within a room suggests just the opposite, an intense inwardness, as if the role that is put on is somehow rooted deeply within the self, not superficial at all but speaking from the self's intimate recesses.

In fact, for Defoe, playing a role is both superficial and authentic. Jack's putting on a role is analogous to the cannibals' taking up the custom of cannibalism or Crusoe's daily routine of climbing the hill to look for signs of the cannibals. Both are customary and in that sense exterior to the self. But, though customary, they are not arbitrary formulations; to the contrary, they are particular behavioral utterances of real, if generalized and amorphous, energies and desires, and in that sense they are expressive of the self's profoundest impulses.

Because our generalized and amorphous energies can so readily be given specific shapes and directions, there is in *Colonel Jack* instance after instance of the easy commerce between playing a role, taking up a custom, or simply projecting an image of the self and the self's actually becoming what it acts out. It was a truth Jack had learned as a young child:

I look'd like what I was … that is to say, like a *Black your Shoes your Honour,* a Beggar Boy, a Black-Guard Boy, or what you please, despicable and miserable, to the last Degree; and yet I remember, the People would say of me, that Boy has a good Face; if he was wash'd, and well-dress'd, he would be a good pretty Boy … I lay'd up all these things in my Heart. (*CJ*, pp. 36–37)

Although something of a physical coward, Jack is thrust with the rest of his troop into the midst of the battle at Cremona, where they acquit themselves well, and this collective action transforms Jack's reality. His compatriots

"Flattered me so much with my bravery as they call'd it … that I fancy'd myself Brave, whether I was or not, and the Pride of it made me Bold, and Daring to the last Degree on all Occasions" (*CJ*, p. 189). In spite of his service to the Pretender, Jack has "no particular attachment" to the cause and has to "pretend a great deal of Zeal," but when the Pretender's troops come to Preston, Jack goes to view them out of "Curiosity" and there an old friend "inspir'd me with new Zeal" and seemingly out of nowhere Jack materializes as a rebel (*CJ*, pp. 199–200, 231). This is the trajectory of Jack's life. He calls himself colonel, and he becomes a colonel. Like those natives Defoe thought would become civilized by being taught the mere forms of civilized behavior, so Jack thinks himself a gentleman, and he acts the role of a gentleman, and he becomes a gentleman.

This easy adoption of roles is dangerous, and it is particularly danger-ous for someone of Jack's temperament. Whereas Crusoe's ruling passions are predominantly individualistic and self-assertive, Jack's are characteris-tically sociable. Crusoe rejects a place in society, while Jack seeks to inte-grate himself into it. Crusoe is too much the master, but Jack too much the servant, and his willingness to subordinate himself, to accept social roles, models, and codes leads him into questionable territory.[78] Lacking an education, Jack is naive and deluded throughout much of his life, and many of the roles he casts himself into thinking they will raise his status turn out to be deficient in some way. When he slips into criminality, Jack puts himself under the tutelage of Will, an "Eminent Pick-Pocket," sim-ply because he is "Eminent" (*CJ*, p. 64). Will becomes Jack's "Guide" and "Master," and Jack patterns his behavior after his (*CJ*, p. 78). "I … always us'd to do any thing he bid me do, went with him without any hesitation"; "I Cloathed my self as he Directed, and we Lodg'd together in a little Garret fit for our Quality" (*CJ*, pp. 76, 65). Jack becomes a colonel for the Pretender, "insensibly drawn in" because he was "well receiv'd," had "a great deal of Honour paid" to him, and these "added to [his] Character" (*CJ*, pp. 199–200).

But if roles can lead Jack into bad and stupid behavior, they also are essential for his self-transformation. After Crusoe saw the bones scattered on the shore, he expressed his primal fears by acting out a kind of role – the habitual action of his daily tour of the hill. This gave his fears a concrete shape, and because it did, Crusoe could become more acutely conscious of his impulses. And when he became conscious of them, he could weigh them, subject them to the rule of reason, and if he found them deficient, he could formulate better ones, ones that more perfectly tended toward the "right Uses" of his needs and desires. So it is with roles in *Colonel Jack*.

Roles articulate energies and impulses and thus make the self legible to the self. By giving inchoate energies concrete shapes, roles bring those energies into consciousness, and this offers the opportunity for Jack to subject them to reason and then to some kind of conscious control.[79]

For example, from childhood, Jack has wanted to become a gentleman, and his ambition to rise pushes him to become a thief. In his naivety, he models his behavior on Will's, for Will has convinced him that they both can become gentlemen by becoming thieves. But once Jack begins to play out the role he has chosen, he comes to see that it is inconsistent with his impulses of kindness and generosity. "Something in me," he says, some "secret Influence," keeps him from hewing to the role (*CJ*, p. 76). The phrasing suggests that he holds himself back because of a rudimentary conscience, a primitive sense of right and wrong he has either innately or one that has been infused in him by his upbringing. But he explicitly rejects these explanations: "As to Principle, … I had no Foundation lay'd in me by Education; and being early led by my fate into Evil, I had the less Sense of its being Evil left upon my Mind." "But," he continues, "when I began to grow of an Age of understanding, and to know that I was a Thief … it came often into my Thoughts that I was going wrong" (*CJ*, p. 77).

"To think," says Moll Flanders, "is one real Advance from Hell to Heaven" (*MF*, p. 230). For Jack, acting out roles brings them into consciousness and makes them objects of thought. The sheer vagueness of Jack's description of his process of thinking out these roles – the "Something in me," the "secret Influence," his final rejection of Will's notion of a gentleman because "my Gentleman … was another thing quite, tho' I cou'd not really tell how to describe it neither" (*CJ*, p. 78) – stresses how coming to a just assessment of roles is made with small, tentative steps while stumbling around in the dark.

And, indeed, roles need to be approached as provisional, malleable, things to be tinkered with, revised, and revised again, for they are valuable only to the extent that they serve the desired end, finding the "right Uses" of our energies. When Jack plays the thief, his ambitions rub against the less Hobbesian impulses of his nature, and so he renegotiates the form his drives and energies take, pushing them in new directions, directions that answer more perfectly to his various needs – needs to which he is still partly blind and of which his evolution from role to role is a sequential clarification. It is not until many years later, when he discovers the "happy Secret" as an indentured servant in Maryland, that Jack is finally able to fashion a suitable form of behavior that at least temporarily resolves the contradiction between his desire to rise and his feeling of kindness and generosity, a contradiction that has dogged him from his earliest days as a thief.

Given the importance of roles in *Colonel Jack,* then, it is not surprising that Jack's growth in mastery entails a developing skill in manipulating them. Indeed, Jack's "happy Secret" of managing the slaves is successful because he creates a fictitious drama in which he plays the stern overseer, pretending to threaten them with dire punishment and then ostentatiously extending his mercy. The slaves are deceived by this performance into developing a sense of gratitude. Jack then stages a similar performance in front of his master. First, he sets the scene, bringing his master to "the Place where the Servants were usually corrected"; there, he has placed "two *Negroes* with their Hands ty'd behind them, as it were under *Sentence*" (*CJ,* p. 129). The slaves "made pitiful Signs to him for Mercy," and the master reproaches Jack: "Alas! Alas! ... why did you bring me this way? I do not love such Sights" (*CJ,* p. 130). When Jack protests that what he has done, he has done in his master's service, the master is appalled:

Hold ... no, no, by no means, any such Severity in my Bounds; remember young Man, you were once a Servant, deal as you would acknowledg'd it would be just to deal with you in his Case, and mingle always some Mercy; I desire it, and let the Consequence of being too gentle, be plac'd to my Account. (*CJ,* p. 130)

The drama succeeds as well as he had hoped ("This is as much as I cou'd desire" [*CJ,* p. 130]). Having gotten his master to command him to deal mercifully with the slaves, having gotten him to have taken responsibility for whatever ill consequences might flow from such merciful treatment, Jack then reveals that he *has,* in fact, treated them mercifully. Thus, the master has been manipulated first to feel horror, then relief, much the same way the slave Mouchat has been manipulated from terror to gratitude.

When the master offers to let Jack buy himself out of his service because he has done such a superb job as an overseer, Jack continues his performance when he expresses his gratitude. "As to buying my Liberty, Sir, *that is to say,* going out of your Service, I had much rather Buy time in your Service, and I am only unhappy that I have but two Year to serve" (*CJ,* p. 143). Jack's submission is so obsequious that his master is taken aback by its palpable insincerity: "Come, come, Col.... don't flatter me, I love plain Dealing, Liberty is precious to every Body" (*CJ,* p. 143).

Now, Jack's theatrical professions of gratitude and submissiveness here are paralleled by Mouchat's, who also abases himself to Jack, *his* master: "he came to me, and kneel'd down to me, and took hold of my Legs and of my Feet, and laid his Head upon the Ground; and Sob'd, and Cry'd, like a Child that had been Corrected" (*CJ*, p. 136). Then, in an extraordinary gesture of gratitude and generosity, he offers his own life to save Jack after Jack stages even another drama to manipulate him, pretending that he himself is going to be hanged by his angry master: "Yes, yes, me be hang, for de poor Master ... *Mouchat* shall hang, the great Master shall hangee me, whippee, any thing to save the poor Master" (*CJ*, p. 138). There is not the slightest indication that Mouchat's submissiveness is a self-conscious performance such as Jack's. "The poor Fellow cry'd most pitifully, and there was no room to Question his being in earnest" (*CJ*, p. 138).

What are we to make of this elaborate parallel that places Jack's triumphant act of self-mastery as a self-conscious and fabricated performance against the sincere, spontaneous reaction of the African slave? In portraying Mouchat as artless, Defoe was almost certainly drawing from Addison's famous portrait of African slaves' "Savage Greatness of Soul."[80] "Frequently ... in our *American* Plantations," Addison claims, there are extraordinary acts of self-sacrifice on the part of slaves: "one hears of Negroes, who upon the Death of their Masters, or upon changing their Service, hang themselves upon the next Tree."[81] Such acts are evidence of a greatness of soul, to be sure, but a "Savage Greatness." The virtues the Africans show in such acts are "Virtues which are wild and uncultivated." They proceed "from a Temper of Mind which might have produced noble Fruits, had it been informed and guided by a suitable Education"; but, in truth, they are but "amazing Instance[s] of Barbarity," examples of "Disorders ... bred in the Minds of those Men whose Passions are not regulated by Virtue, and disciplined by Reason."[82]

"Men's Passions operate variously," Addison concludes, "and appear in different kinds of Actions, according as they are more or less rectified and swayed by Reason."[83] This is exactly the point Defoe is making by contrasting Jack and Mouchat. Jack and Mouchat both have so disciplined their impulses that they can act on the principle of gratitude, but Mouchat's passions, to the degree that they are unreflecting and self-destructive, are the less "rectified and swayed by Reason." He has been educated by Jack into a degree of greatness, but it is still "Savage Greatness," and it is still in need of further refinement and management. In contrast, Jack's passions are more "regulated by Virtue, and disciplined by Reason."

The sign of Jack's relative superiority to the slaves is the fact that his *is* a self-conscious performance. As we saw, the goal of self-discipline, for both Jack and the slaves, is not obedience, but deference, an act of self-government which is based on the subordinate's understanding that the hierarchical structure of society is part of the nature of things, on

his understanding of what his role should be, and on his willing accept-
ance and performance of his role to ensure the smooth functioning of the
whole. The fact that Jack *performs* his deference is evidence of his superior,
more civilized understanding.

Jack's kindness and generosity, uncontrolled by his reason, undermines
the stability of the plantation and thus prevents him from fulfilling the
obligation he owes his master. His "happy Secret" is to perform the role of
an overseer in such a way that he is able to re-establish order on the plantation and repay his debt of gratitude to his master and to do this without
sacrificing that greater debt of gratitude that any "Honest Man" owes, the
debt of behaving charitably to all men. But this performance has one further aim. The passions must be mastered, as we saw in *Robinson Crusoe,*
not simply because they undermine social stability, but also because they
are self-destructive. By not controlling his passions and bringing the plantation to the verge of collapse, Jack potentially undermines the confidence
his master has placed in him and thus works against his own self-interest.
Jack "imprint[s] Principles of Gratitude on [the slaves'] Minds" in part by
showing them "what they might Gain in the End by it," and he has the
confidence that "by talking to them in a plain Reasoning way ... the Sense
of their own Interest would prevail with them first, or last" (*CJ,* pp. 133,
152). Similarly, Jack disciplines his own passions and acts on the principle
of gratitude because he knows what he "might Gain in the End by it." And
thus the full force of the contrast between Jack and Mouchat. Mouchat is
savagely great because he is willing to pay the debt of his gratitude at the
cost of his own life; Jack is less savage because he has creatively performed
a role in which he repays his debt of gratitude while simultaneously acting
in his "own Interest."

In this performance before his master, Jack acknowledges to him his
debt of gratitude: "The Obligation I am under to *your Honour* ... does
bind me to your Interest in the strongest manner Imaginable" (*CJ,* p. 131).
And then, surprisingly, he openly admits that it is in his own interest to act
out of gratitude: "I desire nothing, Sir, but your Favour, and the Advantage
of obliging you" (*CJ,* p. 133). Jack's master is not in the least bit taken aback
by this confession of self-interest. He knows that Jack has stage-managed
him just as he has stage-managed the slaves ("I thought I was too cunning
for you," he admits, "but now I think you have been too Cunning for me"
[*CJ,* p. 131]). But Jack's last piece of stage business simply confirms to the
master his own wisdom in having made Jack an overseer. For by asserting
his gratitude, Jack is promising to serve his master; by revealing that he
knows what side his bread is buttered on and that it is to his advantage

to serve his master, he is pledging to act in his master's interest *because* he knows that it is in his self-interest to do so. No wonder his master, in response to this exchange, sponsors Jack by helping him become master of his own plantation.[84]

Near the end of *Robinson Crusoe*, when Crusoe begins to step back into society, he does so by quite literally playing a role. He acts out an elaborate "Fiction" he has self-consciously created that he is "Governour," pretending to command a large band of armed men (a fiction maintained by the use of offstage sound-effects), theatrically issuing orders and granting pardons (*RC*, p. 256). It is all smoke and mirrors, but in a society where the fashioning and presentation of the self was so deeply dependent on performative and theatrical modes, Crusoe confirms his authority and fitness for the reality of power by acting out the role. This is what Jack does as an overseer.

Defoe's America, like the America of many of the promoters, was a place where individuals could free themselves from the shackles of their old social identities. Jack finds that in the New World he can "begin the World again ... with a Reputation, that nothing past will have any Effect upon," and he holds out to all indentured servants the possibility that they, too, can create a new identity, a "good Character" (*CJ*, pp. 146–147), in America:

I would encourage them upon my own Experience to depend upon it, that if their own Diligence in the time of Service, gains them but a good Character, which it will certainly do, if they can deserve it, there is not the poorest, and most despicable Felon that ever went over, but may after his time is serv'd, begin for himself, and may in time be sure of raising a good Plantation. (*CJ*, p. 146)

By "Reputation" and "good Character," of course, Jack means credit, that *idée fixe* of Defoe's economic thinking. One reason why Defoe was fascinated with credit was because it was an arena in which human beings could negotiate with seeming implacable powers, shaping the economic forces that usually shaped them. Tradesmen "have raised estates out of nothing," Defoe marvels, "by the strength of their Reputation, being sober and diligent, and having with care preserv'd the Character of honest Men."[85] Even when a tradesman fails, credit gives him the power to wipe out the stain and "begin the World again" – Defoe uses the phrase as much in his economic writings as he does in his American novels – because "however great the Infamy ... yet at once he appears with a generous Honesty to discharge his owed Obligations, and pay off the Debts contracted in his Distress, he becomes the Darling, even of Fame it self;

he gains an Applause, infinitely superior to all the Reproach he suffer'd."[86]
Whenever a tradesman behaves honestly, Defoe says,

all his trading Miscarriages are forgotten, all his false Steps are buried in that
one Action of Integrity, and he is call'd an honest Man, nay, the honestest of
honest Men, ever after; without so much as one Reflection of Dishonour upon
the worst of his past Life; He is wash'd clean from every Spot; he is cleaner than
an Innocent, that never offended; for he is spoken of with such an Addition of
Honour to his Character, that a simple Life of Honesty, though in the highest
degree, seldom attains to.[87]

This is exactly what Jack does. By "discharg[ing] his owed Obligations,"
he demonstrates his "generous Honesty"; he is "wash'd clean from every
Spot" and creates for himself the "good Character" of an "honest Man."
On the basis of that good character, his master extends him the financial
credit that will become the basis of his new life.

But if the role of credit in the novel calls attention to Jack's real achievement in creating his own "good Character," it also reveals the constraints
he is operating under. For, though credit is earned, it is extended only on
certain conditions. *Colonel Jack,* as I said, is a secular novel: Jack attains
freedom and mastery in social space, but the forces operating in this space
form a web of constraint and necessity almost as exacting as the forces of
nature and Providence are to Crusoe. "I was left to call myself Mr. Anything, what I pleas'd," claims Jack, but he qualifies this triumphant assertion in his next phrase, "as Fortune and better Circumstance should give
occasion" (*CJ,* p. 34).

Jack becomes master because he seizes the opportunity of the New
World to establish his good credit, but he is able to seize that opportunity
only because his master offers to make credit available to him. Now, he
trusts Jack on the basis of his performance as overseer, but one has to ask
why he singled Jack out from all his other servants to make him overseer
in the first place. What attracts the master's attention to Jack, arouses his
interest, and disposes him favorably enough to him to begin to even think
about helping to promote him from servant to master?

The master's attention is drawn to Jack – and he begins to credit him –
on the basis of two signs he sees: the tears Jack cries when he sees the
transported felon whose life is much like his own and the bill that was
drawn up years earlier in London when Jack deposited his stolen earnings
with the kindly gentleman from the Exchange. Significantly, the master
misreads both these signs.

The master first notices Jack when, having lectured another transported
servant on his past sins, he observes that Jack begins to cry. He tells Jack

that he "saw Tears come from your Eyes, and it was that made me call, to speak to you" (*CJ*, p. 124).

Jack. Indeed Sir, I have been a wicked idle Boy, and was left Desolate in the World; but that Boy is a Thief, and condemn'd to be hang'd, I never was before a Court of Justice in my Life.
Mast. Well, I won't Examine you too far, if you were never before a Court of Justice, and are not a Criminal Transported, I have nothing farther to enquire of you: You have been ill used, that's certain and was it that, that affected you?
Jack. Yes indeed, please your Honour. (*CJ*, pp. 124–125)

Here is a mare's nest. On the one hand, the master is completely wrong. Jack cried not because he felt "ill used," as the master thought, but just the opposite: he was "exceedingly mov'd" because he saw that the "young Rogue, born a Thief, and bred a Pick-pocket" was "like my self" (*CJ*, p. 123), and he is overcome with his own guilt and the master's generosity. On the other hand, the master is not entirely off the mark, for although this is not what he is crying about, Jack *has been* "ill used," kidnapped to Maryland and made an indentured servant. But in this case he is not totally "ill used," either. True, like he says, he "never was before a Court of Justice," like his double, the poor thief, but this is equivocation, for his life of crime is similar enough to that of the other boy that, under the strict terms of justice, he has deserved to be transported.

In the second instance, the master once again credits Jack because he misreads a sign of Jack's guilt as a sign of his innocence. He interprets the bill for the money Jack many years earlier had given to the gentleman from the Exchange as a sign of Jack's honesty and diligence. Again, it is another mare's nest. Jack got the money dishonestly by theft, though the fact that he sought to secure it with a bill *is* a sign of his diligence, of his capacity for self-restraint, and of his impulse to work within the structure of society honestly.[88]

The master's misinterpretation of both these signs and the ambiguity of the reality of what the signs represent make an important point. Here, at the very inception of Jack's transformation in the New World, a role has been given to him that he must live up to if he is to win mastery and freedom. The master has credited him with being an honest, sober, and diligent young man, and if Jack acts up to the role (as he will when he becomes overseer), he will receive the financial credit that will become the basis of his social transformation. This role Jack must live up to is something he must put on, a series of habits and behaviors that are not his entirely; but as a young man who, in fact, has shaped his life, stumblingly and erratically, on the basis of his genuine impulses of honesty, sobriety, and diligence, this role does answer to a reality that is in part his. But most importantly, the role he is given to perform is a constraint to which he must accommodate himself if he is to succeed. He does succeed by an act of will and diligence, mastering himself and thereby creating his own "good Character," but he does so by bending himself to a social model of behavior, a model almost as demanding as the currents and tides Crusoe must negotiate to earn his freedom and mastery.

Jack's transformation from indentured servant to master of a plantation is paradigmatic of a variety of social, psychological, and moral transformations he goes through over the course of the novel. *Colonel Jack* is about Jack's development into a "man" – and that in several senses of the word. He is born a "meer Man," but all other forms of manhood are things he must achieve. By dint of his first theft, he begins to enter adulthood ("I was a Boy, 'tis true, but I thought my self a Man now" [*CJ*, p. 52]). As an adult, he transforms himself into a moral agent – an "Honest Man" – by mastering himself as an indentured servant in Maryland. He then attempts a rise in social status comparable to the financial status he has achieved in the New World by returning to Europe to transform himself into a man of honor, a "gentleman."

Jack's transformations follow the same fundamental pattern as Crusoe's, though their dynamics are almost entirely secular. Like Crusoe, Jack is driven by a number of energies, particularly, in his case, the desire to find a place in the broader social network. These energies are passional, various, contradictory, short-sighted, and too often self-destructive, but still they are the energies that drive forward his growth and transformation. For, once these energies are articulated – formulated as habits, patterns of behavior, roles – reason can press on them and begin to shape them to their "right Uses." Like all of Defoe's protagonists, Jack masters himself, but, more than any of the others, he masters himself by casting himself in roles, sounding them out experientially, assessing them, and then either abandoning them or remodeling them with an eye to finding that form of behavior that best satisfies his various emotional, social, and moral needs. For roles, at best, approximate ideal behavior but, because they can codify false values, roles can also legitimize bad conduct. Thus, the taking on of a role must be done thoughtfully, creatively, and in a spirit of improvisation. Roles are not immutable – nor should they be. Like Crusoe, who comes to see his daily tour of the hill as a bad habit that must be broken so he can recast his fears in some more reasonable form, so Jack, when he comes out of the warehouse an overseer, almost immediately redefines what an overseer is and how an overseer should act. The "Horse-whip that was given him, with his New Office" (*CJ*, p. 132) is the first thing to go, and quite appropriately so, and this doffing of that badge of office and all it represents is just the first step in his creative reformulation of the role of overseer.

The dangers of roles are emphasized again when Jack returns to the Old World a rich man and begins to pursue in earnest his lifelong dream of becoming a gentleman. In part because he has wanted to be a gentleman so badly for so long, in part because he has grown up a penniless boy on the streets and has spent much of his life as a thief, a common soldier, and an indentured servant, Jack plays the roles of a gentleman naively, sometimes stupidly, and almost always blindly. The role dazzles him, so much so that he has difficulty seeing that the gentlemanly code of honor is a cover for violence, predation, and moral vacancy. He abandons the role near the end of the novel and returns to Maryland. Once there, he repudiates his Jacobite past (another delusive role he has played throughout the novel), and he ends his career as a merchant in the Caribbean, trading with the Spanish.[89]

Being a merchant is Jack's last role in the novel – just as it was for both Crusoe and Singleton, who also begin their lives as sinners and criminals but end as merchants and traders. For all three, being a merchant is a sign of their having "civilized" themselves by disciplining their impulses to such a degree that they can at last enter into the web of social interaction. For Defoe, as for many of his contemporaries, commerce and trade were constitutive of civilization, and the merchant was the prime example of a man who had transformed his potentially destructive passions, reconciling individual impulse and self-interest with the public good, harnessing the acquisitive and self-seeking impulses and putting them into the service of the greater good.

And so, at the end of the novel, Jack still has that ambition to rise that has, from the earliest period of his life, made him think he was a gentleman; he still has that impulse toward acquisition and self-promotion that made him a thief; he still possesses that aggression that made him a politically amoral colonel in the Jacobite cause; and, above all, he still has the drive to weave himself into the social web: but now, as a merchant and trader, all these passions are directed into forms of behavior that are social, productive, and certainly far less self-destroying.[90]

Though Defoe thought that "Trade is the most noble way of life," there is no sense at the end of the novel that Jack has achieved some sort of apotheosis.[91] The novel implies throughout that transformation involves the continual fashioning and refashioning of habits, behaviors, roles, codes and forms. Jack's growth is shambling and imperfect, his successes modest, his psychological and moral maturation incomplete, all of which is implied in his failure to become a man in one last way – that is, a male.[92] In marriage, Jack is a signal failure. He is married five times, and five times he is cuckolded, and his last wife – his best wife – turns out to be his first wife, whom he meets again in Maryland when he returns and whom he "remarries." His search for the perfect marriage is circular (as is his search for the perfect role of a gentleman, which similarly leads him from Maryland to Europe and back again), and it is so, I think, to remind us of the limits of mastery. The marriage plot acts as a comic counterpoint to Jack's increasing skill in mastery and achievement. In each marriage, Jack looks for a more and more certain control over his wives, and he is continually frustrated. With his first two wives, he himself bears a good deal of the fault: they are frenchified women to whom he is attracted for the most superficial reasons – they are trophies that mark his assent to the status of a gentleman – and he would have known that the marriages would end in failure had he not been so naive and caught up in his own illusions. But the last wives are different: one cuckolded him when, after many years as a loving and faithful wife, she becomes ill, unbalanced, and alcoholic; the wife who succeeds her "cuckolds" him, too, but years before they were married, and the facts of her affair were hidden from him. If in his first marriages he brought cuckoldry on himself because of his foolish pretensions, in the next two, there is nothing he could have done to know the true nature of his wives.

Cuckoldry becomes the symbol of the limits of our power of mastery. Jack comes to acknowledge that life is "full of Hazards" and filled with "Circumstances dangerous to Mankind, while he is left to choose his own Fortunes, and to be guided by his own short sighted Measures" (*CJ*, p. 230). "Man," he acknowledges, is such "a short sighted Creature" that he "sees … little before him" and "can neither anticipate his Joys, nor prevent his Disasters" (*CJ*, p. 252). One's life is shaped less by one's own will than by "an invisible over-ruling Power," which "Governs all our Actions of every Kind, limits all our Designs, and orders the Events of every Thing relating to us" (*CJ*, p. 264). When his first wife comes back into his life, Jack accepts it as an act of Providence, and he acquiesces to it, just as he will acquiesce to his wife's prudent management of his life in extricating him from the dangers he has put himself into by supporting the Jacobite cause.

Jack reaches these pious conclusions in the last pages of the book, when he finds himself living with the Spanish merchants in Mexico in, as he says, "a kind of Exile," an "agreeable Retirement" where he has "leisure to reflect, and to repent" (*CJ*, pp. 263, 264). He makes good use of this moment – he comes to understand the decrees of Providence and "at last to look with shame and blushes, upon such a Course of Wickedness, as I have gone through in the World" – but he then leaves his "comfortable Retreat," just as he earlier left that equally privileged moment as an indentured servant for whom everything was "immediately provided" (*CJ*, pp. 163, 164). He thrusts himself back into the thicket of the world and returns to London. He has not been able to shape the world entirely to his liking, and he certainly has not shaped himself to perfection, but no matter. There is no end to such shaping.[93]

CHAPTER 4

Moll Flanders *and the misrepresentation of servitude*

The New World and indentured servitude have less of a presence in *Moll Flanders* than in *Robinson Crusoe* and *Colonel Jack*. Moll comes to the Chesapeake twice, first as the wife of a well-off planter, a man who turns out to be her brother, and again at the end of the novel, this time transported as an indentured servant. Though relatively brief, these two episodes neatly structure the novel: each is eight years long and each comes at the end of a thirty-five-year period of Moll's life. Both punctuate her life at crucial moments, defining, in a highly distilled and associative way, her psychological and moral condition.[1]

Perhaps because they are meant to pass summary judgment on Moll, the American episodes confirm with unusual clarity the assumptions about indentured servitude which Defoe made use of in all his fiction. Here, as in his other novels, servitude opens the way to mastery, freedom, and a fuller integration into society at large. This view of indentured servitude is in such contrast to the way actual indentured servants experienced the institution – they saw it as a form of slavery and intense social isolation – that after examining the role of servitude in *Moll Flanders,* I turn to an exploration of the institution itself and then speculate about why Defoe so misrepresented it.

Moll Flanders appears to follow the same trajectory as *Robinson Crusoe* and *Colonel Jack*. Like Crusoe and Jack, Moll is led by her ambition into immoral and criminal behavior. Like Crusoe and Jack, she goes to the New World as an indentured servant, repents of her past behavior, and becomes successful. In all three novels, the protagonists appear to have won an economic freedom earned by their American plantations, a psychological freedom resulting from their having achieved self-autonomy, and a "Christian freedom" that comes with moral reformation. Moll returns to England a wealthy and apparently a reformed woman, with a gentleman for a husband and a rich Chesapeake planter for a son.

But, though her husband may be a gentleman, he is also a lifelong criminal, and his gentility is faintly comic. Her son is the fruit of an incestuous union. And the genuineness of Moll's feelings toward both her husband and son is made problematic by her unabated avarice and ambition. For all her insistence on her moral regeneration, to the end she keeps her eye on the main chance and the bottom line. We are never certain that she is truly repentant.

In short, Moll's experience in the New World is much more ambiguous than Crusoe's or Jack's, and we can see the root causes of this ambiguity in her imprisonment in Newgate, an imprisonment which eventuates in her being sent to the Chesapeake as an indentured servant.

At first glance, Moll's imprisonment in Newgate seems much like Crusoe's confinement on his island "Prison". Both Moll and Crusoe are made "sensible of [their] Condition" (*RC,* p. 123) because of their imprisonment, and this is the first step toward their reformation. Crusoe discovers "Cause to praise [God] for Dungeons and Prisons" because his "Bondage" on the island forces him into "conversing … with my own Thoughts," "opening my Eyes … to see the former Condition of My Life, and to mourn for my Wickedness, and repent" (*RC,* pp. 166, 132, 157, 141). For Moll, too, her prison becomes "a space given me for Repentance" (*MF,* p. 227). She enters Newgate having had "no Sense of my Condition," but there she is "restor'd to the Power of thinking," and her "Reflections … upon the horrid detestable Life I had liv'd" lead to her reformation: "I was perfectly chang'd, and become another Body" (*MF,* pp. 228, 230).

Their prisons make them "sensible of [their] Condition" because both prisons are emblems which depict so concretely and so obviously Moll's and Crusoe's wickedness that they cannot help but understand at last "the horrid detestable" lives they have led. Crusoe's island is a figure for that island-like egocentricity that has characterized the state of his soul long before he ever arrived at the island: absorbed in himself, cut off from family, society, and God. Newgate functions similarly for Moll: it is emblematic of the condition of her inner life. Newgate is "an Emblem of Hell itself" (*MF,* p. 224), and Moll defines "Hell" as a degeneration into a state of insensibility. Newgate is a "dreadful Place" because

Time, Necessity, and Conversing with the Wretches that are there Familiarizes the Place to [the prisoners] … they become reconcil'd to that which at first was the greatest Dread upon their Spirits in the World, and are as impudently Chearful and Merry in their Misery, as they were when out of it. (*MF,* p. 226)

Moll observes this insensibility in the first woman she meets there:

I ask'd her, how the Place look'd to her when she first came into it? just as it did now to me, *says she,* dreadful and frightful, that she thought she was in Hell, and

I believe so still, *adds she, but it is natural to me now, I don't disturb myself about it.* (*MF*, p. 225)

Moll calls this a "Lethargy of Soul," a state in which one is aware but has lost all feeling about what one is aware of, and Moll herself eventually succumbs to this insensibility as she, too, "Familiarizes" (*MF*, p. 228) herself to her condition:

I degenerated into Stone; I turn'd first Stupid and Senseless, then Brutish and thoughtless, and at last raving Mad as any of them were; and in short, I became as naturally pleas'd and easie with the Place, as if indeed I had been Born there. (*MF*, p. 228)

Now, Crusoe and Jack were as "Stupid" as Moll, but Moll is "Stupid" in a way quite different from the ways Crusoe and Jack are. Jack is stupid because he is ignorant. Raised on the streets of London, he is an urban savage who "set out in the World so early" that "when he began to do Evil, he understood nothing of the Wickedness of it"; he "had no sense of Conscience" (*CJ*, pp. 36, 76). Crusoe, on the other hand, does not set out "Stupid" – unlike Jack, he is raised in a pious family – but he becomes stupid because he "degenerates" into a "hardned, unthinking, wicked Creature": "A certain Stupidity of Soul, without Desire of Good, or Conscience of Evil, had entirely overwhelm'd me, and I [had] ... not ... the least Sense, either of the Fear of God in Danger, or of Thankfulness to God in Deliverances" (*RC*, p. 122). From the time he leaves home until the onset of his illness, Crusoe, like Jack, is "without Desire of Good, or Conscience of Evil."

Moll's "Stupidity" is of a different order, one that is exactly emblematized by Newgate. Unlike Crusoe and Jack, Moll is conscious that what she does is immoral, and she is alive to the fact that she is treating others unjustly, cruelly. "The Reproaches of my own Conscience were such as I cannot express, for I was not blind to my own Crime," Moll remarks after one of her immoral dealings (*MF*, p. 113), and such consciousness rarely leaves her. Having delivered Jemy's son, she returns to marry her accountant: "Then it occurr'd to me what an abominable Creature am I! and how is this innocent Gentleman going to be abused by me!" (*MF*, p. 157). When she begins her career as a thief, she is struck with "Horror" at what she has done, "tormented" by guilt at "the wicked Trade" she has involved herself in. Surprised at how "cruel" she has become, disgusted by her own "inhumanity," she condemns her behavior as "base," "dishonourable," "scandalous" (*MF*, pp. 164, 169, 175, 126, 128). Her repeated self-accusations – of vanity, adultery, incest, hard-heartedness, wicked desires,

criminal deeds, bigamy, deception, whoredom, unscrupulous manipu-
lation, sinful impulses, lying, gross indecency, and base designs – reveal
that Moll *knows* that what she is doing is "dreadful and frightful," but she
erects a wall between her knowledge and her feeling so that she has become
"reconcil'd" to what she knows without losing consciousness of what she
knows. Like the other inmates of Newgate, she has become "naturally
pleas'd and easie" with the "Hell" that is her way of life (*MF,* p. 228).

Although Moll says that it is only in Newgate that she has "degenerated" into this insensibility, in fact, she had become "Stupid" years before
she ever was incarcerated. Newgate is an emblem of a state of soul at which
she has already arrived. Moll has partitioned off what she knows about
what she does from what she feels about what she does from the time she
was a very young woman, and her life before her imprisonment is the
history of her progressive and continual hardening.[2] Indeed, her descent
into the "Hell" of insensibility begins in the very first episode when she is
seduced by the elder brother and then coerced into marrying the younger.
She resolves to be never again "trick'd ... by *that Cheat* called LOVE"
(*MF,* p. 66). From that point on, she constructs a life in the teeth of her
own emotions and her own conscience, advancing herself by pushing aside
the claims of morality, by severing the ties of common human sympathy,
by compelling herself to act against her own natural feelings. She acts as
she knows she must act and steels herself against what she feels about how
she acts.

Moll is not ignorant about how immoral or indecent her acts are.
She has split herself. She marries the younger brother in spite of the fact
that "it griev'd me, that I must be the Instrument to abuse so honest a
Gentleman" and in spite of her feeling that she "committed Adultery and
Incest with him every Day in my Desires, which without doubt, was as
effectually Criminal in the Nature of the Guilt, as if I had actually done
it" (*MF,* pp. 64–65). She becomes increasingly more calculating, all the
while acknowledging her own moral poverty and her indecency. But she
dissociates herself from her moral knowledge and her humane sensibilities, not pushing them under to the point of repression usually, but dis-
tancing them just enough to give her freedom to act.[3] When her partner
in crime is caught, Moll is "troubl'd ... exceedingly ... knowing that I
was really the Instrument of her disaster," but she is also "very easie at her
Transportation" because fear that the woman would expose her "took off
all my tenderness" (*MF,* p. 187). When she steals a bundle of goods from
the people whose house is on fire, she thinks of it as "the greatest and the
worst Prize that ever I was concern'd in": "I confess the inhumanity of this

Action mov'd me very much, and made me relent exceedingly, and Tears stood in my Eyes upon that Subject: But with all my Sense of its being cruel and Inhuman, I cou'd never find in my Heart to make any Restitution" (*MF,* p. 175). Her life with the gentleman she meets in Bath was "happy but unhappy," for though she is pleased with the financial security her relationship with him brought, "I was not without secret Reproaches of my own Conscience for the Life I led" (*MF,* pp. 110–111).

Moll's self-alienation is dramatized in the scene where Jemy leaves her when they realize they cannot live together given their financial situation.

> Nothing that ever befel me in my Life, sunk so deep into my Heart as this Farewel: I reproach'd him a Thousand times in my Thoughts for leaving me, for I would have gone with him thro' the World, if I had beg'd my Bread ... *O Jemy!* said I, *come back, come back,* I'll give you all I have; I'll beg, I'll starve with you. (*MF,* p. 135)

All this after having withheld from him the knowledge of how much money she in fact does have and having told him, "I never willingly Deceiv'd him, and I never would" (*MF,* p. 132). He does come back, but Moll does not offer to either beg or starve with him. Indeed, she "was in the greatest Confusion imaginable" and did not know "whether to be glad or sorry" (*MF,* p. 135). He leaves again, this time for good, and Moll makes no move to keep him.

All of Moll's self-contradictions here are ironic, but the point of the irony is not her lack of self-awareness – she knows perfectly well that she is, as she says, "at odds with myself" (*MF,* p. 135) – nor is the point of her irony her hypocrisy, for she is as sincere in being relieved of the financial hardship of living with Jemy as she is in saying she is willing to beg for her bread for them to live together. The point of the irony is that her life is "Hell."

Driven by her occasional need to survive and an abiding ambition to thrive, Moll has narrowed her sense of her self to a very small circle of concerns and needs. Other demands of her fuller self – her moral commitments, her desire for social bonds, the whole compass of her feelings and sentiments – she pushes to the periphery, registering their presence but muting them so that they become manageable. All of her profuse and variegated energies are pressed into the service of a small circle of immediate need and ambition, and those which cannot be pressed into service are set aside. Morality is compromised or evaded, ties of affiliation manipulated, feelings repressed, channeled, or simply faced down, all so that a nub of the self can survive and prosper.[4]

The consequence of the "Stupidity" to which Moll has reduced herself is concisely figured in the first American episode of the novel, where Moll moves to Virginia with her new husband and discovers there that her marriage to him is incestuous.

Because Moll has narrowed her life to a single overweening drive, her relations with other people are largely instrumental and manipulative. She interacts with other people because she must, and she places a barrier between them and herself in order to remain autonomous. Her refusal to integrate herself into the larger human community is symbolized by her incest. In the eighteenth century, incest was most commonly understood as a kind of narcissism, a failure to extend feelings, obligations, and relationships beyond the narrowest of boundaries – an understanding most famously articulated by St. Augustine when he argued that the prohibition of incest existed so that "men ... should be bound together by various relationships; and ... one man should not himself sustain many relationships, but ... the various relationships should be distributed among several, and should thus serve to bind together the greatest number."[5] Incest represented a turning away from the broader social fabric, Bolingbroke explained, and it was prohibited in order to "improve sociability among men, and to extend it as wide as possible."[6] Hutcheson described the ban on incest as a way to "diffuse further among many families the good will and endearment which frequently arises from consanguinity and affinity."[7]

Incest, then, figures forth the "horrid detestable Life" Moll has created for her self – a self cut off from other human beings and from those feelings, values, and moral codes that bind her to other human beings. It is patently ironic that the revelation of her incest occurs in America, for Moll remains blind to its meaning, and so the New World does not become for her a place for moral renewal. That does not occur until she is put in Newgate – where the "Hell" that she herself has become is made so palpable that she cannot help but acknowledge it – and then, as an indentured servant, is sent to the New World, where this time she begins to work out her transformation.

Moll's reformation begins in Newgate when she is forced at last to come to terms with what she evaded in Virginia, her alienation from the human community. The success of Crusoe's and Jack's experience in the New World was marked by their turning away from their selves and weaving themselves into the larger world. Crusoe progressively develops a larger and larger society about him and learns to devote himself to the men for whom he comes to feel responsible. Jack's moral progress was measured by his maturation into an "Honest Man" – "honesty" being, as Defoe said, the "constant Discharge of all good Offices, friendly, kind, and generous Actions" to "the rest of Mankind" (*SR*, p. 69). Moll's conversion, too, begins when, meeting Jemy in Newgate, she develops a sense of obligation and fellow feeling. In an instant, Moll understands that her crimes are "an Offence against God and my Neighbor" (*MF,* p. 225).

I was struck Dumb at the Sight, and knew neither what to say, or what to do; … and I cry'd vehemently for a great while; dreadful Creature, that I am, *said I,* How many poor People have I made Miserable? How many desperate Wretches have I sent to the Devil; This Gentleman's Misfortunes I plac'd all to my own Account …

I was overwhelm'd with grief for him; my own Case gave me no disturbance compar'd to this, and I loaded my self with Reproaches on his Account; I bewail'd his Misfortunes, and the ruin he was now come to, … and the first Reflections I made upon the horrid detestable Life I had liv'd, began to return upon me, and as these things return'd my abhorrence of the Place I was in, and of the way of living it, return'd also; in a word, I was perfectly chang'd, and become another Body.

… [T]he harden'd wretch'd boldness of Spirit, which I had acquir'd in the Prison abated, and Conscious Guilt began to flow in upon my Mind: In short, I began to think, and to think is one real Advance from Hell to Heaven; all that Hellish harden'd state and temper of Soul, which I have said so much of before, is but a deprivation of Thought; he that is restor'd to his Power of thinking, is restor'd to himself. (*MF,* pp. 229–230)

Like Crusoe and Jack, Moll is transformed.

But, of course, it is precisely the question of whether she *is* transformed that is so problematic in *Moll Flanders.* Her "editor" comments that she grew "very Rich" in the New World but adds that she "was not so extraordinary a Penitent, as she was at first" (*MF,* p. 26). A comparison here to *Colonel Jack* is instructive. When Jack comes to America, he really does reform, and his clean break with the past is confirmed when the goods he bought with his ill-gotten money go down in a storm. He is glad for the loss, for that means he can begin utterly anew, and he goes on to construct his new life on the basis of the credit he achieves honestly. Moll does just the opposite: she transfers all her stolen money and goods to the New World and uses them to bankroll her financial success with scarcely a twinge of guilt or a thought of restitution.[8]

The genuineness of her reformation is further muddied by her conduct in the New World. Although she begins to weave herself into the fabric of society when she returns to the Chesapeake at the end of the novel, it is not clear how completely she opens herself to other people or how much she remains dominated by her need for self-autonomy. She comes to the New World, not with a thoroughly renovated outlook but with many of her old self-interested suspicions and withholdings. At first glance, her argument to persuade Jemy to immigrate with her to the Chesapeake appears to be the typical argument made by many promoters of the New World, including Defoe himself:

I thought our mutual Misfortunes had been such, as were sufficient to Reconcile us both to ... living where no Body could upbraid us with what was past ... where we should look back on all our past Disasters with infinite Satisfaction, when we should consider that our Enemies should entirely forget us, and that we should live as new People in a new World, no Body having any thing to say to us, or we to them. (*MF*, pp. 246–247)

But Moll's vision is less a vision of the possibilities of starting a new life on a new foundation than a reiteration of her old anxiety of hiding her identity to preserve her autonomy. When Moll's mother praises the transformative possibilities of the New World, her emphasis is entirely different. She remarks that

many a *Newgate* Bird becomes a great Man, and we have ... several Justices of the Peace ... and Magistrates of the Towns ... that have been burnt in the Hand ... [S]ome of the best Men in this Country are burnt in the Hand, and they are not asham'd to own it. (*MF*, p. 86)

They are "not asham'd to own it" because the brands on their hands are not stigmas but marks of credit, visible tokens of reform, signs of a good character erected by diligence and honesty in the teeth of past failure and weakness. Moll's first journey to Virginia ended in the disaster of incest because no one knew who anyone was or how they were related to anyone else, and incest was an appropriate punishment for her tendency to hide behind false identities and to pursue relationships with self-serving motives and hidden agendas.[9] The fact that she returns to Virginia pleased that "no Body [has] any thing to say to us, or we to them" suggests how little she has changed.

And another fact about her second sojourn in the New World suggests that Moll is not fully reformed: she evades her punishment of indentured servitude. In *Robinson Crusoe* and *Colonel Jack,* servitude dramatizes the moral and psychological reformation of the two protagonists as they master their drives and energies to serve the ends of reason, morality, social obligation, and God. Moll's refusal to submit herself to indentured servitude, then, is a sign of her resistance to reformation, and we know that this obstinacy springs from the very core of her self, from her primal need for autonomy, for the first thing we learn about her is that from earliest childhood she is possessed by an extraordinary "Aversion to going into Service" (*MF*, p. 29). Moll finds the prospect of service "Frightful" because it will make her put her fate into the hands of others and she will lose control over her own life.

They will take me away … and put me to Service, and I can't Work House-
Work … and if I can't do it, they will Beat me, and the Maids will Beat me to
make me do great Work, and I am but a little Girl, and I can't do it. (*MF,* p. 30)[10]

Orphaned and untutored from her earliest years, Moll is buffeted by
large and overpowering social and economic forces. She grows up unpro-
tected in a society characterized by avaricious individualism, a society
whose familial and communal networks have been severely weakened
and whose codes of morality have been brushed aside. Her ability to survive and thrive depends on her becoming autonomous.[11] And yet, though
Defoe is sympathetic toward her predicament, he also understands that
her drive for autonomy undermines the very freedom and mastery for
which she strives and that her self-determination is purchased at too high
and too self-defeating a cost.

In *Robinson Crusoe* and *Colonel Jack,* both protagonists' struggle for
freedom and mastery is defined along two axes. To be free, Crusoe and
Jack must raise themselves from the bottom of the hierarchy of power and
cease to be subject to other people or to external forces. To be free in this
sense means that they must be autonomous enough to move from low
to high, whether materially, economically, socially, morally, or spiritually.
But there is a second axis that defines freedom: freedom is achieved by
moving from outside to inside, by implicating oneself deeper and deeper
into the material, social, cultural, and spiritual matrices that confer power
and status. For in a hierarchical society like Defoe's, to be unfree is not
merely to be at the bottom of the hierarchy but to be outside the hierarchy
altogether. Hence, the struggle for freedom and mastery in Defoe involves
not simply asserting the self against the will of others or against the forces
that be. Rather, freedom and mastery involve simultaneously asserting the
self inward and upward: moving inward by knotting oneself into those
social, cultural, and religious networks that confer power and status and
moving upward in those networks once one has implicated oneself within
them. For this reason, it is obvious why freedom in these novels cannot
be gained by the protagonists simply asserting their will against all that
is arrayed against them. To the contrary, freedom requires an intricate
negotiation of self-assertion and submission: first, they must accept and
submit to the rules of the game to gain admission into the network and
then they must assert themselves within that system to advance upward in
it. Thus, both Crusoe and Jack begin their lives as isolates, men who are
born or who thrust themselves outside their religion, culture, and society, and they succeed in their lives when they regain entrance into those
systems. Jack achieves power and status only after he enters the social

hierarchy by acceding to its values and its codes and standards of behavior; Crusoe masters nature by working within its regime, complying with its demands, and he saves his soul by accepting the rules God has laid down and yielding to His commands. And if they are to achieve any degree of mastery, both Crusoe and Jack must first subdue those irrational energies and egocentric drives that blind them to an understanding of those forces to which they must submit. This complicated negotiation of self-assertion and submission, I have argued throughout this book, is dramatized by Defoe under the figure of indentured servitude.

Moll's evading indentured servitude points to a larger evasion on her part. To a much greater degree than Crusoe or Jack, she refuses to free herself from her drive for autonomy, and she often serves this drive slavishly. As many critics have observed, Moll's excuse that she is forced into a life of crime by necessity wears thin fairly quickly in the novel. "Vice came in always at the Door of Necessity" (*MF*, p. 117), she claims, but she continues her life of crime well after she has any economic need to, stealing "in advance of necessity," as Ian Bell remarks, "in case necessity comes along."[12] Even when there is no rational reason to do so, she is *driven* to steal because she *must* feel secure, and she can feel secure only when her autonomy is ensured. The scene where she steals a horse in spite of the fact that she has no idea how to profit from it is comedic, but typically her compulsion is portrayed more grimly. Moll herself comes to realize that she is in the grips of irrational impulse:

tho' by this jobb I was become considerably Richer than before, yet the Resolution I had formerly taken of leaving off this horrid Trade, when I had gotten a little more, did not return; but I must still get farther, and more … a little more, and a little more, was the Case still. (*MF*, p. 175)

She hopes "that I might perhaps come to have one Booty more that might compleat my Desires; but tho' I certainly had that one Booty, yet every bit look'd towards another" (*MF*, p. 175). More and more, thievery becomes a bad habit to which she mindlessly acquiesces.

Moll is, to use a phrase Defoe used elsewhere, "Damn'd to the Bondage of Mechanick Vice," unable to free herself from the life of crime she thinks will secure her autonomy.[13] She does find some success – "I grew the greatest Artist of my time" (*MF*, p. 180), she says with complacency – but much of this freedom and mastery is specious, for the "informing irony" of the novel, as Richetti points out, is that "she is possessed … by an illusory sense of independence and power."[14] Like all irrational energies in Defoe, Moll's compulsion is self-destructive, for she puts herself continually in jeopardy, pushing herself toward an increasingly certain catastrophe, "hurried on by an inevitable and unseen Fate" (*MF*, p. 224). And so, she ends in prison, a slave to her own need for autonomy.

And there are further consequences. Moll Flanders, like Jack and Crusoe, is an outsider and an isolate. Born at the margins of society, orphaned, wife to many husbands and mistress to many keepers, all of whom abscond or die, mother to many children, all of whom disappear from her life, she is a woman alone. She is denied even the looser network of affiliation, "turn'd out," as she frequently laments, "to the wide World ... with no Friend, no Acquaintance in the whole World" (*MF*, p. 63). To maintain her autonomy, she remains an outsider and an isolate, conducting herself in secrecy, hiding her inner life from everyone. When she participates in society, she participates only as an actress, impersonating someone inside society while in fact standing outside it. Now, both Crusoe and Jack, as we have seen, engage in performances. Crusoe acts out a drama of social power and leadership; it is largely fictitious, but he acts it out to protect the values of that society and to promote its survival. Similarly, when Jack stages his drama of slave management, he publicly pledges himself to his role in society and demonstrates his ability to uphold its values. Both of their performances occur at that moment in their lives when they are moving from being isolated individuals to being social creatures. The purpose of both men's theatrics is to weave themselves into the social matrix by publicly committing themselves to values they honor. But whereas Crusoe and Jack *perform,* Moll merely *acts:* she takes up "new Figures and ... new Shapes every time I went abroad" (*MF*, p. 216), engaging with her society behind a series of masks and deceptions and lies. Her purpose is not to participate in her society, but to exploit it.

And because she remains outside all social, cultural, or religious orders, Moll creates the very "Hell" from which she cannot escape. For she has not lost consciousness of her own lack of humanity, her trespasses against justice, or her violations of fundamental principles of morality. She knows perfectly well what she has done, but in order to be autonomous, she has deadened herself to her own self-accusations. This leads to a hardening, which is at once a deadening of her sensibilities and a paralysis of her will, something Moll has seen in those who have locked themselves up in the Mint,

[men] labouring to forget former things, which now it was the proper time to remember ... Sinning on, as a Remedy for Sin past ... [T]here was something horrid and absurd in their way of Sinning, for it was all a Force even upon themselves; they did not only act against Conscience, but against Nature; they put a Rape upon their Temper to drown ... Reflections ... Having no Principles to

Support him, nothing within him, or above him, to Comfort him; but finding it all Darkness on every Side ... he repeats the Crime, and thus he goes every Day one Step onward of his way to Destruction. (*MF*, p. 70)

Moll herself "repeats the Crime, and thus goes ... every Day one Step onward ... to Destruction" because, in her compulsion to remain autonomous, she keeps herself outside the social and cultural order. But Crusoe and Jack discover that they can achieve freedom and mastery only by moving inside the social, cultural, and religious orders. And for Moll to break out of her "Hell," she must engage with other human beings. Only by working within social and cultural matrices by acting humanely, justly, and morally can she become more humane, just, and moral and in that way cease to "repeat the Crime." This is why her first gestures at reformation come, like Crusoe's, when she breaks out of her mindless habits, "overwhelm'd with grief" for Jemy and for the "many poor People [I] have ... made Miserable" (*MF*, p. 229). She becomes "perfectly changed" (*MF*, p. 230) when she enters into the larger networks of other people, of social obligation, and of the demands of morality and religion.

An indication of Moll's movement toward reformation is her gradually dropping her defenses to reveal to others those feelings and past actions she had tenaciously hidden throughout her life. The novel itself, of course, is an extended confession, and Moll understands her autobiographical impulse to be a "Necessity of Nature" (*MF*, p. 262). "A Secret of Moment should always have a Confident," Moll acknowledges, "a bosom Friend, to whom we may Communicate the Joy of it, or the Grief of it, be it what it will, or it will be a double weight upon the Spirits, and perhaps even insupportable in itself" (*MF*, p. 262). To continue not to speak out, she discovers when she sees Jemy in Newgate, was a "Burden [that] was too heavy for my mind" (*MF*, p. 262). She buckles, and her buckling initiates her reformation.

And after her initial breakthrough, Moll gradually begins to open herself up to the larger social networks she has kept herself apart from, driven by the pressure that comes from those sociable feelings and moral sensibilities from which she has partitioned herself off. The novel thus ends with a protracted series of small revelations that she jerks out of herself, disclosing the truth about herself to the minister in Newgate, her "Mother," her son, and Jemy. But these revelations are painfully halting, gradual, and incomplete. First, she "unlock'd all the Sluices of my Passion" to the minister in Newgate, whose "honest friendly way" of treating her "broke into my very Soul": "I unravell'd all the Wickedness of my Life to him: In a word, I gave him an Abridgement of this whole History; I gave him the Picture of my Conduct for 50 Years in Miniature. I hid nothing from him" (*MF*, p. 235). The minister tries to get her freed from the sentence of transportation, but Moll ceases to encourage him in his endeavors once she meets Jemy and formulates her plan for a life in the New World. "I really was not sollicitous about it, as I was before, but I industriously conceal'd my Reasons for it from the Minister, and to the last he did not know, but that I went with the utmost reluctance and affliction" (*MF*, p. 248).

When she meets Jemy in Newgate, she promises to "tell [him] the particulars" of her life since she last saw him, but she tells him only "so much of my Story as I thought was convenient" and either sidesteps or outright lies about any particulars that would reflect badly on her (*MF*, p. 242). When she asks her governess to help her arrange their voyage to Virginia, she "was forc'd to let her into the whole matter, except only, that of his being my Husband ... As a great Secret, I told her we were to Marry as soon as he came on Board" (*MF*, pp. 251–252). To Jemy, she "faithfully" gives "an Account of my Stock" – except she withholds information about "what I had left with my Governess, in Reserve" (*MF*, p. 252). When she discovers that they had docked near her brother's plantation in Virginia, she "was forc'd to form a Story": she tells Jemy that they cannot settle there because she is afraid to discover herself to some unspecified "Relations" (*MF*, p. 261). She did not "so much as think of breaking the Secret of my former Marriage ... It was not a Story, as I thought that would bear telling" (*MF*, p. 261). About her former marriage, she "let my Husband into so much of it, as I thought would convince him of the Necessity there was, for us to think of Settling, in some other Part of the World" (*MF*, p. 263). When she meets her son, she reveals some of the truth of her life, but she hides the facts about her relation to Jemy by telling him that she is not married and that she is a guest on another plantation. She gives him a gold watch as a token of her love, though "*I did not indeed tell him* that I had stole it" (*MF*, p. 271; Defoe's italics), and when she returns to Jemy, "I related ... all the particulars of this Voyage, except that I called my Son my Cousin" (*MF*, p. 272). When she sees her son the next time, she tells him she has married a gentleman from a neighboring plantation, and she lets him believe that the large cargo she has been sent by the governess and which has been paid for by her criminal earnings belonged to her new husband's estate.

Moll finally does confess to Jemy her incestuous marriage, but even then there is no complete revelation. Though she reveals this shameful secret in the last paragraph of the novel, in the first paragraph of the novel (written, of course, after she has confessed to Jemy), Moll continues to withhold the whole truth, refusing to divulge what she calls elsewhere "the grand Secret, … my true Name" (*MF*, pp. 139–140), a stubborn last resistance, a withholding that seems to border on the irrational:

My True Name is so well known in the Records … at *Newgate* … and there are some things of such Consequence still depending there, relating to my particular Conduct, that it is not to be expected I should set my Name … to this Work; perhaps, after my Death it may be better known; at present it would not be proper, no, not tho' a general Pardon should be issued, even without Exceptions and reserve of Persons or Crimes. (*MF*, p. 27)

Moll's refusal to give up "the grand Secret" suggests that her reformation is not complete. Nor is she able to shuck other habits she has cultivated in her dogged quest for self-autonomy. However sincere her love for her son, she is also dazzled by the prospect of wealth her connection with him will bring, so much so that she entertains fantasies of abandoning Jemy, a potential drag on her fortune. That Moll does not completely reform should not surprise us. Crusoe, whose religious conversion was much more profound than hers, can never resist his wandering impulse, and Jack, after his reformation, enters into illegal commercial ventures in the Caribbean because of his continuing avarice. Yet Moll's incomplete reformation is more disturbing and ambiguous, and the novel as a whole much darker, reflecting, I think, Defoe's recognition that internal forces of need and desire that determine character and behavior are almost as overpowering as the external forces of necessity. The paradox that one can become a slave to the desire for autonomy is at the heart of *Robinson Crusoe,* too. To free himself, Crusoe must become a willing servant, allowing himself to be mastered by God, by the forces of reality, and by the rule of reason. On a figurative level, he becomes a real master only when he becomes an indentured servant. But Moll cannot make herself a voluntary servant. Her need for autonomy is too great, and she can never fully master that need.

Moll does not completely reform because she cannot completely free herself from the compulsions that keep her in bondage, and the sign of her continuing bondage is her refusal to become an indentured servant. In the rich and paradoxical logic of Defoe's American novels, had she become a servant, she would have liberated herself from her slavery to her self-destructive energies.

In *Moll Flanders,* as in *Robinson Crusoe* and *Colonel Jack,* indentured servitude is portrayed as the royal highway to freedom. But for actual indentured servants and for many who were familiar with the real workings of the institution, the idea most often linked with indentured servitude was not freedom but slavery. This contrast between Defoe's fiction and the social reality is so egregious that it needs explaining.

Hugh Jones acknowledged that "the common people [in England] … are under such dreadful apprehensions of the imaginary slavery of the plantations, that they choose for the most part rather to steal, beg, or starve, than go abroad to work."[15] Alsop observed that "among the vulgar in *England*" servants "are stigmatiz'd for slaves."[16] "It hath been a constant report amongst the ordinarie sort of people," Bullock confessed, "that all those servants who are sent to *Virginia,* are sold as slaves."[17] Well into the first half of the 1700s, the words "servant" and "slave" were interchangeable in the Chesapeake colonies. Servants referred to themselves as slaves, and they did so with considerable bitterness.

Why *did* white indentured servants think of themselves as slaves? True, in the colonies physical labor was devalued because of its association with African slaves. Although colonial promoters were extremely uncomfortable to acknowledge it, white servants in the eighteenth century, Carr observes, "were increasingly likely to work besides slaves, a fact that probably downgraded their status."[18] The Earl of Egmont reported what a Carolina merchant told him in 1740: "He said that where there are Negroes, a white Man despises to work, saying, *what, will you have me a Slave and work like a Negroe?*"[19] Still, the differences between African slaves and European indentured servants are obvious. Europeans' servitude was limited in duration, not perpetual, nor did their condition of servitude descend to their progeny. African slaves were wrenched out of their native cultures and were forced to adapt to a wholly alien one. Servants entered a different, but hardly a strange cultural landscape when they came to the New World. Most were not driven to that degree of abject powerlessness that most black slaves were. And, most importantly, they never lost legal claim to their persons. Servants had rights, many spelled out by statute and enforceable by law.[20]

It is difficult to credit the equation many made between indentured servants and slaves. Granted, the conditions of servitude in general were not particularly good. The Chesapeake colonies were "reported to be … a place of intolerable labour, bad usage, and hard Diet," confessed one colonial promoter, and there was a good deal of truth in these reports.[21] Some servants were denied adequate clothing. Elizabeth Ashbridge tells how her master "would not suffer me to have Clothes to be Decent in, having to go barefoote in his Service in the Snowey Weather & the Meanest drudgery, wherein I Suffered the Utmost Hardship that my Body was able to Bear."[22]

Food was often poor, too, and there was little difference between what was fed slaves and servants. "We and the Negroes both alike did fare," wrote James Revel. "A man had really better be hanged then to come a servant into the Plantations, most of his food being homene and water, which is good for negroes, but very disagreeable to English constitutions."[23] A servant in Baltimore County brought suit against his master because the flour he was given contained "Dead worms 3/4 on an Inch long, Clocks, Cock Roaches, Wood Lice, Grasshoppers & Bran, which we are obliged to Sive it all before we can Bake it."[24]

If the quality of the food was often bad, the quantity was often insufficient. Several servants of Richard Preston refused to work and pleaded before court that "Mr Preston doth not allow … sufficient Provisions for th^e inablem^t to our worke, but streightens us soe far that wee are brought so weake, wee are not able to perform th^e imploym^{ts} he putts us upon."[25] The court ordered the servants to receive thirty lashes for refusing to work, though it suspended punishment when they agreed to kneel to beg their master's forgiveness. Governor William Gooch was more sympathetic to the problem. He explained to the Board of Trade that the laws to try hog-stealers were not strictly enforced out of "compassion for servants and slaves who have hard Masters that allow them scarcely any Meat in the Year."[26]

The arduous working conditions could make "the Hardships of an *American* Slavery," as one writer referred to indentured servitude, "infinitely more terrible than a *Turkish* one."[27] Tobacco was a demanding crop that required year-round attention. The work was more burdensome in the Chesapeake than in England, the work day was longer (averaging eight to ten hours compared to the six hours typically found in England), and there were fewer holidays.[28] Much of the most tedious and heavy work was done in the summer in a climate notably hotter and more humid than England's, and since there was less animal power in the Chesapeake than in England, the preparation of the ground was often accomplished by brute manpower.[29]

And there were instances of remarkably harsh treatment. Eddis observed in Maryland that

Negroes being a property for life, the death of slaves … is a material loss to the proprietor; they are, therefore, almost in every instance, under more comfortable circumstances than the miserable European, over whom the rigid planter exercises an inflexible severity. They are strained to the utmost to perform their allotted labor … There are doubtless many exceptions to this observation, yet, generally speaking, they groan beneath a worse than Egyptian bondage.[30]

Court records corroborate this grim assessment. William Drake of Kent County, Maryland, told the court that his master abused him

by tying my two hands and wrists together, hanging me up to ye gunne racks, and whipped me without mercy giving me at least one hundred blows upon my bare skin, and let me hang so long yt ye blood started through and out my fingers and my hands pealed.[31]

In another case, Thomas Bradnox disciplined his servant Thomas Watson for not working hard enough. He gave him "fifty cruel blowes upon the head and sides with a good round hicckory Stick"; Bradnox then "followed him from Morning till Noone with a Stick in his hand to make him fetch wood and beate him more like a dogg then a Christian." He locked him up for six days without bread, and though the other servants saw him forced to drink his own urine, they were so terrified of Bradnox that they could not bring themselves to help their fellow servant. Finally, Bradnox "struck him so violently with his hand on the Brest and face that the blood issued out of his mouth and nose." Watson died.[32]

Still, in spite of numerous individual instances of harsh conditions and brutal treatment, servants as a class were not treated as badly as slaves. Africans were stripped of their names, their ties to families, kin, and clans severed, their cultural inheritance almost utterly destroyed. They were denied all rights and subjected to countless indignities. They were not allowed to form families, and if, by chance, they did, the families could be broken up and dispersed. They were crammed into rude quarters, and, by the early eighteenth century, their work became strictly supervised and regimented. They were assigned the most tedious, repetitious, and onerous tasks. The midday break was shortened, the workday extended into the evenings, Saturday became a full workday. And, as the Chesapeake was transformed from a society with slaves into a slave society, "planters mobilized the apparatus of coercion in the service of their new regime."[33] Beatings, hangings, and dismemberment became more numerous and severe. Indentured servants never sank to this level of misery.[34]

Yet, indentured servants' sense that they were slaves is so pervasive and persistent that one wonders what exactly is at the bottom of it. If the conditions of servants, as bad as they were, were not as severe as those of the Africans, why did they think of themselves as slaves?

A clue can be found in Orlando Patterson's brilliant analysis of slavery. Appalling material conditions, Patterson notes, are not necessarily among the primary "constituent elements of slavery."[35] Rather, the quintessence of slavery, the source of the despair it gave rise to, is the "natal alienation" slaves are forced to undergo and their consequent debasement as "dishon-ored persons."[36] A slave is uprooted from the cultural and social matrix into which he was born and thus is "isolated from his social relations … [and] culturally isolated from the social heritage of his ancestors."[37] Having "ceased to belong in his own right to any legitimate social order," a slave is excluded from "all those areas where power is competed for and status and honor are claimed, conferred, and accepted."[38] Consequently, a slave undergoes a "social death" and becomes "a social nonperson," for it is one's social and cultural matrices that give access to power, that grant status and worth, and that promote respect, and to be removed from these matrices "goes directly to the heart of what is critical in the slave's forced alien-ation": the slave becomes a "dishonored person."[39] "A slave could have no honor because of the origin of his status, the indignity and all-pervasive-ness of his indebtedness, his absence of any independent social existence, but most of all because he was without power except through another."[40]

Patterson's identification of the salient features of slavery is extremely valuable. Of course, just as white indentured servants did not experience the same degree of material deprivation and physical coercion as did black slaves, so they did not suffer to any extent the same depth of alienation and dishonor to which Africans were subjected. But indentured servants were socially alienated and dishonored, and Patterson's insight is valu-able not because it validates the servants' claim that they were treated no better than slaves but because it pinpoints what about their conditions so aggrieved them.

Like slaves, indentured servants suffered a form of natal alienation. To some extent, of course, all immigrants to the New World were torn out of the network of family, friends, and acquaintances and the complex institutional, social, and cultural environment that materially and psycho-logically supported them and defined who they were. But when Thomas Chalkley, setting out from Gravesend for Maryland in 1699, noted that the passengers and their relatives bid one another farewell "as never expecting to see each other any more in this world," he was remarking on some-thing that was particularly true of immigrants to the Chesapeake. Unlike those who settled in New England, newcomers to the tobacco colonies did not come with families, nor did they come from a single locale.[41] All of them – rich and poor, free or bound – came alone, and they entered a new world filled with strangers. In overwhelming numbers, indentured servants were single men and women, almost none having immigrated as part of a family, and more often than not they left an Old World in which they had few if any ties. Statistics are difficult to come by, but on the list of immigrants to the Chesapeake from London between 1682 and 1686, nearly two-thirds of the servants under twenty-one years of age had lost one or both parents.[42]

Further, most servants were in their late teens and early twenties. A substantial proportion, probably around 50 percent, were unskilled. They had not yet established a place in society: they had little if any capital, no land, few possessions, and, if they had a trade, they did not have a high standing in it. Their financial stability fractured by the loss of family, their prospects dimmed by an attenuated network of family and friends, they had already lost many of their roots in their communities.[43]

For many indentured servants, setting out for the New World was merely the last in a series of deracinations. Although a good number of emigrating servants listed London or Bristol as their residences, many had been born elsewhere. In a time of poor wages and poor employment opportunities, they had migrated from place to place, drifting to the more promising urban centers. They failed here, too.[44] And when they arrived in the Chesapeake, they arrived in a land populated by people from different regions who, like themselves, were recently displaced. This new place was not alien, exactly, but because of the death rate, the constant flow in and out of servants, and most especially because it was not where one was born, it was a difficult place to set down roots.

The Chesapeake was not only a land of strangers, but it was a solitary land. People did not cluster in settlements. Plantations were "seate[d] in a stragling distracted Condition," scattered along river banks and creeks and dotting the necks of peninsulas.[45] "There are not fifty houses in the space of Thirty myles."[46] One visitor to the settled region of Virginia remarked that it appeared "wild," "all one continued wood."[47] By 1700, New England had nearly 120 towns; Maryland and Virginia had none to speak of. In the early eighteenth century, both capitals were scarcely villages. Annapolis had "about fourty dwelling houses," and a Swiss traveller observed about Williamsburg that it was at best a place "where a city is intended and staked out to be built."[48]

Even among the long-settled inhabitants, networks of kin, friends, and neighbors were much thinner than in England, and they were thinner still for indentured servants, who were not long settled and who, like slaves, were not allowed to leave their plantations without passes. The unremitting and inflexible demands of the tobacco crop meant that servants' lives were tightly regulated and restricted. Communal activity was rare. Places where inhabitants could gather socially – churches and meeting houses, inns, schools, courts, mills, landings, warehouses, and the shops of merchants and tradesmen – were sprinkled willy-nilly over the countryside. Market days, fairs, and local holidays – in England, occasions for interaction among all members of the community – fell away in the Chesapeake, and much of the body of communal folkways melted away, too. Occasions for any sort of social interaction were rarer than in England, and they were eagerly sought after. The storied hospitality of the mid-Atlantic colonies resulted less from the inhabitants retaining the virtuous customs of their ancestors, which many observers thought, than the sheer loneliness of their lives.[49]

The Chesapeake was so "thinly inhabited," contemporaries complained, that "the Living [was] solitary and unsociable."[50] Though William Fitzhugh resided in Virginia many years, he could never shake off the sense of its sheer alterity and talked often of returning to England: "I am for a Remove to take off that strangeness."[51] William Byrd II, who had a full and active social life, thought Virginia "so lonely a country" that he featured himself a "poor hermit," "buryed alive" in "this silent country."[52]

The feelings of loneliness and estrangement would have been felt particularly strongly by indentured servants, who had lived through a succession of uprootings, each one severing more and more of those threads that knitted them into the social and cultural matrices that gave them a sense of themselves. Margaret Broderick, an indentured servant of William Fitzhugh, so felt the need to "take off that strangeness" that she was compelled to make a connection with past ties, no matter how tenuous. It was her "earnest Desire & Request" to be sold to "Mr Hammersly, who is her father's Country man Towns-Man, & afar off related … She did resolve that neither threats nor persuasions, fair means nor foul should make her do any thing, if she might not be sold to Mr. Hammersly."[53] William Green, a criminal transported as an indentured servant, found himself on a ship departing for America, humiliated and utterly alone:

As for my own part I was very wel dressed, they stripped me of all my Cloaths and gave me lousy rags to put on my back; I cried aloud, and wept amain, but all to no purpose; I had no fond mother to comfort me, no loving friends to pity me: Oh! The scene of misery I was in no one Could express.[54]

After five years, he was sold to a New England ship's captain, and he was forced to leave the only friend he had made in the New World, Anthony Atkinson ("When he found I was going away he weeped bitterly to think that he could not go with me, he said to me, What shall I do when you are gone? I have nobody here to speak to as I have to you").[55] Over the next two years, William managed to save £20 to take Atkinson back to England with him when both their terms expired. Atkinson sailed from

Baltimore to Boston to join his friend. "As soon as the news [of his arrival] reached my ears I was in a transport of joy; I ran immediately on board to see him, he fell on me for joy and wept. Oh! How great was our joys in meeting in this country! ... Oh! the love that was kindled in each heart [was] unspeakable."[56]

In Edward Kimber's *History of Mr. Anderson,* an indentured servant in Maryland laments his "miserable" servitude: "No body owns me – I am an alien and a stranger every where ... To me – *relations dear, and all the charities, of father, son, and brother,* have been, alas! unknown."[57] I do not know whether the pun on "own" is deliberate or fortuitous, but it captures exactly the intuition servants had about the similarity of their condition to that of the "natal alienation" and "social death" of slaves: to be owned as a servant reflected a condition of being unowned – unaffiliated, severed from their familial and social roots. It is not surprising that so many transported felons tried to return to Britain before the end of their sentences, though it meant death to do so.[58]

John Harrower led a relatively agreeable life as an indentured servant in Fredericksburg, Virginia. But he was subject to periodic bouts of loneliness, depression, and drinking. In one such moment, he expressed himself in poetry:

> Both the last nights quite drunk was I,
> Pray God forgive me [of] the sin;
> But had I been in good company,
> Me in that case No man had seen.
>
> Plac'd by myself, without the camp,
> As if I were unclean;
> No freendly soul, does my floor tramp,
> My greiff to ease, or hear my moan.
>
> For in a prison at large I'm plact,
> Boun'd to it, day and night;
> O grant me patience, God of grace,
> And in thy paths make me walk right.[59]

When Harrower says that he is "Plac'd by myself, without the camp, / As if I were unclean," the "camp" he is alluding to is the camp of the wandering Hebrews, who punished the "unclean" by thrusting them outside the camp. The structure of feeling here – the sense of solitariness, alienation, and therefore dishonor – is precisely the same that Patterson identifies as that at the heart of the horror of slavery: to be locked up "in [the] prison" of indentured servitude is, paradoxically, to be placed "without the camp," excluded from the human community and therefore made to feel "unclean," dishonored, and shamed.

Most servants were already "without the camp" even before they immigrated to the New World, and because they came as strangers to a world in which they were excluded from access to the mechanisms to achieve power and establish their worth, they became increasingly more isolated, powerless, and dishonored. Although indentured servitude had been modeled on apprenticeship and service in husbandry, even as it began to take root in the early Caribbean, its adaptations were "sufficiently radical" that it became "a new and different institution":

> The traditional values and ideologies of paternalistic master-servant relations were not retained … The planters did not conceive of their servants socially and emotionally as integral parts of the family or household, but instead viewed them as an alienated commodity which could be recruited and exploited best within the legal framework of traditional servitude.[60]

Galenson observes that economic conditions in the North American colonies led to further adaptations which "produced a fundamental change in the institution, as the rigidity introduced as a result of economic imperatives destroyed relationships basic to the English system of service in husbandry, and resulted in a system in which men were sold as objects."[61]

From the moment he signed his indentures, an indentured servant became property. He could be, and often was, imprisoned until he left for the colonies. Like any other commodity, he could be transferred from one owner to another. He was usually bound to an English agent, but upon arrival in America, his indentures were sold to a second party, and since this was often a colonial agent, he would then be sold to a third owner. ("My Master Atkins," wrote the indentured servant Thomas Best from Virginia, "hath sold me for £150 sterling like a damned slave.")[62] Regarded by their masters as "replaceable goods rather than individuals to be incorporated into families," indentured servants were temporary chattels – slaves only for a space of time, but for that space of time, slaves nonetheless.[63] On tax lists, they were assessed as personal property; in probate inventories, they were listed among livestock and household furniture and were distributed after the death of the master like other items of personal property. A servant could be alienated temporarily to work for a third party, and the profits of his labor were his master's. He could be transferred permanently to another owner to satisfy his master's debt. He could be used to purchase goods. He could be gambled away at a card game.[64]

Forced "without the camp," the indentured servant entered a vicious downward spiral of further exclusion and alienation. He had to struggle to work his way back into the social order so that he might work his way up – up in financial status, up in social rank, up in regard and value; but, having lost power by being placed "without," he had less and less a capacity to engage in that struggle, and so he slipped further outside, and further down.

Servants had rights, and courts in the Chesapeake were not egregiously unfair to them, but too often law followed power. While laws concerning discipline, punishment, and a servant's obligations to his master were extensive, explicit, and detailed, legislation regarding servants' welfare was slight and vaguely worded, leaving the interpretation and implementation to the discretion of the courts. In the "preponderance of ... trials" where masters were charged with the murder or manslaughter of their servants, Richard Morris discovered, "they were acquitted or let off lightly, often in the face of incontrovertible evidence of guilt."[65] Thomas South chased his servant, John Shorte, into a river and stood on the bank impassively as Shorte floundered and cried out for help. Shorte's death by drowning was judged a suicide, and he was denied Christian burial.[66] John Grammer ordered one of his servants to beat another, Thomas Simmons, "neer uppon a hundred stripes wth a Catt of ninetails uppon his bare back," and when he was through, Grammer himself beat him "wth a small ropes end wth a knott att the end of the rope the space of halfe an hour."[67] Simmons died, but Grammer was declared not guilty, for the court decided that the general state of Simmons' health was so bad that "we gather that this person by Course of nature could not have lived long."[68]

Morris also found that in two-thirds of the Maryland cases he studied where complaints of physical abuse or overwork were brought before the courts, servants found some sort of relief, but it usually took the form of an admonishment to the master. Rarely did the court discharge the servant from service. No matter how the case was adjudicated, the results could not have been truly satisfactory for the servant. To bring charges against a master meant openly defying the authority of a person of more power and standing in the community, and the servant risked becoming known as a troublemaker and perhaps jeopardized his chances for work and credit once he became free. If the servant lost, he had to live in a situation greatly exasperated by his having brought suit in the first place, and if he won and his master was merely reprimanded, his day-to-day life might become hellish.[69]

Such a system discouraged servants from bringing complaints to the court in the first place. Consider the cases of Jean Powell, Mary Jones, and Mary Hues, the servants of Henry Smith of Accomack County, Virginia. All three of them were, at various times, severely abused by Smith. They were viciously beaten, denied adequate food and clothing, and overworked. Mary Jones and Mary Hues were both raped by Smith. Smith was pathologically violent and abusive, and not only to his servants. He regularly tyrannized over his wife, beating her and threatening to murder her, and he physically abused her four-year-old daughter from a previous marriage so badly that his wife placed her in the custody of neighbors. Smith openly kept a mistress (herself probably an ex-servant), and when she became pregnant, he colluded with her in an abortion, and then he turned her off his property. He was the father of two bastards. He was accused of causing the death of one of his male servants. As his judges said, he was "one of the most wicked of men."[70]

And yet, against this notoriously wicked man, his servants had little defense. When Jane Powell tried to comfort her mistress after she was beaten, Smith repeatedly struck her with a shoe so severely that "the next day I was not able to lift my hoe."[71] In fact, previous to this Powell had gone to court to seek relief from Smith's "often beating and whipping her without any Occasion given."[72] The court had dismissed her complaint, even though they acknowledged that Smith's abuse of his servants was well known. Nor did they uphold her second complaint against him but simply admonished Smith – who, as Powell would charge in a third suit, "Continuueth his Accustomed Cruellty wth want of Clothes, victualls and hard worke."[73] Mary Jones was so terrorized by Smith (he had imprisoned her on his plantation and unlawfully kept her as a servant for over a year after her term was fulfilled) that for six years she hid the fact that Smith had raped her, revealing it inadvertently only when she was called to court as a witness in another matter. Mary Hues also was raped by Smith. She testified that she had resisted him vigorously "and begged of him for Christ's sake not to ruine her, that she was in a condition bad enough by her service and that he would make her worse than a negro by whoring her."[74] She did not bring charges, in part because when she had earlier tried to go to court to protest his treatment of her, he "very much beat her" and forcibly kept her from going, in part because when after a year's delay she at last did go to court they ignored her, and in part because of what she had seen had happened to her fellow servant: "there was nothing done at Court to Smith for Ravishing Mary Jones but Only she was recorded for a whore, So that the sd Mary Hues could not tell wt to doe durst not Speake of it there for fear of Smiths tiranny."[75]

In 1670, in spite of the overwhelming evidence brought against him, Henry Smith was cleared of the rape charges, and Mary Jones and Mary Hues were ordered "to double there tyme" in order to make up for their being so long absent from work.[76]

If the laws meant to protect servants often worked toward their detriment, those meant to protect the rights of masters did so even more severely, and always with the same consequence: they pushed the servant further outside the network of power and bound him more and more tightly in his servitude. Servants were punished if they breached their contractual obligations, and their punishment almost invariably took the form of having their term of service extended. If apprentices in England took an unauthorized holiday, ran away, or in some way deprived their master of due service, British law required that they merely make up for their lost time; but indentured servants had their time doubled in Virginia, and in Maryland the ratio of the number of days of additional servitude to the number of days of unauthorized absence was an extraordinary ten to one. Servants who felt they had no recourse in the face of an abusive master but to run away were usually punished by the courts with extensions of service, even when they were able to bring evidence of their mistreatment. In Virginia, if a servant lay "violent hands" on his master or overseer, two years of service were added to his indentures. In Maryland, sixteen to twenty months' extra service was the penalty for stealing. If a servant married without consent of the master, he also had to serve more time – sometimes an additional year, sometimes double the time of his stipulated service. Fornication was punished by extending terms of service. Women servants guilty of bastardy had to indemnify their masters for the loss of time or services during their pregnancy and confinement. Abbot Smith found that the typical sentence greatly exceeded the actual amount of time the woman was incapacitated. Taken all together, these penalties could extend the time of service five, even seven, years, and in some cases, the additional time amounted to more than the original term of servitude.[77]

As servants were further alienated by being forced more and more "without the camp," they were, like slaves, dishonored and made to feel, as Harrower says, "unclean." Birth, circumstance, and economic forces had pushed them to the peripheries of their social and cultural networks, and those within the camp saw them as filthy outsiders.

They were stigmatized from the beginning. "We need not doubt," Robert Johnson said in 1609, our land abounding with swarmes of idle persons which having no means of labour to reeleve their misery, doe likewise swarme in lewd and naughtie practices, so that if we seeke not some waies for their forreine employment, wee must provide shortly more prisons and corrections for their bad conditions ... so that you see it no new thing, but most profitable for our State, to rid our multitudes of such as lie at home, and infecting one another with vice and villanie, worse than the plague it self.[78]

Those who are idle because of their own "lewd and naughtie practices" and those who have "no means of labour to reeleve their misery" are tumbled together here, whatever moral distinction one should draw between them eradicated. Like slaves, who were made to undergo a "social death" by being stripped of status and regard, so indentured servants were defined as "dead members of the whole body" of society, as Hugh Jones said of them in 1724, "superfluous persons" – that is to say, no persons at all, at least no persons who count.[79]

Obviously, transported criminals were stigmatized the most. Although Moll's mother says that Chesapeake colonists "make no difference" (*MF*, p. 86) between servants who have voluntarily indentured themselves and transported criminals, her claim is preposterous. All the colonies, from New England to Barbados, resisted accepting felons, and Virginia and Maryland resisted particularly strongly and persistently. Virginia prohibited the importation of felons in 1670 because of the "danger which apparently threatens us, from the barbarous designs and felonious practices of such wicked villains." In 1676, Maryland passed a similar law. "Tis truly hard upon the Province" lamented Cecilius Calvert, "that the Scum and Dregs of the people here sent, should be the Cause of Ruin to Honest men."[80] Almost unanimously American colonists thought these servants were "tricking, thieving and designing rogues" who could never be "brought to get their Livelihood by ... laborious and settled Means."[81] Virginia lawmakers asserted that "most of the felonies ... committed in this colony, are perpetrated ... by persons who have been convicted of felony ... in Great Britain, or Ireland."[82] Transported felons, it was commonly agreed, not only committed "murders, Burglaries, and Other felonies but Debauched the minds and Principles of severall of the Ignorant and formerly Innocent Inhabitants ... so far as to Induce them to Committ Several of the like Crimes."[83] One of the motives for the Transportation Act, in fact, was to make the transportation of felons to America a parliamentary statute so that the colonies would have no choice but to accept them.[84]

Johnson's use of images of pestilence to describe those people who typically became indentured servants ("infecting one another with vice and vaillanie, worse than the plague it self") took on a hypertrophied life in the popular imagination: periodically, panicky rumors swept through communities that the convict servants on an arriving ship were infected with smallpox or jail fever or had already caused an outbreak of deadly disease elsewhere on shore.[85] Other violent figures testify to the sheer visceral repugnance the colonists felt:

BRITAIN! Thou art called our MOTHER COUNTRY; but what good *Mother* ever sent *Thieves* and *Villains* to accompany her *Children;* to corrupt some with their infectious Vices, and murder the rest? What *Father* ever endeavour'd to spread the *Plague* in his Family! ... In what can *Britain* show a more Sovereign Contempt for us, than by emptying their *Jails* into our Settlements; unless they would likewise empty their *Jakes* on our Tables?[86]

One Maryland poet expressed his belief that convict servants were incapable of reform in a particularly revealing metaphor: "As well may Ethiopian Slaves, Wash out the Darkness of their Skin."[87] The convict servant is "unclean," his stain is inborn and ineradicable, and it brands him as a slave.

Nor was it transported criminals alone who were looked upon as so much filth. Indentured servants who came to America voluntarily suffered from a backwash of this contempt. "The generality of the inhabitants" of Maryland, Eddis noted, "generally conceive an opinion that the difference is merely nominal between the indented servant and the convicted felon."[88] Among American creoles, *all* servants, free or criminal, came to be seen as socially inferior and unfit. They were irresponsible, dishonest, dissolute, and disloyal, a "detested Race" of idlers and rogues who had come to the New World because they were incapable of living decent lives in the Old.[89] William Bullock claimed that they would "rather beg than work."[90] Sir Joshua Child asserted that Virginia was

peopled by a sort of loose vagrant people, vicious and destitute of means to live at home (being either unfit for labour, or such as could find none to employ themselves about, or had so mis-behaved themselves by Whoreing, Thieving or other Debauchery, that none would set them to work).[91]

Indentured servants who came to Virginia, according to Hugh Jones, were "the poorest, idlest and worst of mankind, the refuse of Great Britain and Ireland, and the outcast of the people."[92] "The generality of volunteers for transportation are the scuffle and scumme of the people, whose slothe, debauchery and prodigality brings them under those circumstances and if they were not transported to the Plantations it is to be feared many will probably go to Tyburn."[93] Virginia had become, complained one of her citizens, "a Sinke to drayen England of her filth and scum," and Maryland a midden of Britain's "Scum and Dregs."[94]

Servants' sense of their own powerlessness and disrepute came from other directions, too. Having drifted to cities such as London and Bristol in search of work, they met the same economic hardships that had driven them there in the first place, and these same hardships drove them onward to the New World. Their choices were narrowed down by shrinking opportunities, and with each step of their journey, they lost more and more autonomy, caught up in forces that made it seem that they were not exercising their wills but were grabbing at a last alternative as they were going down.[95]

Straitened circumstances and pressing need pushed William Moraley into a stupor of indifference: "not caring what became of me, it enter'd into my Head, to leave *England,* and sell myself for a Term of Years into the *American* Plantations."[96] (Jack is similarly apathetic when he discovers he has been kidnapped to America: "I was grown indifferent ... I had no settled Abode in the World, nor any Employ to get any thing by ... I did not see, but this Service might be as well to me as other Business" [*CJ*, p. 119].) Moraley was not merely impoverished when he bound himself, but hungry, and when he went on board his ship and was fed his first meal,

I began to think myself happy, in being in a way to eat; and on this Account, became insensible of the Condition I had brought myself to ... The small Beer stood upon Deck, and was free for us at all times; so that laying all Reflections [aside], I comforted myself with the Hopes & living well all the Voyage.[97]

By the time he indentured himself, not much mattered but his immediate needs. "A Person like me, oppress'd by Dame Fortune, need not care where he goes. All places are alike to me."[98]

John Harrower also found that he was increasingly powerless to shape his own life. Unable to support his wife and children, he left his home on the Shetland Islands, December 6, 1773, "in order to travel in search of business."[99] His plan, such as it was, was to find employment where he could. Though he was tempted early in his journey to go to North Carolina, when he chanced on a brigantine bound for that colony, "thoughts of being so far from my family prevented me."[100] But, by January 6, having reached Newcastle and found no work, he began to entertain the idea of going to Holland, so he shipped aboard another brigantine with a cargo of coal whose captain "informed me, that he himself was not sure of where he was to go" – possibly Holland, "if not probably to London."[101] But on their voyage south, they happened on two ships – "the one came from Holland

who hade hard getting out by reason of the frost there and the other from
Portsmouth who told us that coals was giving a verry high price there" –
so they sailed neither to Holland nor London but to Portsmouth.[102] "I then
went ashore and immediately set out for London with no more cash in my
pocket 1/8/2d. Str, – I pray, may God provide more for me and for all who
are in strait."[103] He arrived in London on January 18, "like a blind man
without a guide, not knowing where to go being freindless."[104] He began to
look out for "any Business," first answering an advertisement for a bookkeeper in Philadelphia, then offering to go to Maryland as a steward on a
ship.[105] Both possibilities fell through. He then answered an advertisement
to clerk for a London merchant, but he found a dozen applicants before
him, and he "hade litle expectation ... they being all weel acquanted and
I a stranger. I then went to Change to see if any thing would cas[t] up but
to no purpose."[106] Feeling "frendless and forsaken," he began to apply for
a steward's berth on any ship he could find, no matter what its destination, and finally, in desperation, "wrote a petition in general ... offering
to serve any for bare support of life."[107] "But all to no effect, for all pleaces
here at present are entirely carried by freinds and Interest."[108] On January
26, "being reduced to the last shilling," Harrower "was oblidged to engage
to go to Virginia," and on February 7 he was "Indentured for a Clerk and
Bookkeeper."[109] On May 10, his ship anchored in the Rappahannock at
Fredericksberg – on the other side of the world from Holland, where he
originally had set out to go – and two weeks later Colonel Daingerfield
purchased his indentures, setting him to work, not as a clerk or bookkeeper, but as a schoolmaster.

Harassed by circumstance and reduced to pawns of necessity, indentured servants were ashamed of their own weakness. It is not surprising
that they tried to reassert their autonomy. George Alsop confesses at one
point that "Fate" and a "lowness of Estate and Condition" forced him into
servitude, but he blusters in a letter, recasting himself as a hero who, disgusted by the Cromwellian revolution, exiled himself to Maryland as an
act of conscience:

Who then can stay ... to see things of so great weight steer'd by such barbarous
Hounds as these ... What? live in silence under the sway of such base actions, is
to give consent ... I'd rather serve in Chains, and draw the Plough with Animals,
till death shall stop and say, *It is enough.*[110]

Harrower, too, rewrote the story of his emigration. He was driven to
Virginia by economic necessity, but he wrote his brother-in-law, "When
I left the Country, I did not intend going further than Holland, or even
London could I have found bussiness there to my likeing but not finding

that, and the frost being strong in Holland, I was determined to see what I cou'd do in the Western World."[111] The momentary swagger of that "I was determined to see what I cou'd do," the posturing of his "cou'd I have found bussiness to my own likeing" – when, in fact, he had offered to work at *any* job for the "bare support of life" – allow Harrower to recover somewhat from his humiliation by pretending to an autonomy he did not have.

Moraley falls into maddening contradictions when he tries to fix the cause of his "unhappy State of Life" as an indentured servant.[112] It is, he says, entirely due to his own "Inconsideration"; he is an example to others "to take care how they misapply their Talents."[113] And yet, he is "oppress'd by Dame Fortune," a victim to "adverse Fortune," the very "Picture of bad Luck."[114] He accepts responsibility for his own failure ("I neglected to improve my Talents, always preferring the present Time to the future"),[115] but in the very same paragraph he blames his parents for having from his infancy "laid the Foundation of all the Evils that have since befallen me, by [their] over Indulgence."[116] Lacking self-discipline, he threw his advantages away, and in sorrow he "often reflected on the Prodigal Son."[117] Five lines later he sees his life differently: "I have been the Tennis-ball of Fortune,"[118]

But these contradictions make sense. Moraley addresses his memoir to the men of Newcastle, his home town, and he is attempting to curry their favor in order to insert himself back into the social network from which he has been expelled.[119] By insisting that he is the "Picture of bad Luck" and that his "unhappy State of Life" in part is due to circumstances over which he had little control, he shows that he does not have a bad character, that he is not irredeemable; by admitting that his sorry state in part is the result of his own "Inconsideration," he shows that he now accepts the judgment society has made on him, is ready to reform himself, and thus is worthy of readmittance.

And so it is with almost all the indentured servants who have left some record of their feelings. Servitude, they say, was a punishment they had brought upon themselves, but it has also been an opportunity for rehabilitation. "I weare a slave for a time," wrote Charles Rodes to his cousin in England, reflecting on his time as an indentured servant in Virginia. "I know itt was my owne fault. Oh! Sir if I were to talk face to face with you you would say I have under gone more than all the Rodes that ever weare born yet, but all wayes had a good heart."[120] William Roberts wrote to his family to apologize for "all my Misdeeds that I have been guilty of," and he forwards a letter from "a Gentleman of a veary great account" to testify "the character I bear in Maryland": "I hope by Gods Blessing to live an honest Life if it is a hard one Thank God I have got an honnest Character as aney young man that Ever crost the Seas."[121] Elizabeth Ashbridge admits that her misfortune came about "through disobedience brought upon myself," but "It is good that I have been afflicted," she says; God has allowed her to suffer "for my Good."[122] Like Jack, they tell their life stories as ways of performing deference: they *have* assimilated the values of society, they insist; they *are* changed people. My own opinion is that most of these admissions of responsibility and avowals of reform were sincerely felt, but even in cases where a servant was saying what he felt he was expected to say, the social dynamic is the same: servants systematically have been driven "without the camp" and therefore denied access to power, standing, and respect; to establish power and standing – perhaps, hopefully, even to ascend in the social hierarchy – they had first to reintegrate themselves into the social matrix from which they had been excluded. To move up, they had first to move in.

As it turned out, they faced formidable barriers to reintegrating themselves, even after they were free from their indentures. By Defoe's time, Chesapeake society was becoming increasingly stratified, and the social distance between master and servant was widening. A native-born colonial elite had emerged, and its members had begun to assert themselves as a distinct social class. Rank and social order had become more visible and more rigid – "more like that in England."[123] "There appears to have been a strengthening of traditional English attitudes toward social hierarchy … and a hardening of attitudes toward the poor. Social divisions widened and became increasingly fixed."[124] The native-born of all classes began to harbor attitudes and behaviors of social distance between themselves and those who came to America to serve them. In 1701, Nicholson noted this shift in attitude: "Natives … begin to have a sort of aversion to others, calling them strangers."[125]

In such an atmosphere, transported criminals had almost no chance to work themselves back into the social network and thus regain a sense of worthiness. Although initially Virginia granted them the same rights accorded to voluntary servants, so strong was the stigma against them that these rights were soon curtailed, and they became more and more excluded from the rest of the white community. Nor did they have an easy time finding a livelihood when their indentures were completed. "Those who survive the term of servitude seldom establish their residence in this country," observed Eddis;

the stamp of infamy is too strong upon them to be easily erased; they either return to Europe and renew their former practices; or, if they have fortunately imbibed habits of honesty and industry, they remove to a distant situation, where they may hope to remain unknown, and be enabled to pursue with credit every possible method of becoming useful members of society.[126]

But voluntary servants had almost an equally difficult time. As we saw in Chapter 1, indentured servitude, which once had promised the poor that they could eventually move upward, now "kept a majority of its laborers in perpetual bondage."[127] After servitude, prospects were poverty or emigration, not upward mobility. As a result, they could no longer gain entry into the social and economic orders that would confer power and status. Most of them were unable to sink roots deep enough to gain them respect in their new communities by becoming householders, husbands and wives, mothers and fathers, masters and mistresses. To survive, they had to drift onward to the frontier, continuing a life of perpetual rootlessness, migration, and alienation.[128]

When Moraley received his freedom dues, he observed dryly that his master "accouter'd me in an indifferent Manner, and gave me my Discharge, to find out a new Way of Living."[129] He could find nothing to take hold of. He drifted from place to place, trying his hand at being an iron worker, a cowherd, a watchmaker, a tinker, an itinerant clock cleaner, a household servant, and a field worker. But he could not find entry into the colonial social and economic network. He felt "People's Good-nature beginning to cool," and he realized that "the Life [was] not ... likely to last long."[130] One morning, while he was forging a horseshoe, he heard of a possibility of a berth on a ship that had just docked. "I ... immediately left the Horse Shoe unfinished, and went to the Ship."[131] He struck a bargain with a captain to work his way home to England. His American adventure was over.

This seems an appropriate ending to Moraley's career in the New World, the unfinished horseshoe a symbol for a life that failed because of his lack of persistence. It is inconceivable that Robinson Crusoe would walk away from anything unfinished, and Jack and Moll are colonial successes because, unlike Moraley, they persisted. But they persisted because they thought that hard labor in the colonies would allow them to work themselves back into the social structure that had alienated and dishonored them, and, having worked themselves back into that social structure, they could work themselves up to a standing of relative power and respect. In reality, as one skeptical colonial observer noted about immigrants to the Chesapeake, "not finding what was promised, their courage abates, & their minds being dejected, their work is according."[132] Moraley walked away from his unfinished horseshoe because he did not believe finishing it would lead anywhere, and therein lies the difference between indentured servitude in the Chesapeake and indentured servitude in Defoe's fiction.

Beverley reported two rumors about indentured servitude in the Chesapeake: "It has been so misrepresented to the common people of England as to make them believe that the servants in Virginia are made to draw in cart and plow, as horses and oxen do in England, and that the country turns all people black who go to live there."[133] The belief that indentured servants were reduced to the status of Africans and animals was pervasive. Alsop, too, says that it was commonly thought that "those … transported over thither, are sold in open Market for Slaves, and draw in Carts like Horses."[134] "Like horses you must slave," complained another indentured servant, "and like galley-slaves you will be used."[135] Such associations were made almost automatically. Humut Godfrey and his wife Margaret, indentured servants in Prince George's County, Maryland, were driven unmercifully by their overseer. When Margaret protested, the overseer threatened to whip her, and she shot back that she "was not a slave." Angered, the overseer bound her with a rope, and Godfrey protested she should not be "tied like a dog."[136]

To return to the original question, then, why did indentured servants think themselves slaves? Well, in part because their material conditions were similar to those of Africans and in part because the institution of servitude had evolved in such a way that servants were considered commodities and property. But the fact they felt they were treated as both slaves *and* animals suggests that their resentment sprang from a deeper reservoir of anger and shame at having been driven outside the camp and deemed unclean, degraded to a less-than-human status. Because they were deracinated and then excluded from readmission to social networks that were avenues to power and status, because they were robbed of agency, because they were stripped of a sense of their own worth, what they resented most was, as Patterson says about slaves, their "social death."

Elizabeth Ashbridge's master tried to pressure her into a sexual relationship, and when she resisted, in retaliation he trumped up a charge and "sent for the Town Whipper to Correct me."[137]

[He] ordered me to strip; at which my heart was ready to burst … I then fixed my Eyes on the Barbarous man [her master], & in a flood of Tears said: "Sir, if you have no Pity on me, yet for my Father's Sake spare me from this Shame … & if you think I deserve such punishment, do it your Self."[138]

It was not the physical pain Ashbridge feared, but the "Shame," "for I could as freely have given up my Life as Suffer such Ignominy."[139] Slaves and animals were whipped, and even though she avoided the whipping in the end, so shamed was she, so humiliated that "my Credit was gone," she walked up to her garret to hang herself.[140]

Thomas Hellier was born into a respectable family, received a good education, married well, and then squandered his money and ended up on the docks of London, where a sea captain offered to take him to Virginia as a servant. "I replied, I had heard so bad a character of that Country, that I dreaded going thither, in regard I abhored the Ax and the Haw. He … promised I should be onely employ'd in Merchants Accompts, and such Employments to which I had been bred."[141] In Virginia, after he was sold to Cuthbert Williamson, he received other promises: "*Williamson* promised me I should be employed in teaching his Children."[142] But he was put to work in the fields with a hoe.

Though my labour at the Home was very irksome … I was however resolved to do my utmost endeavour at it, yet that which embittered my life, and made every thing I took in hand burdensome to me, was the unworthy Ill-usage which I received daily and hourly from my ill-tongued Mistress; who would not only rail, swear and curse at me within doors, whenever I came into the house, casting on me continually biting Taunts and bitter Flouts; but like a Ghost would impertinently haunt me, when I was quiet in the Ground at work.[143]

No longer able to endure their usage, Hellier ran away. He was captured and returned to the Williamsons, six weeks added to his indentures. Hellier's mistress continued "taunting me with her odious and inveterate Tongue."[144] "I began to cast about and bethink my self, which way to rid me of that hell on Earth … Betimes in the Morning, I put on my best Cloaths, then got my Ax."[145] He killed the Williamsons and a fellow servant who rushed to save them.

Hellier frames his life as an indentured servant as a story of betrayed expectations and of dishonor. After twice being promised a situation suitable to his station and education, he was forced into the fields, servant to a man who was not even an equal. (Williamson was originally a tenant before he acquired his own small plantation, and he was, so implied Revd Paul Williams, who ministered to Hellier during his last days, of "low Mean Education, and obscure base Original.")[146] To become a servant to such a man was bad enough, but to endure the "biting Taunts and bitter Flouts" of his wife – a woman! – was the final degradation. And so, in his act of violence, he asserted his worth and status. That is why, when he took up the ax, he put on his "best Cloaths": they showed him for what he really was.

Memoirs of an Unfortunate Young Nobleman is filled with the details of the physical horrors of servitude, but the horror that is returned to again and again is not the hunger and pain but the fear of degradation – to a slave and to an animal. The young nobleman of the title is treated "absolutely as an Ox or an Ass."[147] The master "seemed to take a savage Pleasure in adding to the misery of [his servants'] Condition by continual ill usage, and to do every thing in his Power to degenerate them from the human Species, and render them on a Level with the mute Creation."[148] The young nobleman "lamented more the being deprived of an Education suitable to his Birth than all the Hardships he endured," the "Improvements of the Mind," the "Talents he had received from God":[149]

A deep Sense of his Misfortunes had now took hold of him – the ardent desire he had from Nature to attain those Accomplishments he had an Idea of … He knew what he *ought to be,* and to think he never *cou'd be* what he ought and wished to be, was a Dagger to his Soul, which gave Wounds too severe for any thing in the Power of those he was among to heal.[150]

Memoirs of an Unfortunate Young Nobleman is an account of the notorious case of James Annesley, whose uncle had him kidnapped and sold into servitude in order to deny him his inheritance and title. Of course, it is dangerous to extrapolate from this young nobleman's experiences what was felt by other indentured servants, a statistically negligible number of whom were of his status. But the trope of being tricked, seduced, or kidnapped was a staple of narratives of indentured servitude, and over the course of two centuries these told and retold a "long-lived mythology" of betrayal, stories of gullible servant girls seduced by their masters, of husbands selling their wives into servitude in order to be with their mistresses, of mothers trepanning servant girls their sons had fallen in love with, of men seduced on board a ship by beautiful women and carried off to Virginia.[151] The stories, fictional and nonfictional, were told of all classes, not only of the upper-class Annesley but of the well-to-do and middle-class protagonists sold into servitude in the novels of Aubin, Chetwood, and Kimber, of the socially more humble author of *An Apology of the Life of Bamfylde-Moore Carew,* of the lower-class men and women in numerous popular ballads and broadsides, and of Defoe's orphans and criminals, Jack, kidnapped to the Chesapeake, and Bob Singleton, who was stolen "by one of those Sorts of People who … make it their Business to Spirit away little Children … to sell them to the Plantations."[152]

The actual number of people illegally coerced into servitude was not particularly high. But, as John Wareing argues, even though the majority of indentured servants were not "kidnapped by force," most were nevertheless "trepanned by spirits" or "recruited illicitly" in the sense that they were tricked into immigrating: enticed by false promises of employment, plied by drink, lured aboard ship, hoodwinked by false tales, and, above all, persuaded by promises of extraordinary opportunities spread by recruiting agents and writers of promotional pamphlets.[153] And so the widespread stories of patently illegal coercion speak less to the relatively small number of forced abductions than to a more general sense of betrayal brought about by the exaggerations, promises, and lies.

The characterization of indentured servants as the "scuffle and scumme of the people" was a considerable overstatement.[154] "Servants who emigrated to the Chesapeake comprise a representative cross section of the ordinary working men and women of England," James Horn concludes. "They came from the middle and lower echelons of that section of society that contemporaries labeled 'the Commons': the ordinary people who made up the vast majority of England's population and who were obliged to work with their hands to earn a living."[155] A large proportion of them were farmers, both yeomen and husbandmen, skilled laborers, and agricultural workers. And although many were at the lower margin of British society, and although many had fallen on hard times, as a class, they were hardly the rogues, whores, idle vagabonds, and dregs they were characterized as being.[156] Even convict servants were not what they were said to be, depraved malefactors who would overwhelm the colonies in a wave of crime and violence. Most of the convicts who were transported were not guilty of serious crimes, nor were they habitual criminals, nor did they disproportionately continue their criminal activity in America.[157]

Such people as these certainly did not expect to be treated in ways many servants were treated, and (given the intense propaganda of the colonial promoters) most probably had expectations that they would become something more than slaves. William Moraley was humiliated by his servitude in the New World, and when he writes about his misfortunes, he greatly overstates his early education and pampered upbringing, his father's wealth, his mother's genteel family, all as ways to justify his sense of betrayed expectations, expectations which perhaps not everyone in his society would think appropriate for a person of his relatively low rank. Elizabeth Ashbridge intimates that she had some such expectations, too, when she says of the "Sufferings of my Servitude,"

it would make the most strong heart pity the Misfortunes of a young creature as I was, who had a Tender education; for tho' my Father had no great estate, yet he Lived well. I had been used to Little but my School, but now it had been better for me if I had been brought up to more hardship.[158]

Her apologetic feint ("tho' my Father had no great estate") suggests that she feels she is appropriating an explanation for a feeling she may not have thought was entirely socially legitimate (her father appears to have been a ship's surgeon, not a particularly respected or prestigious position). But she appropriated the explanation anyway, for after all, she *did* have expectations, and they *were* disappointed, and even if some in her society did not readily allow such expectations to women of her class, she *had* suffered because they were disappointed.

"This day," reports John Harrower after his ship landed in Virginia,

severalls [sic] came on board to purchase servts. Indentures and among them there was two Soul drivers. They are men who make it their bussines to go on board all ships who have in either Servants or Convicts and buy sometimes the whole and sometimes a parcell of them as they can agree, and then they drive them through the Country like a parcell of Sheep untill they can sell them to advantage.[159]

The phrase "Soul drivers" was not Harrower's. It was in common use, probably because its violent yoking of the idea of the soul with the image of the slave- or animal-driver pinpointed so exactly the source of that feeling of being swindled which many indentured servants experienced, their sense of their degradation to slavery and their betrayed potential, the sting of the casual dismissal of their worth, the pain of being reduced to social nonpersons.

I have made as stark as possible the contrast between how indentured servitude was experienced by actual servants and how that experience was portrayed by Defoe. It is not simply that servants responded to servitude one way and that Defoe imagined it differently. It is that they thought of indentured servitude completely oppositely. Defoe's tales tell of men and women who are delivered from their material, psychological, and spiritual bondage. Beginning as solitaries, stupid and degenerate, they master their irrational energies and adverse circumstances and raise themselves up to become more fully human and more fully integrated into society. Actual servants typically followed the opposite trajectory. For them, servitude did not lead to mastery. It was a story of a life increasingly constrained by crass contingency and animal need, a life bottoming out in a stupor of indifference, intransigent solitude, and social alienation. Servitude was a continual, and usually unsuccessful, struggle to become a full person in the teeth of shame and intense social disapprobation. Crusoe will *not* be an animal, Jack will *not* be a slave, and indentured servitude delivers them from these fates. Actual indentured servants felt their servitude reduced them to animals and slaves.

As we have seen, slavery – and indentured servants' sense of themselves as slaves – was defined along two axes, the first low and high, the second out and in. To be a slave is to be at the bottom of the hierarchy of power and lacking the means to move economically, socially, or psychologically from low to high. And to be unfree also is to be outside the hierarchy altogether, excluded from the social and cultural networks that confer status, power, and respect. Slaves and servants suffered dishonor not simply because they were at the mercy of their masters but because, having been uprooted from their own cultures and forced to marginal positions in new ones, they were outside the social order and made incapable of gaining status, power, and respect for themselves. Now, this is precisely the same structure of circumstances in which Crusoe, Jack, and Moll find themselves. All three are quintessential outsiders, and to the degree that they are successful in mastering their lives and in moving up, they simultaneously are successful in moving into the social and cultural networks from which they have been excluded. Because of this deep similarity between indentured servants and his protagonists, one would think that Defoe would have been more sensitive to the servants' complaints that they had been made slaves. He certainly was aware of their sentiments. "The Inhabitants of the Colony," he has Moll's mother say, "were brought over … to be sold as Servants, *such as we call them* … but they are more properly call'd *Slaves*" (*MF*, pp. 85–86). Jack thinks of himself as suffering the "miserable Condition of a Slave" when he is an indentured servant (*CJ*, p. 121).

And yet, in spite of the fact that Defoe harbored some doubts about transportation and indentured servitude, and in spite of the fact that he allowed those doubts occasionally to surface in his novels, he usually tucked them away in unnoticed corners. He rarely failed to use any occasion to promote indentured servitude and to justify transportation.

Why was Defoe so optimistic, even in the face of his own doubts? First, I think, he felt that indentured servitude in the New World, for all of its uncertainty, offered at least a better chance for a successful life than did England, especially for the poor. Moll's mother's story of how pickpockets in England rose to positions of prominence and responsibility in Virginia and Jack's rise from a street criminal in London to a wealthy plantation owner in the Chesapeake both testify to the economic restraints of England, and Jack's difficulties in achieving gentility when he returns to the Old World point to the kind of social restrictions with which Defoe was impatient, a system of attitudes and values that made it difficult for traders and merchants such as himself to be fully accepted in their society.[160] At the end of his life, Defoe explored these ironies and injustices in

The Compleat English Gentleman, but for all its mordancy, that work does not have the sheer subversiveness of the earlier *Moll Flanders* and *Colonel Jack,* where the New World acts as a satiric foil to England. "Virginia," says Jack, was "the only Place I had been bless'd at, or had met with any thing that deserv'd the Name of Success in" (*CJ,* p. 220). America, with its possibilities of freer upper mobility and looser class restrictions, represented something of an ideal for Defoe, and he thought it offered opportunities for his countrymen to raise themselves financially and socially by hard work, self-discipline, and persistence.

But if he was optimistic about America because the opportunities it offered appealed to him as a social and economic thinker, indentured servitude appealed to him more as an artist. Although *Robinson Crusoe, Colonel Jack,* and *Moll Flanders* have a good deal to say about life in the New World, America serves a more important function in his novels as a setting for the drama of spiritual reformation and moral and psychological growth, and in this scheme, indentured servitude played an important figurative role. Consider, for instance, the sanitizing of the Preston rebels that occurs in *Colonel Jack.* In point of fact, the actual Preston rebels who were sent to the Chesapeake vigorously protested their being sold into servitude and brought suit in the colonies on the grounds that, though they "implored [the King's] clemency" and had made "petition[s] for mercy," they had not signed indentures and so by law were not obliged to serve the seven years to which they were sentenced.[161] The Preston rebels' protests call attention to the fact that at bottom transportation was coerced exile and slavery, a fact *Colonel Jack* not simply covers over but turns on its head. For in the novel the Preston rebel is Colonel Jack himself, and, far from resisting servitude and protesting the injustice that has been done to him, he eagerly searches out a pardon and swears eternal gratitude for the King's mercy. Indentured servitude plays such an important symbolic role in the larger drama of mercy, gratitude, and reformation that Defoe envisions in his American novels that he allows the complex historical particulars of the institution to be trumped by its meaning as an emblem.[162]

And yet, even as an emblem, indentured servitude had real-world economic implications for Defoe, and this is the third reason why he portrays it so favorably in his novels. The commonplace that *Robinson Crusoe, Colonel Jack,* and *Moll Flanders* are celebrations of the ambition of rising is not entirely true. Although Defoe eagerly supported the economic and social advancement of traders and merchants (such as himself), his views toward the increasingly mobile society that England had become were ambivalent. As Peter Earle reminds us, Defoe "was not a democrat but a Whig."[163] Defoe's society was hierarchical, and he could not conceive of it as existing without continuing subordination and deference. A year and a half after *Colonel Jack* appeared, Defoe published *The Great Law of Subordination Consider'd*, a tract which in some ways is a fitting coda to his novels of American servitude. It is a "conservative, if not reactionary" piece, its rhetoric often overwrought, particularly when Defoe touches on the topic of the degeneration of contemporary England.[164] "Order is inverted, Subordination ceases, and the World, seems to stand with the bottom upward," all because the sense of proper hierarchy and subordination has decayed.[165] As a consequence, "in *England* the Poor govern, and the Rich submit."[166] It is a new and a frightening world where "Servants ... set up to be Masters, and govern even the Masters themselves."[167] England is now ruled by "a general Spirit of Insolence and Dishonesty"; those who should act with deference are pushing themselves forward, possessed with "mistaken Notions of ... LIBERTY ... abusing that *Liberty* to indulge their Wickedness; suggesting that Liberty is a Freedom to Crime, not a Security against Oppression and Injustice."[168]

None of this is out of keeping with *Robinson Crusoe, Colonel Jack,* and *Moll Flanders.* To the degree that these novels are about ambition and rising, they legitimate such energies only after they have been safely contained by self-discipline. Crusoe's and Jack's climbing is approved because both men have introjected the proper attitudes toward subordination and deference – to God, to nature and reality, to society at large – and if we are not entirely comfortable with Moll's reformation and rise at the end of the novel, it is because we are not completely convinced that she has fully accepted those attitudes. Only after his protagonists have accepted their need for servitude does Defoe think it safe for them to become masters, and indentured servitude is central in all three novels because it is a symbol of the voluntary subordination of the self.

Conclusion: Defoe, cannibals, and colonialism

In *Robinson Crusoe*, *Colonel Jack*, and *Moll Flanders*, the punishment of transportation and indentured servitude is construed as merciful because servitude offers an opportunity for moral reformation and material achievement. This is in keeping with the official public mythology that surrounded transportation: a felon petitioned for mercy of his own free will (supporters claimed), the king graciously responded to the felon's admission of his guilt by granting a pardon, and the felon acknowledged the king's paternal care with gratitude. This myth had little foundation in fact. Convicted felons asked for mercy whether they were guilty or not; justices drew up lists of those whose sentences they recommended for commutation, usually not giving the reasons why they deserved mercy; and the king signed the lists without review. There is no record of a single case where the recommendation of mercy was refused. From beginning to end, the whole bureaucratic process was "purely formal."[1]

The felon's plea for mercy was hardly a choice that was made freely. Although Jack's master says that transportation for criminals was a "Favour they had receiv'd ... granted them on their own Request and humble Petition" (*CJ*, p. 121), that legal fiction was so threadbare that Defoe could not help but express his skepticism elsewhere. Moll emphasizes the reality of coercion that lies beneath the fiction of a voluntary "Request." Transportation, she says, "indeed was a hard Condition in it self, but not when comparatively considered; and therefore I shall make no Comments upon the Sentence, nor upon the Choice I was put to; we shall all choose any thing rather than Death" (*MF*, p. 239). Defoe knew there was something fantastical about the claim that transportation was merciful – the very claim he used to fabricate the plots and to weave the symbolic meanings of his American novels. The Transportation Act was not an expression of the King's merciful disposition. It was drafted in response to an alarming rise in the incidents of robbery, violent crime, and public disorder. By using transportation as a punishment, the Act addressed deficiencies in the courts' power to adequately penalize offenders whose crimes were serious but not heinous enough to merit death, and it did so in a particularly tidy way by sweeping some of England's most pressing social problems whole to the shores of America. The reformation of criminals was certainly "not a major consideration" of the Act, "its overriding purpose [being] neither rehabilitation nor deterrence, but ridding Britain of dangerous offenders."[2] Once felons reached the colonies, Ekirch dryly observes, "authorities rarely betrayed any interest in their future prospects."[3] Although Defoe often expresses his belief that transported criminals can benefit greatly from their sentence of servitude in America, he was not taken in by the formulaic rhetoric about the Act's benevolent intentions nor was he blind to the adversities the rhetoric papered over. Moll concludes that transportation is "a severity that was esteem'd a Mercy" (*MF,* p. 240), and Defoe himself says bluntly that criminals are "sent over [to America] by Force, and as a Pretence of Mercy to save them from the Gallows."[4] And after having dramatized Jack's gratitude to a just and merciful king who has commuted his death and after having praised George I for his leniency to the rebels in transporting them, Defoe gives voice to the "Miserable People" who surrendered after the battle of Preston and allows their disbelief to call into doubt whether gratitude and mercy have anything at all to do with indentured servitude: "Several hundreds of them ... were at their own Request transported, *as 'tis vulgarly Express'd,* to the Plantations, *that is to say,* sent to *Virginia,* and other *British* Collonies, to be sold after the usual manner of condemn'd Criminals" (*CJ,* p. 232; Defoe's italics).

We have seen these contradictions again and again. In the midst of Defoe's spirited presentation of indentured servitude and life in the colonies, we hear his oblique concessions and querulous hesitancies. And so, if we have asked why Defoe portrayed indentured servitude so positively when he knew its many drawbacks and failures, we must now ask the opposite: having so many reasons to portray indentured servitude so optimistically, what are we to make of his allowing his doubts to surface so often? Nor is it a question we need to ask about indentured servitude alone. For, the more one examines the matter, the clearer it is that not only indentured servitude but the whole complex of ideas that Defoe explored under the figure of indentured servitude – self-restraint, mastery, civilization, the project of colonization itself – is fretted through with this kind of ambiguity.

Getting a handle on these ambiguities is not easy in part because Defoe's novels, even when they deal explicitly with colonial matters, are not always the most reliable places to go to ascertain his beliefs about colonization. They are, at once, both too broad in focus and too narrow.

Defoe does not write "colonial novels" in which he takes a wide-ranging, comprehensive, and coherent view of England's colonial ventures. More often, his focus is narrow and disciplined. He writes about this specific colonial matter and that specific colonial matter. Much of his attention in *Robinson Crusoe* is taken up with conversion as a colonial policy, and *Moll Flanders* and *Colonel Jack* are preoccupied with encouraging emigration, defending the Transportation Act, and promoting indentured servitude. But even a cursory reading of Defoe's economic writings makes it obvious that of far greater interest and importance to him was the relationship between the colonies and trade and commerce. Trade and commerce are the central themes of *A New Voyage round the World,* but they are touched on only briefly at the end of *Colonel Jack,* and they barely receive a hearing in *Moll Flanders* and *Robinson Crusoe.* The problem with this narrow focus is not simply that Defoe's colonial thinking comes to us piecemeal but that, by focusing on one colonial issue, Defoe inadvertently distorts his views on another. A Caribbean island periodically visited by cannibals is an excellent setting to stage the "paradigmatic" colonial drama of the confrontation between the civilized Christians and the heathen savages, but it plays havoc with Defoe's complex ideas about the colonial economy. In *Colonel Jack,* Defoe proposes a system of slave management in order to dramatize the psychological transformation an immigrant must go through to become successful, but in doing so, he has had to suppress his strongly held convictions about the Christianization of the slaves.

At the same time as Defoe's focus can be very narrow, it can also be quite dispersed. Defoe has a number of interests in his novels. No matter how important the New World episodes are in *Moll Flanders* and *Colonel Jack,* they serve a variety of purposes, and it is not always clear in particular instances what those purposes are. For instance, one of the common objections against transportation was that those with money could buy themselves out of their punishment, evade their sentence of transportation, and return to England before their terms were completed to continue their lives of crime.[5] Defoe appears to entertain this objection when he has Moll's governess ask, "Did you ever know one in your Life that was Transported, and had a Hundred Pound in his Pocket" (*MF,* p. 240). And, in fact, Moll does use her earnings from her criminal activities to buy herself out of her indentured servitude. And it gets worse. Transported criminals typically were held in leg irons between decks for the twelve-week voyage to the Chesapeake, a mode of transportation as uncomfortable as it was dangerous, since one out of five failed to survive the voyage over.[6] Moll uses her tainted money to purchase a comfortable "Cabbin …

in which was very good Conveniences to set our Chest, and Boxes, and a Table to eat on" (*MF*, p. 254). "In this Condition very Chearful, and indeed joyful at being so happily Accomodated as we were; we set Sail" (*MF*, p. 257). Does Defoe dramatize these abuses only to take the sting out of the fear of evasion and recidivism in the end by having Moll and Jemy remain in America for the lengths of their terms, thus implying that the prospects of financial success were so good in the colonies that transportation was by and large a workable system? Or is he making a comment on Moll's moral state and psychological habits? Or is he setting the tone for the new turn in Moll's fortunes? It is difficult to know for certain.

Even in a work rather tightly focused on colonial concerns such as *Robinson Crusoe,* issues are muddied by Defoe's shifting his attention elsewhere. I have argued that the centrality of conversion in the *Crusoe* books reflects Defoe's support for a specific Anglo-Indian policy that was in the process of being formulated at the very time he was writing. But a good case has been made that at least some of the conversion material specifically refers to the Bangorian and Salter Hall controversies, controversies so tangential to colonial matters as to be nugatory.[7] And although Crusoe's dealing with those who inhabit his island often seem to play out Defoe's sense of the proper relationship between colonist and native, Manuel Schonhorn has shown that Defoe uses them as occasions to speculate about the nature of sovereignty, the correct relationship between sovereign and subject, and the sources of political power, matters important to England's internal affairs but not directly related to colonial policy.[8]

And then there is the problem of propaganda. Consider the way Defoe makes a case for colonizing the Patagonian peninsula.[9] He presents the area as a perfect place for settling. The Spanish title to the land is dubious, and there are so few inhabitants that the English could settle there unmolested or, push come to shove, could easily seize the land. There are Indians, but they are not numerous, and anyway they are an "innocent harmless People," "honest, quiet, and free from Design," and "as to Violence against any Body, they entertained no Thought of that Kind" (*NV*, pp. 192, 194–195, 199). They hate the Spanish so much for their past cruelties that if the English "would but come in ... and support them in their Rising against them, they would soon rid their Hands of the whole Nation" (*NV*, p. 152). The climate is temperate, the country "rich, pleasant, fruitful, wholesome, and capable of every thing for the Life of Man, that the Heart could entertain a Wish for" (*NV*, p. 216).

And there is gold, fabulous amounts of gold, gold in the sands of the lake shores, gold "in all the little Gullies and Rills of Water," gold "come down from the Mountains on every Side" (*NV,* p. 206). "Gold lay in every Ditch," so much gold it might be had by "picking it up off the Dunghill," so much gold "to make the World say they had enough" (*NV,* pp. 208, 206, 216).

All this gold is perplexing. Defoe was skeptical about colonies that sustained themselves by extracting wealth from the ground. Spain, after all, had numerous possessions in the New World, all of them founded on "Mines of Gold and Silver," yet they had little to show for it.[10] "To this Day, after almost 200 Years of peaceable Possession," the Spanish have not "brought the most fruitful and richest Provinces and Districts of *America* to be much more productive than they were before."[11] In contrast,

the *English* tho' planting near 100 Years after them, and taking ... the Fag-end of the Discovery, the northern, cold, and barren Parts, without Silver and Gold, without Mine or Mineral, without any apparent Product; yet how has the improving Genius of the *English* brought Gold out of their Dross.[12]

In those "barren Countries" and on those "trifling little Spots of Islands, not thought worth looking at by the *Spaniards,*" the English have created "the richest, the most improved, and the most flourishing Colonies in all that Part of the World."[13] England's colonies prospered because they were based on commerce and trade; Spain's were stagnant because they were based on gold.

True, Defoe alerts his attentive readers to the dangers of gold. He portrays the Spanish colonists as enervated by all this mineral wealth. With so much gold within hand's reach, asks one of the Spaniards, why should they cultivate the land, develop commerce, engage in trade? Anyone, he says, "will reap the Harvest which has the least Labour and Hazard attending it, and the most Profit" (*NV,* p. 191). The effect of the gold on the English is equally as calamitous. "The sight of the Gold, made them stark mad" and so filled them with "avaricious Rage" that they became "ungovernable," losing sight of their practical goals and their own safety (*NV,* pp. 232, 239, 231).

And yet, even taking into account these cautionary gestures, one suspects that Defoe is using the promise of gold disingenuously, perhaps cynically. The existence of gold in the region was one of the few details he did not find in the sources he used, and the picture he presents of its abundance is so absurdly overwrought that it is difficult not to conclude as Novak has that Defoe "stressed the prospect of gold as a bait to increase the effectiveness of his propaganda."[14] He wanted the tip of South America for Britain, and what better way to motivate adventurers and settlers to enter the high-stakes game of colonizing than to insinuate that unthinkable wealth was to be had effortlessly?

This propagandistic strain in Defoe can make it difficult to decipher his real feelings. And yet, the way he tenders the prospect of easy wealth here while simultaneously warning of its dangers suggests that there may be another, additional factor at work. Given what was known about South America at the time, it was not unlikely that gold would be found in Patagonia, and although Defoe did not think it wise that an entire colonial system be founded on mineral wealth, he certainly would welcome the additional bullion to England's coffers. And so he gives voice to his hope – and then he gives voice to his fear. What is striking about Defoe's treatment of gold in *A New Voyage round the World* is that it is played out in the same rhythms as his utterances about indentured servitude – that onrush of optimism, hurrying forward an enthusiastic fantasy that has some toehold in reality, and then the seeping in of doubt, the undertow of pessimism, and these two contrary currents of feeling rubbing one against the other, discordant and unreconciled.

There is a doubleness that seems to be fundamental to Defoe's mentality, and it is this doubleness I want to explore here, the way his thinking, not only about indentured servitude but also about the core issues of England's colonizing enterprise, is caught up at once in the flow of his optimism and the counterflow of his more sober doubts. To get some purchase on these ambivalences, I want to put his novels in the context of some contemporaneous fiction that was also set in America, and then I want to turn briefly to a body of nonfictional works that appears to have had some influence on Defoe and his contemporary novelists, the Barbary and American captivity narratives.

Penelope Aubin's *The Life of Charlotta Du Pont, an English Lady* (1723) and William Chetwood's *The Voyages, Dangerous Adventures, and Imminent Escapes of Captain Richard Falconer* (1720) are set in the extended Caribbean of Defoe's America, and, like *Robinson Crusoe*, both are providential novels that have defining moments of cannibalism.

The plots of all of Aubin's novels braid together story after story of captivity – the captivity of Europeans by heathens and savages, but also their imprisonment in dungeons, citadels, convents, holds of ships, guarded rooms, fortified houses, debtors' prisons, and desert islands in the Caribbean. These captivities test the faith of her protagonists and demonstrate the power of God. As Aubin herself summarizes the intent of her plots,

Thus Providence does, with unexpected Accidents, try Men's Faith, frustrate their Designs, and lead them thro a Series of Misfortunes, to manifest its Power in their Deliverance; confounding the Atheist, and convincing the Libertine, that there is a just God, so boundless is his Power, that none ought to despair that believe in him.[15]

"We have nothing more to do, to be happy and secure from all the Miseries of Life," she concludes, "but to resign our Wills to the Divine Being; nor does Providence ever appear more conspicuously than on such Occasions."[16]

Providence conspicuously drives the plot of *Charlotta Du Pont*. The lovers Belanger and Charlotta are separated after a pirate attack, he ending up in Virginia, she in the Spanish West Indies, where, to preserve her virtue, she marries Antonio de Medenta, son of the governor of Santo Domingo. Belanger learns of her marriage, and, unable to control his passion, he sets sail with his friend, Lewis de Montandre, to contact her surreptitiously. But de Medenta catches wind of their meeting and has him and de Montandre imprisoned. This turns out to be a providential blessing ("it was a Providence that [Belanger] was at that time fetter'd, or else his despair might have drove him to destroy himself"), and de Montandre finds an even greater blessing in it.[17] Trying to reclaim Charlotta was a foolish impulse, he tells Belanger, and this imprisonment is punishment for his lack of self-restraint. And yet, he continues, it is "a Mercy," too, because it is an occasion for repentance. "Here we may live free from the Temptations of the World," says de Montandre,

and learn the state of our own Souls; nay, converse with our Maker by Contemplation, and enjoy that Peace of Mind, that we were Strangers to whilst we liv'd at large … *Charlotta* has already, doubtless, suffer'd for your Imprudence; and in pursuing her, you have offended Heaven, who having thus punish'd you, on your Submission will (I doubt not) free you hence.[18]

Belanger appears to have learned his lesson. "'I merit all that I can suffer … My God, thy ways are marvellous; in thee I'll trust, and strive to bring my stubborn Will to submit to thine.' The first Transports of his Passion being thus conquer'd, he began to be resign'd."[19]

But he is not resigned for long. He takes up the offer of a friendly warden to help them escape, but, after fleeing the island, they end up adrift in the Caribbean on a boat – another variation of a prison where, once again, they are tested, for they have no food.

And now they began to reflect, that it had been better for them to have continued Prisoners, than have expos'd themselves to such Miserys. Thus Experience tells us, that when we have obtain'd our Wishes, not easy in the state Providence has plac'd us in, we are more unhappy than we were before.[20]

Both near death, de Montandre offers himself up as food so Belanger can survive. Belanger is appalled.

"Let us redouble our Importunity to God to send us Deliverance." Before the Words were out of his Mouth a Wave toss'd a large Dolphin into the Boat, which they kill'd with the oars, and fell to eating, sucking the warm Blood and raw Flesh more greedily than ever they had done the most delicious Food prepar'd for them.[21]

And so they are delivered.

It is significant that this sequence culminates in a scene of cannibalism. De Montandre's offer to give up his body to Belanger is a supreme form of self-sacrifice, and Belanger's rejection of his friend's offer is much the same. For both, it is a sign of their final mastery of their appetites and passions, their triumph in the last test Providence has posed for them. That it takes place in the Caribbean, a region synonymous with cannibalism, is equally as significant. For a book that is set here, *Charlotta Du Pont* shows remarkably little interest in the natives; its focus is almost entirely on the English, French, and Spanish colonists and on the civilization they have wrought in America, with its "Castles" and "Courts" and nobles who "liv'd like ... King[s]," a civilization in its manners and morality indistinguishable from that of Europe.[22] The few times the natives appear (most notably, the Caribs on the banks of the Orinoco, not far from the island Crusoe would have inhabited) they are "Cannibal-Savages."[23] There is a colonial subtext in *Charlotta Du Pont,* though muted: Europeans have silently displaced the savages in their native land, and it is just they should have done so, for Europeans possess that highest attribute of civilization, self-mastery, and for this they are favored by Providence.

Much the same colonial drama is played out in Chetwood's *Richard Falconer* in a lengthy and ingeniously structured series of episodes that also revolve around cannibalism. Early in the novel, Falconer is shipwrecked on a Caribbean island, where he manages to survive alone for several weeks. A second boat is driven on the island, with four British sailors. Among them is Randal, an older man who becomes Falconer's spiritual mentor and moral guide.

Falconer is not impious like the young Crusoe, but he is callow, and though he admits his sin when he is shipwrecked and submits himself to Providence, he is unable to sustain his belief, for his faith is unsteady and his control over his passions uncertain. Seeing that Falconer "despair[s] of a

Redemption" from the island, Randal chides him, telling him that he himself has no doubt in "the Mercy of God in working out our Deliverance," and to drive home his point, he gives an account of two other times he has been a castaway and how Providence has delivered him.[24]

Years earlier, Randal recounts, he was tossed up on an island in the Baltic, his only companion a dog and her six pups. Pressed by hunger, he kills the pups and, although "it went very much against me," ate them, feeding the offal to the dog and her one remaining pup, "who eat of it heartily, and making no Scruple tho' their own Flesh and Blood."[25] Providentially delivered from the island, Randal boards another ship, and he is cast away again, this time on Virginia's Eastern Shore. Here he endures another captivity. For he is seized by Indians – cannibals who threaten to "drink [his] Blood, and feed upon [his] Flesh."[26] Once again, he is providentially delivered.

Randal dies soon after he tells these two tales of his deliverances. Falconer and the rest of the men repair the boat that brought them, but, on the eve of their departure from the island, they all get drunk, and a hurricane carries Falconer away from the island alone – as punishment for his failure to control his appetites, Falconer realizes. By the time he is able to make his way back to the island, the men, near starvation, have dug up Randal's body and eaten it.

This sequence of episodes makes several important equations and distinctions. Both the dogs and the Indians are willing cannibals, and this similarity reduces the Indians to the status of animals. The Europeans engage in cannibalistic acts, too. Falconer is dismayed by what they did. "Horror … overcame my Reason," he says, but in the end his reason masters his repulsion, and he excuses their cannibalism because they acted under the pressure of extreme need and then only "with a great deal of Reluctance."[27]

The men's resisting of their animal needs and Falconer's mastery of his understandable, but violent emotional response find their echo in Randal's death. "That poor Wretch that helped to support our Misfortunes when alive with his sage Advice," says Falconer about his mentor, "now was a means of preserving their Lives, tho dead."[28] Chetwood's invoking of the Eucharist, like Aubin's invoking of it in the case of de Montandre, makes an important point about the European colonial venture. The men's struggle against their appetites, Falconer's rational command of his passions, and Randal's symbolic self-transcendence distinguish Europeans from the savages. Over the course of the novel, Chetwood surveys the American Indian tribes from Newfoundland to the Caribbean. They have no redeeming qualities. The Virginian Indians are cannibals, and they are preternaturally stupid. The Indians of Florida are implacably hostile, and those of Cuba worship the Devil. The Newfoundland Indians are incapable of being converted: "when attempted to be taught, they would Answer[,] We are contented with our own God, neither do we desire any other."[29] It is not surprising that in the episode that concludes the novel, Falconer is captured by those "Cannibals, or Man-Eaters," the Caribs.[30] Falconer escapes and, like Crusoe, makes one of them a servant. But when he tries to convert him to Christianity, he finds that "all the arguments I cou'd use was of no Effect; for Heathenism was so rooted in him, and all the other *Indians,* that it will be the greatest Difficulty imaginable to bring 'em to embrace Christianity."[31]

Aubin's and Chetwood's use of cannibalism as the definitive mark of difference between Europeans and New World natives and their lack of interest in or outright dismissal of the possibility of the conversion of the savages would seem to distinguish them from Defoe. After all, the spiritual and moral drama of *Robinson Crusoe* is driven by the perception of the similarity between Crusoe and the cannibals – a similarity which, once perceived, provokes Crusoe to struggle against the savage within in an effort to convert himself, a similarity that obliges him, once he has converted himself, to convert the savages. And yet, is there all that much difference between them? After all, Chetwood's Europeans become cannibals only out of necessity, but that is true of Defoe's European cannibals, too. The survivors of the ship that was wrecked off the coast of his island would resort to cannibalism, Crusoe speculates, only when compelled by hunger. The same is true of the starving young woman in *Farther Adventures* – and, anyway, she only *conjectures* that she could become a cannibal. Defoe claims that "Man ... devours his own Species, nay his own Flesh and Blood" out of "Avarice, Envy, Revenge, and the like" (*SR*, pp. 130–131), but this is a figure of speech.

When the mutineers land on the island, Friday is convinced that they plan to eat their captives. "*No, No,*" Crusoe replies. "*I am afraid they will murther them indeed, but you may be sure they will not eat them*" (*RC*, p. 243). The irony that Europeans are as cruel as cannibals, perhaps even surpass them in their barbarity, is easy to hear in this exchange, and it is reminiscent of the irony one hears in Montaigne's "Of Cannibals." But there is also an unvoiced demur. Even among those, such as Montaigne, who were willing to entertain seriously the similarities between Europeans and savages, there is a final refusal to admit to the fact of European cannibalism.[32] So it is here. Crusoe is driven by savage, ravening appetites, and by speaking about him figuratively as a cannibal, Defoe is giving us access to his psychology and moral status, but it is all figurative. Friday is a cannibal; Crusoe is only like one.

Crusoe's first reaction when he stumbles across the remains of the cannibal feast is to vomit "with an uncommon violence" and then to thank God that he "was distinguish'd from such dreadful Creatures as these" (*RC*, pp. 178–179), and his struggle to come to terms with his own savage impulses of revenge against the cannibals is rooted in this conviction that he is capable of being something more than his savage impulses and that his ability to master those impulses is precisely what distinguishes him from them.

The fact that Europeans are not literally cannibals does not contradict Defoe's belief that they are the same as savages *by nature.* For all human beings are something more than their natures: their identities are determined by their cultures and especially by the presence or absence of God. God has never abandoned Christian Europeans as He has the savages, and the culture of Christian Europeans – their institutions, social structures, and morality – have been created under His superintending presence. Europeans can commit acts of cannibalism, of course, but they are infrequent, certainly not customary, and they are committed only in the most extreme situations. The presence of God and the structures of European culture have caused Europeans to master such appetites.

In contradistinction, savages are not pressed, either by God or by their culture, to rise above their impulses or the force of their passions. Even under the influence of Europeans, they cannot quite cross that invisible line that distinguishes Europeans and savages. Mouchat is willing to lay down his life to save the life of his master. Friday is willing to do the same thing for Crusoe, and so is Xury ("*If wild Mans come,*" he says to Crusoe, "*they eat me, you go wey*" [*RC*, p. 74]). Such gestures bespeak their "Savage Greatness," and to Defoe, they are signs of a potential that, someday, may be wrought up to the highest form of civilized behavior, but they are also signs that, for now, these three non-Europeans remain passional, self-destructive, and irrational creatures. That irrational stratum of their energies does not make them different from Europeans, but their failure to master themselves on their own or to determine the "right Uses" of their passions justifies the continuing imposition of European culture and religion on them so that they may, ultimately, become the same as Europeans in fact as they are the same in nature.

In spite of the effort Crusoe makes to overcome the prejudices of his past thinking and to come to a balanced judgment of the savages' cannibalism, in spite of the fact that he reaches the reasoned and principled conclusion that he must abandon his "bloody Schemes for the Destruction of innocent Creatures," in the end, Crusoe does slaughter them, twice. The first time he does so because he is prompted by a divinely inspired dream, a "clear Call from Heaven" (*RC,* p. 184). The second time he does so because he must save the life of a European Christian. As much as for Aubin and Chetwood, there is a line Defoe will not cross. For all the similarities between savages and Europeans, because of the presence of God and the supremacy of their culture, Europeans are distinguished from the cannibals – literally.

Still, to entertain the idea that there are similarities between Europeans and savages, even conditionally and cautiously and behind the protective buffer of figuration, is no negligible concession, and I suspect the willingness to do so helps account for some important differences between the way Defoe approached colonial matters in his novels and the way Aubin and Chetwood did.

Aubin's *Charlotta Du Pont,* as I said, takes place in the extended Caribbean of Defoe's American novels: Virginia, Bermuda, Jamaica, Hispaniola, on several uninhabited islands, and even on the Orinoco among cannibal savages. But about half way through, the action unexpectedly shifts to Tunis, and the novel takes on the contours of a Barbary slave narrative. After about fifty pages, just as abruptly, the novel returns to the Caribbean. The same toggling between Barbary and the Caribbean occurs in *Robinson Crusoe,* of course. Crusoe is a literal slave in Sallee, and then, within a few pages, he becomes a figurative slave on his Caribbean island.

When Aubin switches her scene from the Caribbean to Barbary, there is little sense of disruption. The change in locale is abrupt, but it is by no means radical – in fact, there seems to be no change at all. The same things happen in Tunis that happened in the Caribbean: European men and women are held captive, often made slaves, imprisoned in various ways, and, after their faith is tested, through a series of daring adventures and extraordinary coincidences (all of which are attributed to Providence), they are delivered. In Aubin, what happens among the cannibals of the New World is pretty much what happens in the seraglios of Barbary. What is important for Aubin is the fact of captivity and imprisonment, and she changes the setting for the sake of pleasing variety, but wherever she sets her tales, she tells the same story again and again.

In *Robinson Crusoe,* the change from the Barbary Coast to the Caribbean is quite different. In Sallee, Crusoe is made to "do the common

Drudgery of Slaves," "look[ing] after [the] little Garden" of his master, suffering solitude because he has "no Body to communicate" with (*RC,* p. 16). He procures himself a slave, Xury, who "assisted [him] … faithfully," and together they face the threat of being devoured by beasts and cannibals (*RC,* p. 27). The Sallee episode, obviously, foreshadows Crusoe's captivity on the island, and therefore it has a function unlike anything we see in Aubin: the episode both reveals Crusoe's spiritual condition and dramatizes his failure to reflect upon it. He has been warned of his sinfulness, of God's anger, and of his impending punishment twice before – by the two storms – and, after the Sallee episode, he will be warned a fourth time when in Brazil he finds himself alone again, unable to communicate with anyone, working the ground and acquiring slaves. Each time, the warning becomes more literal, detailed, and explicit, and yet Crusoe continues to ignore it. Even when he is cast away, he still does not see the emblematic significance of the island. It takes a vision of an angel to spell out its meaning in downright prose before Crusoe understands that he is estranged from God and man, a slave to sin, and in need of deliverance.

The Sallee episode points to an important difference between Defoe's narratives and the colonial novels of Aubin and Chetwood. In the novels of Aubin and Chetwood, the characters are made captives of savages or are imprisoned in various ways in order to test their faith in God and their willingness to submit themselves to Providence. Crusoe's captivity, however, is less a test than a trial in the wilderness. Of course, he ultimately does have to learn to submit himself to Providence, but the first and most important trial he must undergo is a trial of self-recognition, a coming to the awareness of his own savage depravity.

This is no trivial distinction, and I think it has important consequences for how the writers of the period responded to the colonial project, and I think, too, that it helps account for some of the ambivalences and contradictions we find in Defoe's thinking about colonialism.

One can see how significant the difference between the test and the trial in the wilderness is in the two kinds of captivity narratives that appear to have some influence on the novels of Aubin, Chetwood, and Defoe, the Barbary and American captivity narratives, that popular genre of nonfictional accounts of Europeans held captive among the heathens and savages of northern Africa and North America. Indeed, one reason why Aubin and Defoe could toggle so seamlessly between the two regions is because both the Barbary and the American narratives used imprisonment and captivity among the savages to tell the same story as they did of slavery, redemption, and deliverance, dramas in which "the power and providence" of God were "made manifest" and in which Europeans were subjected to "God's trials," the purpose of which was "to cleanse the dross from the gold and bring us out of the fire again, more clear and lovely."[33] In the Barbary captivity narratives, however, "God's trials" are not the trials in the wilderness that involve the kind of revelation of the sinful self that we see in *Robinson Crusoe*. The pains of slavery and the afflictions meted out by the Muslims were tests to be endured: they were evils inflicted on true believers to challenge their faith as they awaited God's mercy and deliverance. The captive's forbearance under suffering and duress becomes a mark of the strength of his belief in God.

The Barbary captivity narratives, as Snader shows, "contain surprisingly little in the way of explicit religious commentary."[34] They tend toward the "secular rather than the sacred," and "although the motifs of captivity and travail invited application to Christian beliefs concerning sin and salvation, the texts only rarely make these applications explicit."[35] The American captivity narratives are quite a different matter. While the Barbary narratives "downplay the elements of spiritual autobiography," in the American narratives, captivity by the Indians becomes an occasion for intense self-examination.[36] "In the Puritan vision, captivity among the heathens corresponds to the Christian's captivity to sin and to the world, and the captive must learn that reliance on worldly satisfactions leads to inevitable disappointment, while reliance on God's providence furnishes internal peace."[37] Captivity is a punishment because it is God's chastisement for having fallen away from Him, but it is a mercy, too, because captivity provokes self-examination, and with the growing consciousness of one's own depravity comes the opportunity for a renewal of faith. From this springs the Christian's "deliverance" ("deliverance" and "redemption" are ubiquitous in the titles of American captivity narratives), deliverance from the literal bondage in the wilderness and their spiritual bondage to sin and the vanity of the world.

Because captivity was seen as a trial in the wilderness, the savage Other potentially was experienced differently in the American than in the Barbary captivity narratives. In the latter, the Muslim Other is heretical, inhumanly cruel, sexually deviant, and irrational, and when the captive is tested, he defines his Englishness and Christianity by resisting (with the help of Providence) the temptations and coercions of the Orient.[38] But in the American captivity narratives, the savage Other can become a mirror that reflects the hidden savagery of the punished sinner.

One can see this most clearly in Mary Rowlandson's *Sovereignty and Goodness of God,* an account of her captivity by the Wampanoag in 1676, published in 1682. Like Crusoe, Rowlandson comes to understand her trial in "the vast and howling wilderness" to be a providentially ordained punishment for her lukewarm faith, and, like Crusoe's trial in the wilderness, it is a punishment that was also a mercy:

I ... remembered how careless I had been of God's holy time, how many Sabbaths I had lost and misspent and how evilly I had walked in God's sight, which lay so close unto my spirit that it was easy for me to see how righteous it was with God to cut the thread of my life and cast me out of His presence forever. Yet the Lord still showed mercy to me and upheld me, and as He wounded me with one hand, so He healed me with the other.[39]

The drama of Rowlandson's self-recognition is played out through numerous scenes of eating. The savages are "inhuman creatures" who, like "ravenous beasts," descend on Rowlandson and her family to "devour" them.[40] The more Rowlandson is subjected to deprivations among the savages, the more she becomes like them. The food they eat, she says, is "filthy trash," but soon she too is eating horses' feet and intestines, unborn fawn, and bear – and not merely eating, but relishing them.[41] Her punishment in the wilderness has given her a "wolfish appetite," and she enjoys what before would "turn the stomach of a brute creature": "Though I could think how formerly my stomach would turn against this or that and I could starve and die before I could eat such things, yet they were sweet and savory to my taste."[42] She comes to recognize that she, too, is a brute creature, her appetites as depraved as those of the savages who have captured her, and that she is a heathen like them, too, since her faith is only skin-deep. In the climax of her degeneration, she becomes an utter savage:

The squaw was boiling horses' feet; then she cut me off a little piece and gave one of the English children a piece also. Being very hungry, I had quickly eat up mine, but the child could not bite it, it was so tough and sinewy but lay sucking, gnawing, chewing, and slabbering of it in the mouth and hand. Then I took it of the child and ate it myself and savory it was to my taste. Then I may say as Job, chap. 6: 7, "The things that my soul refused to touch are as my sorrowful meat."[43]

Rowlandson's recognition of her savage self unnerved her. Even many years after her captivity, she could not live with the easy assumptions of the quotidian.

I can remember the time I used to sleep quietly without workings in my thoughts all nights together, but now it is other ways with me ... Oh, the wonderful power of God that mine eyes have seen, affording matter for my thoughts to run in that when others are sleeping mine eyes are weeping![44]

Even worse, her trial in the wilderness called into doubt the whole colonial enterprise of the New England Puritans. They had, they thought, been called to the New World to create the New Canaan, but the attacks of the savages were a sign that God had abandoned them. For Rowlandson's captivity had forced her to become aware of her own depravity, and in her depravity she saw a reflection of the savage depravity and heathenism of her coreligionists and the hollowness of their colonial pretensions. They all had fallen away from God, they all had lost their belief, and now their project has come to ruin:

> The enemy came upon our town … like so many ravenous wolves, rending us and our lambs to death. But what shall I say? God seemed to leave his people to themselves and order all things for His own holy ends. "Shall there be evil in the city and the Lord hath not done it? They are not grieved for the affliction of Joseph, therefore shall they go captive with the first that go captive." It is the Lord's doing, and it should be marvelous in our eyes.[45]

The New England Puritans found in the story of their migration and settlement of the New World a redemptive design played out within the patterns of scripture, and in the captivity narrative they had formulated rhetorical and symbolic patterns that were central to *Robinson Crusoe*: the confrontation with the savages; the survival in the wilderness; the punishment of captivity and the mercy of God's deliverance; the despair of self-recognition followed by the joy of inner renewal, all of which were imagined with the same spiritual resonances we find in Defoe. But, in pointing to these obvious, broad parallels, I do not want to claim even another source for *Robinson Crusoe*. It is possible that he was acquainted with some of the writings that grew out of the trauma of the American colonists' confrontation with the savages, but what similarities there are between American captivity narratives and *Robinson Crusoe* are more likely accounted for by a shared religious tradition that predisposed Defoe and the American Puritans to think about the nature of man and of man's relationship to God in the same way and, especially, a shared literary tradition of spiritual biography and autobiography and of providential histories.[46] The point of comparison to which I want to call attention is much more simple. Like Rowlandson, Defoe was convinced of the savage depravity of the self, and if he could bring himself to think of Crusoe and other Europeans only figuratively as cannibals, even that had consequences. As with Rowlandson, such a possibility could call into doubt the colonial endeavors by civilized and Christian Europeans and undermine his own optimism about self-mastery, reason, and civilization.

Will Atkins was left on the island at the end of *Robinson Crusoe* as punishment for his mutiny. He is a brutish and idle man, driven by his animal
energies, lacking self-restraint, contemptuous of all civilized values, and
his story recapitulates Crusoe's history, for Will too gradually embraces
civilization and religion and, in the end, becomes a model member of the
European settlement. He and his two companions become civilized when
they come face to face with the fury of the cannibals. Like Crusoe, they
find an image of their own brutishness in the Other. After their confrontation, they are "delivered" by the Spaniards.

This Deliverance tam'd our *English* Men for a great while; the Sight had fill'd
them with Horror, and the Consequences appear'd terrible to the last Degree,
even to them, if ever they should fall into the Hands of those Creatures, who
would not only kill them as Enemies, but kill them for Food, as we kill our
Cattle. And they profess'd to me, that the Thoughts of being eaten up like Beef or
Mutton, tho' it was suppos'd it was not to be till they were dead, had something
in it so horrible, that it nauseated their very Stomachs, made them sick when they
thought of it, and fill'd their Minds with such unusual Terror, that they were not
themselves for some Weeks after.
    This, as I said, tam'd even the three *English* brutes. (*FA*, p. 44)

The language circles around itself here. The thought of being treated
as animals provokes the English "brutes" to stand on their humanity and
civilize themselves, but the very act of civilizing themselves, rather than
raising them out of the realm of animals, mysteriously precipitates them
back into it, for they are "tam'd" as if they were mindless animals. Of
course, earlier Defoe dealt with precisely this same tension by drawing
an analogy between Crusoe and the goats. In *Robinson Crusoe,* Defoe
resolved this tension by developing the contrast between mindless animal
behavior and Crusoe's reasoning, self-reflection, and mindful choosing.
But the recurrence of the tension here, the insistent repetition ("This, as
I said …"), the bluntness of the language ("tam'd"), and the pointedness
of the paradox hint at the possibility that our commitment to human and
civilized values may be driven by energies that are neither distinctively
human nor civilized.

    These tensions are compounded. When the cannibals come to the
island a final time, the Europeans retreat, leaving two of their dead in the
field, "and the Savages when they came up to them, kill'd them over again
in a wretched manner, breaking their Arms, Legs, and Heads, with their
Clubs and wooden Swords, like true Savages" (*FA*, p. 67). The Europeans
attack again that night and rout the cannibals, and when they return to
the field of battle in the daylight,

they found several of the poor Creatures not quite dead, and yet past recovering Life; a Sight disagreeable enough to generous Minds: for a truly great Man, tho' obliged by the Law of Battle, to destroy his Enemy, takes no Delight in his Misery.

However, there was no Need to give any Orders in this Case; for their own Savages, who were their Servants, dispatch'd those poor Creatures with their Hatchets. (*FA*, p. 69)

On the one hand, we see here the contrast Defoe has been insisting on all along. The savage cannibals, driven by ungoverned rage and revenge, act out their passions brutally and irrationally (the men are dead already). The Europeans, by contrast, have contained those passions in a cultural code (a "Law of Battle") which they discipline themselves to follow ("obliged ... to destroy his Enemy"), and this difference, signaled by self-restraint and the submission of the self to higher codes, is precisely what separates the savage from the civilized, the brute from the human. After they dismember the dead bodies, the cannibals "shouted twice in token of their Victory"; when the Europeans killed their enemy, they took "no Delight in his Misery" (*FA*, pp. 67, 69).

Yet Defoe is palpably anxious about the line he is attempting to draw here, his anxiety revealed not only in his refusal to speak out forthrightly about the brutality of the deed, but in the way one nervous gesture of exoneration treads rapidly on the heels of another: the Europeans felt pity for the "poor Creatures"; they took "no Delight in [their] Misery" – indeed, it was a "disagreeable" sight to see them suffer so; they did what they did only because they were "obliged" to do so by the laws of warfare, and what they did in no way diminished their humaneness, for what they did was evidence of their "generous Minds"; and anyway, the poor cannibals were "past recovering Life"; and anyway, the Europeans did not kill them, their "own Savages" did; and anyway, they actually did not tell their "own Savages" to do anything at all: they were their "Servants," and "there was no Need to give any Orders in this Case."

And more. Atkins now becomes responsible for saving the European settlement. For though these cannibals are defeated, a large body of survivors remains on the island, and if they are allowed to return to their homeland, Atkins reasons, "the Colony was undone" (*FA*, p. 70) for they will bring back an even larger force of cannibals. Atkins is the only one who sees what the Europeans must do: "they must destroy the [cannibals], or be all of them destroy'd themselves" (*FA*, p. 70). The Spanish resist, but Atkins "shew'd them the Necessity of it, so plainly, that they all came into it" (*FA*, p. 70). And so, under the leadership of Atkins, the Europeans

begin to hunt down the savages "like wild Beasts," "killing and wound-
ing" them, reducing them to "the utmost Misery for want of Food, and
many were afterwards found dead in the Woods, without any Hurt, but
meerly starv'd to Death" (*FA,* pp. 70, 71). "The Extremity and Distress
they were reduc'd to was great, and indeed deplorable" (*FA,* p. 71). When
the savages have dwindled "in Number to about 37," the Europeans begin
to treat with them and "at last tame them" (*FA,* p. 71). They are shuf-
fled off to a reservation in a distant corner of the island and are left alone
"provided they would give Satisfaction that they would keep to their own
Bounds" (*FA,* p. 72).

I do not want to press on these passages, asking them to bear more
weight than they can bear. Defoe did not fully share our own sensibilities about the brutal treatment of the New World Indians, nor did he
have the skepticism many of us profess to have about the superiority of
European civilization to the native cultures of the Americas. Civilizing
and Christianizing the savages was pretty much an unalloyed good in
Defoe's mind, and savage society had for him few, if any, redeeming qualities. If there is a cost to the natives for the triumph of civilization, Defoe
does not seem to have seriously questioned, as Atkins phrased it, "the
Necessity of it."

That "Necessity," though, like that "tam'd" in the earlier passage, suggests some stress fractures in Defoe's sense of things. Although he may
not have questioned the cost to the natives of being civilized, he appears
to be nervous about the cost of civilization to the Europeans. In *Farther
Adventures,* after the battle with the Cochin-Chinese natives, Crusoe
broods over his long history of confrontation with savages:

I was sick of killing such poor Savage Wretches, even tho' it was in my own
Defence, knowing they came on Errands which they thought just, and knew
no better; and that tho' it may be a just Thing, because necessary, for there is no
necessary Wickedness in Nature, yet I thought it was a sad Life, which we must
be always oblig'd to be killing our Fellow-Creatures to preserve, and indeed I
think so still. (*FA,* p. 158)

The source of Crusoe's melancholy is that he is a free, humane, self-
restrained, civilized being caught up in the machinery of necessity, and
though he is morally untainted ("for there is no necessary Wickedness in
Nature"), he still feels wicked, for the battle between civilization and savagery is not entirely comprehensible ("they came on Errands they thought
just"), and the differences between what Crusoe is compelled to defend
and the savage Other against whom he must defend it blurs. Crusoe
(and Defoe) believe that the hallmark of a civilized and Christian man

is freedom, the freedom to think out and choose, to freely assimilate into himself the values of civilization and to voluntarily act on them, but here Crusoe is forced to defend civilization without thinking or choosing. Like Atkins, he is simply "oblig'd" to go through the paces of some vast, blind, violent ceremony. It has all the feel of savagery.[47]

Perhaps, in fact, much of this business of freedom, choice, and human dignity is illusory. In his mid-seventies, some twenty years after leaving his island, Crusoe puts roots down in England for good. He identifies his new, settled life as a "Life of Composure" and adds a rather perplexing parenthesis: "for now, and not till now, I may say that I begun to live, that is to say, a sedate and compos'd life" (*SR*, p. 129). But if it is only now, at the end of his life, that he has found true composure, what are we to make of those earlier moments in *Robinson Crusoe* when he claimed he had composed himself, and, having composed himself, achieved "Mastership" over himself and events? Were these moments of genuine composure based on a reasoned insight into the truth of God or nature or society?

The more you examine these moments – particularly those surrounding the appearance of the cannibals – the more they seem shot through with self-deception and delusion. For instance, in the years immediately before he sees the footprint, Crusoe struggles mightily to compose his rebellious energies and to submit himself to the will of God. "I work'd my Mind up, not only to Resignation to the Will of God in the present Disposition of my Circumstances; but even to a sincere Thankfulness for my Condition" (*RC*, p. 154). "Thus I liv'd mighty comfortably," he claims a few pages later, "my Mind being entirely composed to resigning to the Will of God, and throwing my self wholly upon the Disposal of his Providence" (*RC*, p. 157).

In this Government of my Temper, I remain'd near a Year, liv'd a very sedate retir'd Life … and my Thoughts being very much composed as to my Condition, and fully comforted in resigning my self to the Dispositions of Providence, I thought I liv'd really very happily in all things, except that of Society. (*RC*, p. 163)

Yet, he appears to misread the intentions of Providence. For the appearance of the footprint, as is clear to us, though not to Crusoe at first, is a sign that Crusoe should not resign himself to isolation on the island (as he convinced himself in his "composure") but to prepare himself for his re-entry into society.

In fact, what is so startling about the last half of the novel is how thoroughly Crusoe continues to misread Providence, how the more he resigns himself to the will of God and throws himself into pursuing what he considers the course he is meant to take, the more he is blind to the role he is actually playing, a fact emphasized by the sheer raggedness of the conclusion, full of false starts and plotlines abandoned in mid-stride. Crusoe has a dream that he is furnished with a friendly cannibal, with whom he would "certainly venture to the main Land; for this Fellow will serve me as a Pilot" (*RC,* p. 203), and when his dream materializes with the coming of Friday, he assumes that this is the course he is meant to follow. But just when he teaches Friday to navigate the boat they build together, within a few months of venturing out, the cannibals come again, bringing Friday's father and the Spaniard. Crusoe changes plans abruptly. Assuming that he is now "the Instrument of [the Spaniard's] Deliverance," he sends Friday's father back to retrieve the Spaniard's compatriots and bring them to the island, where all of them will build a large vessel "for a Voyage to any of the Christian Colonies of *America*" (*RC,* pp. 237–238). Then, just when he expects the Spaniards to return, a ship *does* drop anchor off his island – but it is, of course, the English ship seized by mutineers, and, once again, Crusoe rereads the providential scheme and changes his actions midstream.

As ragged as they seem, there is a symbolic pattern to these events. Crusoe offended against his father, now he reunites father and son; Crusoe was in need of providential deliverance, now he is the instrument of providential deliverance; Crusoe sinned against hierarchy and legitimate authority, now he is instrumental in re-establishing both. Another pattern is divine: God, using Crusoe as His instrument, delivers Friday, the Spaniard, the English, and He finally delivers Crusoe himself. But the outcome of these chains of events is not at all what Crusoe planned or disciplined himself to work towards, and the disquieting fact about the plot of *Robinson Crusoe* is that the more Crusoe seems to become an agent, temperamentally composed to such a degree that he has mastered his egocentric energies and has submitted himself to Providence, the less he seems to shape or even to understand his own destiny. The more Crusoe thinks, chooses, and acts, the more he seems a pawn in a pattern of which he cannot see the lineaments. "So little do we see before us in the World," Crusoe concludes,

and so much reason have we to depend chearfully upon the great Maker of the World, that he does not leave his Creatures so absolutely destitute, but that in the worst Circumstances they have always something to be thankful for, and sometimes are nearer their Deliverance than they imagine. (*RC,* p. 244)

Yet the jaunty optimism that comes with this knowledge, and the knowledge that leads to such composure, is unsettled too. After Crusoe sees the cannibals, he thinks about how he has "walk'd about in the greatest Security, and with all possible Tranquillity" when in fact he was in "real Danger," when "nothing but a Brow of a Hill, a great Tree, or the casual Approach of Night, had been between me and the worst Kind of Destruction," and he thinks

> How infinitely Good that Providence is, which has provided in its Government of Mankind, such narrow bounds to his Sight and Knowledge of Things, and though he walks in the midst of so many thousand Dangers, the Sight of which, if discover'd to him, would distract his Mind, and sink his Spirits; he is kept serene, and calm, by having the Events of Things hid from his Eyes, and knowing nothing of the Dangers which surround him. (*RC*, p. 201)

But this has been played out before, in a much more somber and chilling key:

> There sat a Creature like a wild Cat upon one of the Chests, which when I came towards it, ran away a little Distance, and then stood still; she sat very compos'd, and unconcerned, and look'd full in my Face ... I presented my Gun at her, but as she did not understand it, she was perfectly unconcern'd at it ... I tossed her a bit of Bisket ... and she went to it, smelled of it, and ate it, and look'd (as pleas'd) for more. (*RC*, p. 98)

After reading this passage, it is difficult to know whether achieving composure is an act of reason, freedom, and choice that manifests that which is exquisitely human in us or if it is just sheer animal stupidity.

Defoe admitted that he had "a Mind Impatient of Confinement," and his intellectual restlessness, that dogged and obstinate doubleness of his mind, is evident in the way he worries and worries the enigmas of freedom, choice, self-restraint, and civilization which are huddled together under the figure of indentured servitude, and then how he undermines his optimism about colonialism itself.[48] If he does not solve any of their mysteries or resolve many of his own doubts, as his inability to quiet his contradictory responses suggests he does not, at least he clarifies some of their ambiguities and contradictions.

Notes

I DEFOE'S AMERICA

1 Papenfuse and Coale, *Historical Maps of Maryland,* pp. 11–31.
2 C. A. Johnson called attention to this error in "Two Mistakes in *Moll Flanders.*" Defoe gets the compass bearings of the Chesapeake right elsewhere (*A General History of Discoveries*, p. 209) and, curiously, he made the same kind of error in his description of the region around Dorking, Surrey, in *A Tour thro' the Whole Island of Great Britain.* As John Robert Moore observes, although he was extremely familiar with the area, he consistently got the compass directions wrong by 90 degrees (*Daniel Defoe,* pp. 28–32).
3 Dollerup, "Chronology of *Moll Flanders.*"
4 Morgan, *American Slavery, American Freedom,* pp. 244–245; Rutman and Rutman, "More True and Perfect Lists," pp. 48–49; Horn, "Moving On in the New World"; Morgan and Rushton, *Eighteenth-Century Criminal Transportation,* p. 133; Ekirch, *Bound for America,* pp. 141, 173. The Northern Neck was the most popular destination for transported criminals when *Moll Flanders* was published, not when Moll herself went to the Chesapeake. As often has been pointed out, this episode is anachronistic: during the period Moll is sent to Virginia, the colony refused to accept transported criminals.
5 Clemens, "Economy and Society"; Clemens, *The Atlantic Economy,* pp. 47–51. Moll says that her land was "purchased of the Proprietors of the Colony" (*MF,* p. 267). Since Maryland was a proprietary and Virginia a royal colony, the land she purchased had to have been in Maryland, and it had to have been in Somerset County, the only county in Maryland south of Phillips Point.
6 Clifford, "Daniel Defoe and Maryland."
7 Hatfield, *Atlantic Virginia,* p. 61; Berkley, "Extinct River Towns of the Chesapeake Bay Region." Lord Baltimore remarked on "the greate want ... of a sufficient number of store houses" (*Archives of Maryland,* vol. VIII, p. 43).
8 Foley and Waller, *Elliott's Island,* pp. 12–14; Roundtree and Davidson, *Eastern Shore Indians,* pp. 84–124; "A List of Men, Women, Children & Slaves in the Province of Maryland, in 1704," *Archives of Maryland,* vol. XXV, p. 256; Clemens, "Settlement and Growth."
9 Assembly Proceedings, October–November 1683, *Archives of Maryland,* vol. VII, p. 256.

10 Jones, "Maryland in 1699," p. 371. For discussions of the history of town creation in Maryland, see Reps, *Tidewater Towns*, pp. 92–116; Menard, "The Tobacco Industry in the Chesapeake Colonies," pp. 133–134; Morriss, *Colonial Trade of Maryland*, pp. 89–90; Carr, "The Metropolis of Maryland." Phillips Point was never mentioned in any of the town-creation Acts.

11 Carroll, "Maryland Quakers in the Seventeenth Century"; Carroll, "Quakerism on the Eastern Shore of Virginia"; Torrence, *Old Somerset,* pp. 85–111. Coincidentally, the land nearest Phillips Point was originally owned by a prominent Quaker, John Edmundson. Like the "honest Quaker" Moll meets at Phillips Point, his plantation was elsewhere – he owned numerous tracts of lands on Maryland's Eastern Shore: Mowbray and Mowbray, *The Early Settlers of Dorchester County*, vol. II, pp. 6–12, 24, 29, 32; McAllister, *Land Records of Dorchester County*; Edmundson and Roberts, "John Edmundson."

12 Gray, *History of Agriculture*, vol. I, pp. 277–278; Morriss, *Colonial Trade of Maryland,* pp. 15–20. G. A. Starr has called attention to this passage in his edition of *Moll Flanders*, p. 407n. "As to Rice," Defoe wrote in 1728, "it is a new Trade, being the Product of one Colony only, namely of *Carolina,* and has been brought over [to England] in Quantity but a few Years" (*Plan of the English Commerce*, p. 252).

13 Sutherland, "Early Troubles."

14 In regard to what Defoe did and did not know about the region, I think it worth noting that, although Moll is extremely successful, her expenses and profits are all within the realm of possibility. She and Jemy paid £35 for land to establish "a sufficient Plantation to employ between fifty and sixty" servants and slaves, and in the end their plantation brought in "at least, 300*l*. Sterling a Year" (*MF,* pp. 267, 274). A landowner needed about 20 acres per hand to sustain a profitable output of tobacco (Earle, *Evolution of a Tidewater Settlement System,* pp. 24–30). For "a sufficient Plantation to employ between fifty and sixty" servants and slaves, then, Moll would need to buy a minimum of 1,000 acres. In 1686, about the same time Moll's plantation was bringing in £300 a year, William Fitzhugh remarked that his plantation of "a thousand Acres" earned £300 per annum (Fitzhugh to Dr. Ralph Smith, April 22, 1689, in Fitzhugh, *William Fitzhugh and His Chesapeake World,* pp. 175–176). Would £35 buy 1,000 acres of land? Given land values on the Eastern Shore, such a price is not unreasonable. In Accomack County, the Virginia county immediately south of Somerset County, in 1673, John Custis sold four tracts totaling 1,900 acres for slightly more than £100 and, in 1679, Samuel Sandford, Defoe's factor in the Chesapeake, purchased 2,500 acres for "fifty pounds lawful money of England" (Ames, *Studies of the Virginia Eastern Shore,* pp. 25–29, 39). Since Somerset County was frontier territory, even cheaper land could be found there. How much labor would Moll need to earn £300 a year? Since in the 1670s, a male servant could cultivate about 1,900 pounds of tobacco and thus bring in £8 to £9 (Menard, "Economy and Society," Table VII-2), Moll would need about thirty laborers. (The Fitzhugh plantation that earned £300 per year had twenty-nine

laborers.) But, based on the calculations of labor and profit ratios Clemens and Walsh have made, my best estimate is that Moll may have needed as many as fifty laborers, and hence her projection of a workforce of "between fifty and sixty" is plausible (Clemens, *The Atlantic Economy*, pp. 85, 87, 153; Walsh, "Plantation Management"). How much would it cost to purchase this much labor? At the very least, it would cost Moll £400 if she bought the least amount of the least expensive laborers (fifty white servants) at their lowest price in the 1670s (£8); at the very most, it would cost a bit more than £1,400 if she bought the largest number of the most expensive laborers (sixty black slaves) at their most expensive price (a little more than £23). For land and labor, then, at most Moll would have to pay about £1,500, which, as it happens, is precisely the amount of money Thomas Bray estimated it would take in 1702 to purchase an estate in Maryland that would bring in £300 a year (Thompson, *Thomas Bray*, p. 68). Since Moll had over £700 available to her in her first year in Maryland, and since she had eight years to build up an estate, there is little question that with careful management she could create the plantation Defoe claims she did. And eight years probably would have been enough. Consider the case of Anne Toft, who resided near Defoe's factor, Samuel Sandford. In 1660, as a young widow of seventeen, she had patented 800 acres. Ten years later, she had parlayed her holdings to over 20,000 acres and went on to build one of the largest empires on the Eastern Shore (Whitelaw, *Virginia's Eastern Shore*, vol. II, pp. 1149–1153; Ames, *Studies of the Virginia Eastern Shore*, p. 25).

15 Defoe, *The Great Law of Subordination Consider'd*, p. 114. The research on the number of servants who came to the Chesapeake is extensive, but the best summaries can be found in Horn, "Servant Emigration to the Chesapeake"; Horn, "British Diaspora"; Carr and Menard, "Immigration and Opportunity"; Galenson, *White Servitude in Colonial America;* Menard, "British Migration to the Chesapeake"; and Morgan, *Slavery and Servitude*, pp. 44–45.

16 Orders of the Council of State, August 14, 1656, *Calendar of State Papers, Colonial Series, America and West Indies*, vol. I, p. 447. Hereafter *CSP Colonial*.

17 Orders of the Council of State, August 14, 1656, *CSP Colonial*, vol. I, p. 447; Smith, *Colonists in Bondage*, pp. 136–203.

18 Ekirch, *Bound for America*, pp. 23, 114–116; Kaminknow and Kaminknow, *Original Lists*.

19 Menard, "British Migration to the Chesapeake," p. 127.

20 Hunter, *The Reluctant Pilgrim*; Starr, *Defoe and Spiritual Autobiography*.

21 Quoted in Menard and Carr, "Lords Baltimore," p. 204.

22 Hammond, *Leah and Rachel*, p. 295; Alsop, *Character of Maryland*, p. 49.

23 Jones, *Present State of Virginia*, pp. 64, 101, 130.

24 Nairne, *Letter from South Carolina*, p. 66. The prevalence of this sentiment in promotional tracts is discussed in Greene, *Intellectual Construction of America*, pp. 73–78.

25 Jones, "The Colonial Impulse"; Lefler, "Promotional Literature of the Southern Colonies."

26 Oldmixon, *British Empire in America*, vol. I, pp. 425–426.

27 Alsop, *Character of Maryland*, p. 61.

28 Alsop, *Character of Maryland*, p. 56.

29 Hammond, *Leah and Rachel*, p. 299.

30 Hammond, *Leah and Rachel*, pp. 296–297.

31 Wilson, *Account of Carolina*, p. 165.

32 Durand, *Huguenot Exile*, pp. 111–112.

33 Alsop, *Character of Maryland*, p. 33.

34 Reavis, "Maryland Gentry."

35 Menard, "From Servant to Freeholder," p. 42.

36 Menard, "From Servant to Freeholder," p. 40.

37 Menard, "From Servant to Freeholder, p. 55.

38 Walsh, "Charles County," pp. 182–183. Menard has written comprehensively about this period in his *"Economy and Society,"* pp. 213–277. Similar conclusions have been reached about servants who arrived in the middle decades of the seventeenth century: Menard et al., "Opportunity and Inequality."

39 Moray, "Letters," p. 160. The opportunities in Virginia during this period have been assessed in Sosin, *English America and the Restoration Monarchy*, p. 155; Morgan, *American Slavery, American Freedom*, p. 209; Games, *Migration and the English Atlantic World*, pp. 105–114; Wertenbaker, *Planters of Colonial Virginia*, pp. 73–83.

40 The chronology of *Colonel Jack* is irresolvably self-contradictory. According to one way of calculating, he began his plantation in the mid- to late 1690s. He was born *c.* 1672. (He was "almost 10 Year old" when his nurse died, and her husband "had been drown'd a little before" in the *Glouster*, which sank in 1682 – *CJ*, p. 37.) He was an established planter by the first years of the eighteenth century, when he says he was "above 30 Year old" (*CJ*, p. 150). Since he completed three years of his contracted five years of servitude before his master set him up, and since he spent an unspecified period after that nursing the growth of his plantation, he probably would have been spirited to Maryland in the early 1690s. However, counting backwards from his long sojourn in Europe gives us an earlier date. Jack's fourth wife dies soon after the battle of Preston, 1715, and a short time after her death, he returns to Maryland "after a Ramble of four and Twenty Years" (*CJ*, p. 221). Since he had cultivated his plantation for at least twelve years before he left for Europe (*CJ*, p. 151), he would have begun his career as a planter in the early 1680s. Whichever timeline we follow, Jack owned his plantation in the 1690s and in the first two decades of the eighteenth century, and I make all my calculations within these, admittedly hazy, boundaries.

41 Menard, "From Servant to Freeholder"; Menard et al., "Opportunity and Inequality"; Carr and Menard, "Immigration and Opportunity."

42 Governor Lord Culpeper to Secretary Coventry, July 8, 1680, *CSP Colonial*, vol. X, p. 568; Gray, *History of Agriculture*, vol. I, pp. 259–276; Menard,

"Farm Prices of Maryland Tobacco"; Menard, "Tobacco Industry in the Chesapeake."

43 Beverley, *History of Virginia,* pp. 76, 78.
44 Quoted in Morgan, *American Slavery, American Freedom,* pp. 241–242.
45 Quoted in Breen, "Changing Labor Force," p. 6.
46 Berry and Moryson, *Rebellion in Virginia,* p. 113; Washburn, *The Governor and the Rebel,* pp. 17–39.
47 Lord Culpeper to the Lords of Trade and Plantation, December 12, 1681, *CSP Colonial,* vol. XI, p. 156.
48 Carr and Jordan, *Maryland's Revolution of Government.*
49 Jack's master's plantation is "up a small River or Creek, which falls into *Potowmack* River"; through "his Interest with the Lord Proprietor," he buys land for Jack "very near" his own plantation (*CJ,* pp. 120, 145). The only three Maryland counties along the Potomac in Defoe's time were St. Mary's, Charles, and Prince George's, but Prince George's was not founded until 1695. Migrants came to the area earlier, of course, but they settled on the rich land near the Patuxent river and avoided the less fertile land along the Potomac until the early eighteenth century (Kulikoff, *Tobacco and Slaves,* p. 97). Since Jack's master's plantation was already well established by the time Jack arrived there in the 1680s or 1690s, it is more likely that he was living in Charles or St. Mary's County.
50 Walsh, "Servitude and Opportunity," p. 122 and Tables 5.3 and 5.4; Menard, "From Servant to Freeholder," pp. 57–59 and Table 1.
51 Menard, "Farm Prices of Maryland Tobacco"; Menard, "Tobacco Industry in the Chesapeake," pp. 122–123; Carr and Menard, "Immigration and Opportunity," p. 224; Carr and Menard, "Wealth and Welfare," p. 96 and Figure 2.
52 Rutman and Rutman, *A Place in Time,* p. 188; Jordan, "Political Stability," pp. 243–273; Menard and Carr, "Lords Baltimore," p. 210; Walsh, "Charles County," pp. 339–364; Clemens, "Economy and Society," pp. 163–167.
53 Main, "Maryland and the Chesapeake Economy"; Main, *Tobacco Colony,* pp. 48–96; Menard et al., "Opportunity and Inequality"; Earle, *Evolution of a Tidewater Settlement System,* pp. 106–119; Parent, *Foul Means,* pp. 9–54.
54 Morgan, *American Slavery, American Freedom,* pp. 218–221; Fischer and Kelly, *Bound Away,* p. 75. One quarter of the landowners in Virginia owned half the land by 1700. "In the five best tobacco-growing counties, … the top quarter owned 70 percent of the land" (Parent, *Foul Means,* p. 36).
55 Blair and Locke, "Virginia: An Appraisal", p. 155.
56 Wyckoff, "Land Prices in Seventeenth-Century Maryland"; Clemens, "Economy and Society," p. 158.
57 Craven, *White, Red, and Black,* pp. 29–30; Rutman and Rutman, "More True and Perfect Lists," pp. 59–62; Menard, "Economy and Society"; Menard, "Immigrants and Their Increase," pp. 97–98; Menard, "British Migration to the Chesapeake."
58 Walsh, "Servitude and Opportunity," pp. 118–119; Menard, "From Servants to Slaves," pp. 371–373 and Table 7; Dowdey, *The Virginia Dynasties,* p. 125;

Russo, "Self-Sufficiency and Local Exchange," pp. 406–408; Galenson, "Economic Aspects of the Growth of Slavery," pp. 265–292 and Table 1.

59 Menard, "Economy and Society," p. 227.

60 Menard, "From Servant to Freeholder"; Walsh, "Servitude and Opportunity," p. 118; Walsh, "Charles County," pp. 167–168; Kulikoff, *Tobacco and Slaves*, pp. 85–92.

61 Wertenbaker, *Planters of Colonial Virginia*, p. 98; see also pp. 96–100, 122–123; Morgan, *American Slavery, American Freedom*, pp. 226–227; Rutman and Rutman, *A Place in Time*, pp. 75–76; Deal, *Race and Class in Colonial Virginia*, p. 130.

62 Carr and Menard, "Immigration and Opportunity," p. 234.

63 Carr and Menard, "Immigration and Opportunity," p. 236.

64 Governor Nicholson to the Board of Trade, March 27, 1697, *Archives of Maryland*, vol. XXXIII, pp. 87–88; Walsh, "Charles County," pp. 163–167, 447–455; Walsh, "Staying Put or Getting Out"; Horn, "Moving On in the New World"; Earle, *Evolution of a Tidewater Settlement System*, pp. 50–54; Clemens, *The Atlantic Economy*, pp. 54, 162–163; Fischer and Kelly, *Bound Away*; Menard, "Economy and Society," pp. 99, 201, 260, 307, 399, 417–419; Anderson and Thomas, "Growth of Population and Labor Force." The most comprehensive examination of the progressive shutting down of opportunity for servants, immigrants, and the poor in the Chesapeake in the eighteenth century is Kulikoff, *Tobacco and Slaves*, pp. 45–161.

65 Roberts, "Letters," p. 124.

66 Roberts, "Letters," p. 124.

67 Roberts, "Letters," p. 125.

68 Roberts, "Letters," p. 125.

69 Roberts, "Letters," p. 125.

70 Roberts, "Letters," p. 126.

71 Roberts, "Letters," p. 126.

72 Roberts, "Letters," p. 128.

73 Roberts, "Letters," p. 128.

74 Roberts, "Letters," p. 129.

75 I have drawn this thumbnail sketch from James Horn's reconstruction of Roberts' life and from Roberts' letters printed in Roberts, "Letters."

76 Carr and Menard, "Immigration and Opportunity," p. 235.

77 Carr and Jordan, *Maryland's Revolution of Government*, p. 181; Main, *Tobacco Colony*, pp. 152–153 and Table IV.1; Burnard, *Creole Gentlemen*, pp. 265–270.

78 Given the standard in Maryland at the time, Moll's and Jack's holding in land and labor would put them in the top 5 percent of the population: Land, "Economic Base and Social Structure," p. 642; Burnard, *Creole Gentlemen*, pp. 36–38 and Tables 2.5, 2.6.

79 Defoe, *Review*, January 19, 1712.

80 Defoe, *Review*, December 2, 1707.

81 Defoe, *Review*, January 1, 1708.

82 Defoe, *Plan of the English Commerce*, p. 122 (italics reversed).

83 Defoe, *Plan of the English Commerce,* pp. 285–286.
84 Defoe, *Plan of the English Commerce,* p. 319.
85 Defoe, *The Complete English Tradesman, Volume 1,* pp. 242–243.
86 Defoe, *Plan of the English Commerce,* p. 318.
87 Defoe, *Review,* December 2, 1707.
88 Novak, *Economics and the Fiction of Daniel Defoe,* p. 140; Dharwadker, "Nation, Race, and Ideology of Commerce," p. 64; McVeagh, "Defoe and Far Travel," p. 124. The most incisive examination of Defoe's fiction and colonization is Downie, "Defoe, Imperialism, and Travel Books Reconsidered."
89 Earle, *Evolution of a Tidewater Settlement System,* pp. 43–47. In 1728, Defoe was very optimistic about the Chesapeake economy: "The Plantations in *Virginia* and *Maryland* are increased to such a Magnitude, that I am told they produce now from eighty to an Hundred Thousand Hogsheads every Year; a Quantity so great, compar'd to what has formerly been produced, that if it be all disposed of, no Man can say the *Virginia* Trade is not infinitely increased" (*Plan of the English Commerce,* pp. 268–269).
90 Walsh, "Charles County," pp. 365–378; Land, "Economic Base and Social Structure," pp. 639–654; Horn, "Adapting to a New World," pp. 146–150. "Wealth and social class are the same thing in Virginia ... In Virginia, careers are open to talents, and Jack rises to his proper level ... Defoe is not nostalgic for a moneyless world, quite the opposite. The great attraction of America for him is that so much money can be made there, so relatively easily, which is to say merely by hard work. If Defoe is nostalgic for anything, it is a world where wealth stands in direct relation to work, and where earned wealth and an individual's status – which is to say, economic activity and perceived social worth – are exactly congruent" (Faller, *Crime and Defoe,* pp. 189, 194).
91 Roach, *Cities of the Dead.*
92 Faller, *Crime and Defoe.*

2 MASTERING THE SAVAGE: CONVERSION IN *ROBINSON CRUSOE*

1 Defoe, *Political History of the Devil,* p. 97.
2 Harvey, *The Inward Wits;* Anderson, *Elizabethan Psychology and Shakespeare's Plays.*
3 "As for [the cannibals] eating human Flesh, I take it to be a Kind of martial Rage rather than a civil Practice, for 'tis evident, they eat no human Creatures, but such as are taken Prisoners in their Battles" (*SR,* p. 137). Friday says about the cannibals, "*They no eat Mans but when makes the War fight;* that is to say, they never eat any Men but such as come to fight with them, and are taken in Battle" (*RC,* p. 222). Most of Defoe's contemporaries agreed. Charles de Rochefort, for instance, asserts that they "eat the flesh of their Enemies ... to satisfie their indignation and revenge, and not out of any delicacy they find in it" (Rochefort, *The History of the Caribby-Islands,* p. 266). After surveying early accounts of Carib cannibalism, Neil L. Whitehead concludes that "the

sources are remarkably consistent in defining [Carib cannibalism] as a limited, ritual act only associated with victory in battle" (*Lords of the Tiger Spirit,* p. 180; see also pp. 175–180).

4 Lawson, *New Voyage to Carolina,* p. 173.
5 Cushman, *Reasons and Considerations,* p. 243.
6 Defoe, *Plan of the English Commerce,* p. 306.
7 Starr summarizes the relation between Providence and will: "Providence … not … simply 'provides' for man, but rather … it affords him – if he is attentive and obedient to its dictates – the means of providing for himself. Thus Providence does not excuse man from action, but calls him to it and sustains him in it" (*Defoe and Spiritual Autobiography,* pp. 189–190). Geoffrey Sill has discussed the centrality of the drama of Crusoe's struggle to rationally control his passions in his *The Cure of the Passions and the Origin of the English Novel,* pp. 86–106.
8 What I describe as the dynamic of sameness and difference is a variation of what Tzvetan Todorov has identified in *Conquest of America* as the duality of "the prejudice of equality" and "the prejudice of superiority" that drove much of the European response to New World natives from Columbus on.
9 Vincent, *True Relation of the Battle,* sig. Bv.
10 Whitaker, *Good Newes from Virginia,* p. 24.
11 Francis Le Jau to the Secretary of the Society for the Propagation of the Gospel in Foreign Parts (SPG), October 20, 1709, in Le Jau, *Carolina Chronicle,* p. 61.
12 Hakluyt, *Writings and Correspondence,* vol. II, p. 368.
13 Tynley, *Sermon,* p. 29.
14 Sergeant, *Letter,* p. 16.
15 Burton, *Anatomy of Melancholy,* p. 56.
16 Strachey, *True Reportory of the Wracke,* p. 1030.
17 Strachey, *Historie of Travell into Virginia,* p. 24.
18 Johnson, *Nova Britannia,* p. 14. The idea was a commonplace: Kupperman, *Indians and English,* pp. 16–40; Oberg, *Dominion and Civility,* pp. 18–22. Defoe himself pressed this historical parallel, justifying English colonization by arguing that the Roman conquest of Britain was "the kindest Thing that could have befallen the *British* Nation, since it brought in the Knowledge of God among the *Britains,* and was a Means of reducing a heathen and barbarous Nation to the Faith of Christ, and to embrace the Messias" (*SR,* p. 211).
19 Strachey, *Historie of Travell into Virginia,* p. 24.
20 Gray, *Good Speed to Virginia,* sig. C2r.
21 Quoted in Cogley, *John Eliot's Mission to the Indians,* p. 247.
22 Winthrop, *Life and Letters,* p. 312.
23 Seed, *American Pentimento,* pp. 29–44.
24 Johnson, *Nova Britannia,* p. 22.
25 Johnson, *Nova Britannia,* p. 22. The putative ease of conversion was another commonplace of colonial thinking: Oberg, *Dominion and Civility,* pp. 50–54.
26 Vincent, *True Relation of the Battle,* sigs. B1r–B1v.

27 Pagden, *Lords of All the World,* p. 87.

28 Hakluyt, *Writings and Correspondence,* vol. II, pp. 211, 214.

29 Hakluyt, *Writings and Correspondence,* vol. II, pp. 216, 237.

30 Hakluyt, *Writings and Correspondence,* vol. II, p. 334.

31 Ralegh, *The Discoverie of Guiana,* p. 194.

32 Ralegh, *The Discoverie of Guiana,* p. 196.

33 Ralegh, *The Discoverie of Guiana,* p. 165.

34 Ralegh, *The Discoverie of Guiana,* pp. 172, 184.

35 Ralegh, *The Discoverie of Guiana,* pp. 121, 123–124.

36 Ralegh, *The Discoverie of Guiana,* p. 165.

37 Ralegh, *The Discoverie of Guiana,* p. 198.

38 Defoe, *Plan of the English Commerce,* pp. 303, 120–121.

39 Defoe, *Plan of the English Commerce,* p. 305.

40 Defoe, *Plan of the English Commerce,* p. 303.

41 Defoe, *Plan of the English Commerce,* p. 303.

42 Defoe, *Plan of the English Commerce,* p. 305.

43 Defoe, *Plan of the English Commerce,* p. 306.

44 Cogley, *John Eliot's Mission to the Indians,* p. 170.

45 Canny, "Origins of Empire," pp. 31–32. In his "England's New World and Old," Canny examines in detail this decline of religious motivation.

46 Lords of Trade to Secretary Stanhope, November 18, 1715, *Documents of Colonial New York,* vol. v, p. 467.

47 Colonel Peter Schuyler to Governor Robert Hunter, February 5, 1717/1718, *Documents of Colonial New York,* vol. v, p. 507.

48 Council of Trade and Plantations to Secretary Stanhope, November 18, 1715, *CSP Colonial,* vol. XXVIII, p. 345. Relations between the British and the Iroquois are examined in Jennings, *Ambiguous Iroquois Empire*; Aquila, *The Iroquois Restoration*; and Richter, *The Ordeal of the Longhouse.*

49 Governor Nicholson to the Board of Trade, August 20, 1698, *Archives of Maryland,* vol. XXIII, p. 500.

50 Defoe, *Review,* June 20, 1704; Defoe, *Two Great Questions Considered,* p. 36.

51 Defoe, *Two Great Questions Considered,* p. 38.

52 Defoe, *Review,* January 19, 1712.

53 Richard Harris to Mr. William Popple, Secretary to the Board of Trade, March 11, 1715, *CSP Colonial,* vol. XXVIII, p. 116.

54 Charles Rodd to his employer in London, May 8, 1715, *CSP Colonial,* vol. XXVIII, p. 169.

55 Governor Spotswood to the Lord Commissioners of Trade, June 4, 1715, *Letters,* vol. II, pp. 115–116.

56 Samuel Eveleigh to Messrs. Boon and Berresford, October 7, 1715, *CSP Colonial,* vol. XXVIII, p. 297.

57 Council of Trade and Plantations to Secretary Stanhope, July 7, 1715, *CSP Colonial,* vol. XXVIII, p. 221.

58 Abel Kettleby and other planters and merchants trading to Carolina to the Council of Trade and Plantations, July 18, 1715, *CSP Colonial,* vol. XXVIII,

p. 236. Oatis, *A Colonial Complex*, and Ramsey, *The Yamasee War*, both investigate the complex causes of the war.

59 Caleb Heathcote to Governor Robert Hunter, July 8, 1715, *Documents of Colonial New York*, vol. v, p. 430.

60 Caleb Heathcote to Lord Townsend, July 12, 1715, *Documents of Colonial New York*, vol. v, p. 432.

61 Governor Spotswood to the Board of Trade, February 1, 1719/1720, *Letters*, vol. ii, p. 329.

62 Council of Trade and Plantations to Secretary Stanhope, July 19, 1715, *CSP Colonial*, vol. xxviii, p. 238.

63 Thomas Bannister to the Council of Trade and Plantations, July 15, 1715, *CSP Colonial*, vol. xxviii, p. 524.

64 Crane, *The Southern Frontier*, p. 206.

65 "State of British Plantations," *Documents of Colonial New York*, vol. v, p. 622.

66 "State of British Plantations," *Documents of Colonial New York*, vol. v, p. 623.

67 Steele, *Politics of Colonial Policy*, pp. 165–170.

68 Secker, *Sermon*, p. 44.

69 Richard Harris to Mr. Popple, March 11, 1715, *CSP Colonial*, vol. xxviii, p. 116.

70 White, *Planter's Plea*, pp. 27, 35–36.

71 The New England Company to John Endecott, April 17, 1629, in *Chronicles of the First Planters*, p. 149; Matthew Cradock to John Endecott, February 16, 1629, *Chronicles of the First Planters*, pp. 133–134. Cogley, *John Eliot's Mission to the Indians*, pp. 1–22, has explored the prevalence of what has been termed the "affective model" of Puritan missionary activity – the belief that the Indians could be won over by virtue of their admiration for the colonists' moral rectitude and civilized behavior.

72 The fear of Indianization has been exhaustively documented by many scholars, but a thorough discussion can be found in Slotkin, *Regeneration through Violence*, pp. 1–222.

73 John Yeo to Archbishop Gilbert Sheldon, 1679, quoted in Thompson, *Into All Lands*, p. 8.

74 These fears were expressed by the General Assembly of Connecticut in 1677 as they deliberated ways of resettling towns that had been abandoned in the Indian wars; quoted in Axtell, "Scholastic Philosophy," p. 359.

75 Quoted in Thompson, *Into All Lands*, p. 70.

76 Quoted in Pascoe, *Two Hundred Years of the SPG*, vol. i, p. 21.

77 Hubbard, *History of the Indian Wars*, vol. ii, pp. 256–257.

78 Berkeley, *Works*, vol. vii, p. 345. Defoe was not impressed by the spiritual condition of the Americans: "*America* is throng'd with Christians, God wot, such as they are; for I must confess, the *European* Inhabitants of some of the Colonies there … very ill merit that Name" (*SR*, p. 204). He also remarked that "no such Thing as Religion of any Kind whatsoever has ever been heard of" in northern Scotland and added, "no more than was found in the

Northern Continent of *America,* indeed not so much" (*Review,* December 20, 1709).

79 Butler, *Awash in a Sea of Faith,* pp. 37–66.
80 Secker, *Sermon,* p. 5.
81 Berkeley, *Works,* vol. VII, p. 359.
82 Petition of the Council and Assembly of the Settlements in South Carolina to the King, February 3, 1720, *CSP Colonial,* vol. XXXI, p. 333.
83 Letter of unnamed South Carolina missionary to the SPG, October 20, 1710, quoted in Pascoe, *Two Hundred Years of the SPG,* vol. I, pp. 15–16.
84 Letter of unnamed SPG missionary, January 9, 1708, quoted in Kennett, *Sermon,* p. 30n.
85 Reverend Alexander Forbes to the Bishop of London, July 21, 1724, in Perry, *Historical Collections,* vol. I, p. 327. Frank J. Klingberg cites numerous missionaries in South Carolina in the early decades of the eighteenth century who saw the bad example of the white colonists as the most serious obstacle to the conversion of the Indians: "Indian Frontier in South Carolina."
86 Nelson, "Anglican Missions in America," p. 696.
87 Willis, *Sermon,* p. 17.
88 Quoted in Pascoe, *Two Hundred Years of the SPG,* vol. I, p. 68. I have drawn my information about the missionary activities of the SPG from several sources: Nelson, "Anglican Missions in America"; Pascoe, *Two Hundred Years of the SPG*; Thompson, *Into All Lands*; Butler, *Awash in a Sea of Faith*; Calam, *Parsons and Pedagogues*; Klingberg, *Anglican Humanitarianism*; Woolverton, *Colonial Anglicanism*; Schlenther, "Religious Faith and Commercial Empire"; Goodwin, "Christianity, Civilization, and the Savage"; and Wood, *Black Majority,* pp. 131–142.
89 Bray, *Life and Works,* p. 137.
90 Wilcocks, *Sermon,* pp. 14–15.
91 Burnet, *Of the Propagation of the Gospel in Foreign Parts,* pp. 20–22.
92 Berkeley, *Works,* vol. VII, p. 345.
93 Berkeley, *Works,* vol. VII, p. 358.
94 Berkeley, *Works,* vol. VII, p. 122.
95 Eliot is quoted in Winslow, *Glorious Progress,* p. 18. For the belief among the English that Indians must be civilized before they were converted to Christianity, see Axtell, *The Invasion Within*; Canny, "The Ideology of English Colonization"; Woolverton, *Colonial Anglicanism,* pp. 103–104; Kellaway, *The New England Company,* pp. 5–8; and Beaver, "Methods in American Missions."
96 Defoe, *Plan of the English Commerce,* pp. 121, 303.
97 Such rhetoric is conventional, but in this instance I am quoting from Burnet's *Of the Propagation of the Gospel in Foreign Parts,* p. 12. A comprehensive account of the Black Legend can be found in Maltby, *The Black Legend in England.*
98 Rummell, "Defoe and the Black Legend." The need for fair and just treatment of the natives is mentioned several times in *A New Voyage round the World,* but there is one particularly significant episode (pp. 101–106) that

appears to allude specifically to Ralegh's call for self-restraint and just treatment. When the crew finds two naked Indian women, they clothe them and
ostentatiously send them back to their village unmolested. In gratitude, the
natives open a trading relation with the English.

99 Hulme, *Colonial Encounters*, pp. 186–187.
100 Snader, *Caught between Worlds*, p. 139. See, too, Azim, *Colonial Rise of the
    Novel*; Green, *Dreams of Adventure, Deeds of Empire*, pp. 1–96; and McInelly,
    "Expanding Empires, Expanding Selves."
101 Defoe, *Plan of the English Commerce*, p. 285.
102 Pennington, "The Amerindian in English Promotional Literature."
103 The importance in Defoe's fiction of portraying natives as peaceful as a con-
    dition of profitable settlement has been explored by Haskell, "Antagonistic
    Structure," pp. 15–56. The Carib threat has been discussed by Boucher,
    Cannibal Encounters.
104 Defoe, *A General History of Discoveries*, p. 214.
105 Downie, "Defoe, Imperialism, and Travel Books Reconsidered."
106 The idea that Defoe was using *Robinson Crusoe* to float a scheme to settle the
    continent opposite Crusoe's island was originally proposed by Moore, *Daniel
    Defoe*, pp. 223–224, and has been most recently argued for by Downie,
    "*Robinson Crusoe*'s Eighteenth-Century Contexts." Much of the force of
    this argument is based on the assumption that Defoe announced his inter-
    est in such a colony in *An Historical Account of the Voyages and Adventures of
    Sir Walter Raleigh* (1720), but the ascription of this pamphlet to Defoe has
    been disputed by Furbank and Owens, *The Canonisation of Daniel Defoe*, pp.
    164–167.
107 For my brief discussion of conditions in the Caribbean, I am indebted to
    Burns, *History of the British West Indies*; Bridenbaugh and Bridenbaugh,
    No Peace beyond the Line; Thorton, *West-India Policy under the Restoration*;
    Beckles, "The 'Hub of Empire'"; and Dunn, *Sugar and Slaves*.
108 Ligon, *A True & Exact History*, pp. 108, 22. John Oldmixon observed about
    Barbados that by 1650 "the People that went thither from *England*, could not
    be so mean as those that transported themselves to other Parts of *America*,
    because to raise a Plantation required a Stock of some Thousands of Pounds"
    (*The British Empire in America*, vol. II, p. 14).
109 Governor Francis Russell to Lords of Trade and Plantations, March 23, 1695,
    CSP Colonial, vol. XIV, p. 446.
110 Governor Daniel Parke to Mr. Secretary Hedges, October 4, 1706, *CSP
    Colonial*, vol. XXIII, pp. 254–255.
111 Dunn, *Sugar and Slaves*, p. 164; see also pp. 149–187.
112 In these last three sections of this chapter, I am trying to flesh out two of
    Peter Hulme's most provocative statements: *Robinson Crusoe* is "less a 'real-
    istic account' of English colonialism in the Caribbean than a parable of the
    anxiety surrounding the … 'composition of the self'"; "The threat from the
    cannibals … [should] be read … as a graphic image of the *decomposition*
    of the self" (*Colonial Encounters*, p. 196). My assumption that in *Robinson
    Crusoe* and other of Defoe's novels the Other becomes "an image of the

protagonists' own earlier, weaker self" has been adumbrated by Maddox, "On Defoe's *Roxana*," p. 266.

113 Defoe, *Review*, March 5, 1706.
114 Defoe, *Jure Divino*, p. 71.
115 Defoe, *Review*, September 15, 1711.
116 Defoe, *Political History of the Devil*, p. 283.
117 Jager, "The Parrot's Voice."
118 Strachey, *Historie of Travell into Virginia*, p. 24.
119 The most thorough analysis of Crusoe's struggle to conquer his passions and of the novel's rhythms of imprisonment, slavery, and deliverance is in Blewett, *Defoe's Art of Fiction*, pp. 28–54.
120 Richetti, *Defoe's Narratives*, p. 39.
121 Richetti, *Defoe's Narratives*, p. 45.
122 Richetti, *Defoe's Narratives*, p. 53. As Starr has argued, "Providence does not excuse man from action, but calls him to it": "it indicates solutions rather than simply performing them, it evokes effective action rather than obviating it, and confers human responsibility rather than precluding it" (*Defoe and Spiritual Autobiography*, pp. 189–190). Defoe puts it a bit more bumptiously. "I am for freely and entirely submitting all Events to Providence," he says, but it does not follow that one should be "supinely and unconcernedly passive, as if there was nothing warning, instructing, or directing in the Premonitions of God's Providence; and which he expected we should take Notice of, and take Warning by … To be utterly careless of ourselves … and talk of trusting Providence, is a Lethargy of the worst Nature; for as we are to trust Providence with our Estates, but to use at the same Time, all Diligence in our Callings, so we are to trust Providence with our Safety, but with our Eyes open to all its necessary Cautions, Warnings, and Instructions" (*SR*, pp. 185, 190).
123 Gibson, *Two Letters of the Bishop of London*, p. 11.
124 Defoe, *The Great Law of Subordination Consider'd*, pp. 51, 61, 53.
125 Defoe, *The Family Instructor, Volume 2*, p. 134.
126 As Starr points out, in Crusoe's wanderings leading up to the island episode, "by obeying inclination rather than reason and duty," Crusoe makes choices on the basis of an illusory freedom; "these 'decisions' … mark the … enslavement of his will" and, consequently, "throughout these wanderings, he is mastered by events rather than master of them" (*Defoe and Spiritual Autobiography*, pp. 87–88).
127 Defoe, *Political History of the Devil*, pp. 423, 426; Defoe, *Jure Divino*, p. 69.
128 Defoe, *A Hymn to the Mob*, in *The True-Born Englishman and Other Poems*, p. 424.

3 SERVITUDE AND SELF-TRANSFORMATION IN *COLONEL JACK*

1 Davis, *The Problem of Slavery*.
2 Berlin, *Many Thousands Gone*, pp. 115–119. Jon Butler provides an excellent overview of Anglicanism and slavery in *Awash in a Sea of Faith*, pp. 129–163.

3   Francis Le Jau to the SPG, March 22, 1709, in Le Jau, *Chronicle of Le Jau*, p. 55.
4   Quoted in Jordan, *White over Black*, p. 184.
5   Joseph Ottolenghe to the SPG, September 9, 1751, quoted in Klingberg, *Anglican Humanitarianism*, p. 20n27.
6   Baxter, *Christian Directory*, p. 557.
7   Tryon, *Friendly Advice*, pp. 109, 116.
8   Godwyn, *The Negro's & Indian's Advocate*, p. 13.
9   Fleetwood, *Sermon*, pp. 13–14.
10 Butler, *Sermon*, p. 13.
11 James Blair to Edmund Gibson, Bishop of London, July 20, 1730, quoted in Tate, *The Negro in Eighteenth-Century Williamsburg*, p. 74.
12 The slaveowners' fears and the reformers' responses to them are reviewed in Davis, *Problem of Slavery*, especially pp. 85–90, 101–102, and 203–211; Jordan, *White over Black*, pp. 179–215; Butler, *Awash in a Sea of Faith*, pp. 132–133; Calam, *Parsons and Pedagogues*, pp. 50–51; Van Horne, *Religious Philanthropy and Colonial Slavery*, pp. 26–29; Parent, *Foul Means*, pp. 236–249; Bennett, *Bondsmen and Bishops*; and Anesko, "So Discreet a Zeal."
13 Secker, *Sermon*, p. 22.
14 Gibson, *Two Letters of the Bishop of London*, p. 11.
15 Fleetwood, *Sermon*, pp. 16–17.
16 Berkeley, *Works*, vol. VII, pp. 346, 122.
17 Robert Jenny to David Humphreys, November 19, 1725, quoted in Jordan, *White over Black*, p. 182.
18 Le Jau to the Secretary of the SPG, June 13, 1710, in Le Jau, *Chronicle of Le Jau*, pp. 76–77.
19 Tryon, *Friendly Advice*, p. 217.
20 Godwyn, *Negro's & Indian's Advocate*, pp. 124, 128 (mispaginated as pp. 108 and 112).
21 Elias Neau to John Chamberlayne (*c.* May 1711), quoted in Klingberg, *Anglican Humanitarianism*, p. 131.
22 Defoe, *Plan of the English Commerce*, p. 253.
23 Defoe, *Review*, January 10, 1713.
24 Defoe, *Review*, February 22, 1709.
25 Defoe, *Review*, February 17, 1709. Important discussions of Defoe's views on slavery can be found in Andersen, "Paradox of Trade and Morality"; Novak, *Economics and the Fiction of Daniel Defoe*, pp. 20, 65, 90–92, 104, 144, 167n2; Kaplan, "Daniel Defoe's Views on Slavery and Racial Prejudice"; and Knox-Shaw, "Defoe and the Politics of Representing the African Interior." The long-standing critical discussion about how "ironic" or "ambivalent" Defoe is in his fictional treatment of slaves and slaveowners has been canvassed by Keane, "Slavery and the Slave Trade"; in general, I agree with his conclusion that "Defoe's attitude toward slavery and the slave trade can hardly be said to differ from that of Crusoe" (Keane, "Slavery and the Slave Trade," p. 108).
26 In *The Family Instructor, Volume 2*, p. 217, Defoe argued that African slaves, like the cannibals in *Robinson Crusoe*, were essentially the same as white

Europeans. "They exercise all the Faculties of the Soul ... as we do; ... they have Understanding, Memory, the Power of Reasoning; Knowing things absent and future, and can act and operate upon immaterial Objects," and they are able to "repent of their Sins," for they "are capable of all we are capable of, both here and hereafter." "They go to Hell, too ... if they either do not know GOD, or do not obey GOD," and thus it is incumbent on Christians to educate and convert them.

27 Defoe, *Religious Courtship*, p. 216.
28 Defoe, *The Family Instructor, Volume 2*, p. 135.
29 Defoe, *The Family Instructor, Volume 2*, pp. 209–210.
30 Defoe, *The Family Instructor, Volume 2*, pp. 218, 211.
31 As Peter Coldham has pointed out in "The 'Spiriting' of London Children to Virginia," the practice of kidnapping and selling children and youths into indentured servitude was met with intense popular outrage. By making Jack the victim of spiriting, Defoe could count on his readers being sympathetic and granting him a real degree of innocence.
32 William Byrd to John Boyce, Baron Boyle of Broghill, May 20, 1729, in Byrd, *Correspondence*, vol. 1, p. 394.
33 Byrd, *History of the Dividing Line*, p. 2.
34 Byrd, *History of the Dividing Line*, pp. 54, 110, 92.
35 Byrd, *History of the Dividing Line*, pp. 304, 92.
36 Beverley, *History of Virginia*, p. 319.
37 Martyn, *Impartial Inquiry*, p. 5.
38 *An Account, Shewing the Progress of the Colony of Georgia*, p. 18. The fear of New World idleness has been thoroughly explored in Bertelson, *The Lazy South*.
39 Mountgomery, *Design'd Establishment of a New Colony*, p. 13; Jones, *Present State of Virginia*, pp. 87–88.
40 Defoe, *A Tour thro' the Whole Island of Great Britain*, p. 203.
41 Martyn, *Reasons for Establishing Georgia*, p. 182.
42 Rundle, *Sermon*, p. 207.
43 Thomas, "Historical Account of Pensilvania," p. 339.
44 Oglethorpe, *New Account of South Carolina and Georgia*, p. 141.
45 Governor Alexander Spotswood to the Bishop of London, October 24, 1710, in Spotswood, *Letters*, vol. 1, pp. 27–28. The prevalence of this argument has been discussed by Shields, *Oracles of Empire*, pp. 19–20 and 36–55.
46 Defoe's suspicions about withdrawal from the world have been elucidated by Blewett, "The Retirement Myth in *Robinson Crusoe*."
47 Behn, *The Widdow-Ranter*, pp. 258–259.
48 Ward, *Trip to Jamaica*, p. 16.
49 Defoe, *The Great Law of Subordination Consider'd*, p. 70.
50 Defoe, *The Great Law of Subordination Consider'd*, p. 68.
51 Defoe, *The Great Law of Subordination Consider'd*, pp. 40, 71.
52 Defoe, *The Great Law of Subordination Consider'd*, p. 45.
53 Defoe, *The Great Law of Subordination Consider'd*, pp. 171, 173, 175.

54 Defoe, *The Great Law of Subordination Consider'd*, p. 189.
55 Defoe, *The Great Law of Subordination Consider'd*, p. 125.
56 Defoe, *The Great Law of Subordination Consider'd*, p. 125.
57 Defoe, *The Great Law of Subordination Consider'd*, p. 125.
58 Defoe, *The Family Instructor, Volume 2*, p. 126. The whippings and beatings of Major, Captain, and Colonel Jack make no lasting impression on them nor do they deter them from their crimes: Armstrong, "I Was a Kind of an Historian."
59 Locke, *Some Thoughts Concerning Education*, pp. 144, 138.
60 Locke, *Some Thoughts Concerning Education*, p. 138.
61 Locke, *Some Thoughts Concerning Education*, p. 222.
62 Locke, *Some Thoughts Concerning Education*, pp. 161–162. Laura A. Curtis has investigated the similarities between Defoe's and Locke's educational theories: "Defoe's Domestic Conduct Manuals."
63 Pocock, "The Classical Theory of Deference," p. 516.
64 Locke, *Some Thoughts Concerning Education*, p. 103.
65 Locke, *Some Thoughts Concerning Education*, p. 112.
66 Locke, *Some Thoughts Concerning Education*, p. 112.
67 Locke, *Some Thoughts Concerning Education*, p. 112.
68 Locke, *Some Thoughts Concerning Education*, p. 255.
69 Locke, *Some Thoughts Concerning Education*, p. 142.
70 Locke, *Some Thoughts Concerning Education*, p. 223.
71 Locke, *Some Thoughts Concerning Education*, p. 168.
72 Defoe, *The Family Instructor, Volume 2*, pp. 135, 130.
73 The contradictions of Jack's system of slave management as well as its underlying violence have been astutely analyzed by Boulukos, *The Grateful Slave*, pp. 75–94.
74 Defoe, *The Evident Approach of a War*, p. 39
75 Defoe, *The Evident Approach of a War*, p. 39.
76 The phrase (and the insight) is Blewett's from *Defoe's Art of Fiction*, p. 101. The importance of gratitude in Defoe's thinking and his conception of it as a "natural virtue" is explored in Novak, *Defoe and the Nature of Man*, pp. 113–128.
77 At base, these impulses, though directed outward, have a strong egocentric component. Virginia Birdsall has convincingly shown that behind many of Jack's generous actions and fueling his drive to enter society and thrive lie such self-seeking motives as the desire for status, power, respect, and self-esteem: *Defoe's Perpetual Seekers*, pp. 121–142.
78 Roberts, "Introduction" to Defoe, *Colonel Jack*, pp. xii–xiii.
79 My sense of roles in *Colonel Jack* is different from John Richetti's. He argues that Jack "plays so many roles that he remains essentially apart from them all": "The radical secret of *Colonel Jack* is that its hero is impersonating throughout, playing at even the most sordid and threatening reality he lives in, always the master of experience because he is somehow existentially prior to it." Since Jack is "essentially apart" from the roles he plays, Richetti

concludes, he "is presented fully formed"; "Jack never changes, never in any essential way": *Defoe's Narratives,* pp. 145–191; quotes from pp. 147, 162, 151, and 172. I am arguing that, to the contrary, the roles Jack plays answer, though imperfectly, impulses that are essential to him. By playing these roles and experiencing their imperfection – that is, their failure to perfectly express his needs – he creates for himself opportunities to change himself.

80 Addison and Steele, *The Spectator,* vol. II, p. 339 (no. 215, November 6, 1711).
81 Addison and Steele, *The Spectator,* vol. II, p. 339 (no. 215, November 6, 1711).
82 Addison and Steele, *The Spectator,* vol. II, p. 340 (no. 215, November 6, 1711).
83 Addison and Steele, *The Spectator,* vol. II, p. 340 (no. 215, November 6, 1711).
84 Jack's master's behavior is itself a mixture of sociable feeling and self-interest, too. He buys Jack a plantation of 300 acres and gives him "30*l.* a Year Wages for looking after one of his own Plantations." The plantation his master purchases for Jack is very near his own plantation, and "he told me plainly, that I was not beholding to him for it at all; for he did it, that I might not be oblig'd to neglect his Business for the carrying on my own" (*CJ,* p. 145).
85 Defoe, *The Complete English Tradesman, Volume 1,* p. 76.
86 Defoe, *The Complete English Tradesman, Volume 2,* p. 98.
87 Defoe, *The Complete English Tradesman, Volume 2,* p. 99.
88 James Thompson points out that "at this point in its narrative, the bill … [has] been converted from material capital to symbolic capital" and it "serves as the authenticating sign of [Jack's] worth … [T]he bill … convinced the master that Jack is a man of property; thereby the master's goodwill is secured": *Models of Value,* pp. 109–110.
89 As Blewett has shown in *Defoe's Art of Fiction,* pp. 95–100, Defoe consistently associated the Jacobite cause with delusion, and he attributes Jack's attachment to the cause to his naivety.
90 For Defoe's belief in the power of trade and commerce, see Meier, *Defoe and the Defense of Commerce,* pp. 40–45. For the widespread assumption that trade and commerce were forces of peace, benevolence, and civilization, see Weinbrot, *Britannia's Issue,* pp. 254–295. In pointing to the contrast between Jack's activities as a merchant and trader and his earlier criminal behavior, I am taking my lead from Lincoln B. Faller, who makes this argument persuasively throughout Chapters 5 and 6 of his *Crime and Defoe.* Still, as Novak shows, Jack's trading activities in Mexico were illegal and thus his behavior retains a taint of criminality (*Economics and the Fiction of Defoe,* pp. 122–127), and I would speculate that, by characterizing Jack's trading as both productive and tainted, Defoe catches the liminal nature of roles themselves, which shape the energies of our lower nature and direct them to higher ends, but the energies that are shaped are still energies of our lower nature. That same mixture of productivity and criminality characterizes Singleton's and Crusoe's final merchant ventures as well as Moll's successful management of her plantation, which she purchases with the money she has gained from her criminal activities.
91 Defoe, *Review,* January 3, 1706.

92 Zimmerman, *Defoe and the Novel*, pp. 126–154.

93 The implication that the unfolding of the self through a series of imperfect roles is a process that will never end in resolution accounts for the
peculiar texture of *Colonel Jack*, which has been characterized by George
A. Starr as proceeding by exploring competing norms, values, and standards, pitting them one against the other "dramatically but inconclusively."
Concomitantly, Jack himself develops sporadically, incompletely ("His
career is marked by a series of windfalls and losses, not steady gains"), and
often he does not develop at all. Like the novel itself, Starr suggests, Jack's
trajectory is "a case history of extensive but unresolved groping for mean-
ingful values" (*Defoe and Casuistry*, pp. 82–110; quotes from pp. 87, 97, and
110).

4 *MOLL FLANDERS* AND THE
MISREPRESENTATION OF SERVITUDE

1 The two episodes have been analyzed by Camaiora, *The American Episodes.*
Though we agree in our general conclusions, my analysis takes a different
tack.

2 Starr, *Defoe and Spiritual Autobiography*, pp. 126–162.

3 Zimmerman, *Defoe and the Novel*, pp. 75–106.

4 The most subtle treatment of this facet of Moll is Richetti, *Defoe's Narratives*,
pp. 94–144. He observes that Moll "is most fully herself when she keeps
something of herself … aside and ready for future possibilities" because
she not only "remains apart from the world" but also "stands apart from
[her own] spontaneous experience" (Richetti, *Defoe's Narratives*, pp. 105,
102–103).

5 St. Augustine, *City of God*, vol. II, pp. 78–79.

6 Bolingbroke, *Works*, vol. V, p. 179.

7 Hutcheson, *Moral Philosophy*, p. 252. Nelson, "Incest in the Early Novel."
Other aspects of the incest theme are explored by Wilson, "Science, Natural
Law, and Unwitting Incest," pp. 249–270; and Pollak, *Incest and the English
Novel*, pp. 110–128.

8 For an investigation of how important ideas of restitution were for a sense of
the sincerity of repentance, by both Defoe and his society at large, see Suarez,
"The Shortest Way to Heaven?"

9 "The main message encoded in most scenarios involving incest" in eighteenth-century texts, argues Nelson, "is that while a rootless individual may
learn to make a virtue of belonging to no family, the lost or forsaken kin-
group will reach out across the miles to punish the transgressor. In *Moll
Flanders* the heroine's discovery that her Virginia marriage is incestuous
is in some ways equivalent to Robinson Crusoe's exile on an uninhabited
island: both are, in part, punishments visited on the protagonists for exult-
ing in their freedom from family and regional loyalties" ("Incest in the Early
Novel," pp. 147–148).

10 Moll's "compulsive fear" of "being in the power of others" and her need "to control her own destiny" has been explored by Krier, "A Courtesy which Grants Integrity."

11 Chaber, "Matriarchal Mirror."

12 Bell, *Defoe's Fictions,* p. 138.

13 Defoe, *Jure Divino,* p. 72. Sill, *Cure of the Passions,* pp. 114–121.

14 Richetti, *The Life of Daniel Defoe,* p. 252.

15 Jones, *Present State of Virginia,* pp. 131–132.

16 Alsop, *Character of Maryland,* p. 99.

17 Bullock, *Virginia Impartially Examined,* p. 13.

18 Carr, "Emigration and the Standard of Living," p. 322.

19 The Earl of Egmont is quoted in Jordan, *White over Black,* pp. 129–130. Sobel, *The World They Made Together,* p. 48; Walsh, "Charles County," p. 203.

20 Smith, *Colonists in Bondage,* pp. 226–252; McCormac, *White Servitude in Maryland*; Ballagh, *White Servitude in Virginia.*

21 Hammond, *Leah and Rachel,* p. 284.

22 Ashbridge, *Some Account of the Life,* p. 152.

23 Revel, "Poor Felon's Account," p. 191; Mr. George Larkin to the Council of Trade and Plantations, December 22, 1701, *CSP Colonial,* vol. IX, p. 693.

24 Quoted in Lancaster, "Almost Chattel," p. 353.

25 Provincial Court Proceedings, 1663, *Archives of Maryland,* vol. XLIX, p. 9.

26 Governor William Gooch to the Board of Trade, May 10, 1750, quoted in Morgan, *Slave Counterpoint,* p. 136.

27 Annesley, *Unfortunate Young Nobleman,* vol. I, p. 63.

28 Morgan, *Slavery and Servitude,* p. 22. Menard estimates even longer working hours – from ten to fourteen hours a day, six days a week ("Economy and Society," p. 91).

29 Carr et al., *Robert Cole's World,* pp. 69–70. Rhys Isaac gives a detailed description of the yearly cycle of work that had to be performed on a tidewater plantation in *The Transformation of Virginia,* pp. 24–27.

30 Eddis, *Letters from America,* p. 38.

31 Case cited in McCormac, *White Servitude in Maryland,* p. 64.

32 Provincial Court Proceedings, 1658–1662, *Archives of Maryland,* vol. LVI, pp. 501–502.

33 Berlin, *Many Thousands Gone,* p. 164; see also pp. 109–149.

34 Berlin, *Many Thousands Gone,* p. 164; see also pp. 109–149.

35 Patterson, *Slavery and Social Death,* p. 13.

36 Patterson, *Slavery and Social Death,* p. 5.

37 Patterson, *Slavery and Social Death,* p. 5.

38 Patterson, *Slavery and Social Death,* p. 296.

39 Patterson, *Slavery and Social Death,* pp. 8, 5, 7.

40 Patterson, *Slavery and Social Death,* p. 10.

41 Thomas Chalkley is quoted in Middleton, *Tobacco Coast,* p. 1; Horn, "Servant Emigration to the Chesapeake," p. 68.

42 Horn, *Adapting to a New World,* p. 62; Grubb, "Fatherless and Friendless."

43 Galenson, *White Servitude in Colonial America,* pp. 23–78.

44 Menard, "British Migration to the Chesapeake," pp. 123–126; Wareing, "Migration to London and Transatlantic Emigration"; Horn, "Servant Emigration to the Chesapeake."

45 Langston, "On Towns and Corporations," p. 101.

46 "Answer of the Lord Baltimore to the Queryes about Maryland," *Archives of Maryland,* vol. v, p. 266.

47 John Clayton to "a Doctor of Physik," April 24, 1684, in Clayton, *Parson with a Scientific Mind,* p. 4.

48 Jones, "Maryland in 1699," p. 372; Muchel, "Report," p. 126.

49 Rutman and Rutman, *A Place in Time;* Horn, *Adapting to a New World,* pp. 237–239; Graham, "Meeting House and Chapel"; Walsh, "Community Networks in the Early Chesapeake"; Earle, *The Evolution of a Tidewater Settlement System,* especially pp. 62–100; Breen and Innes, *"Myne Owne Ground",* pp. 56–67; Breen, *Tobacco Culture,* pp. 45–55; Bruce, *Social Life in Virginia in the Seventeenth Century,* pp. 218–244; Bushman, "American High-Style and Vernacular Cultures," pp. 370–373; Carson, *Colonial Virginians at Play,* pp. 1–8.

50 Clayton, "Letter to the Royal Society," p. 21.

51 William Fitzhugh to Nicholas Hayward, January 30, 1686/1687, *William Fitzhugh and His Chesapeake World,* p. 203.

52 William Byrd to John Boyle, Baron Boyle of Broghill, July 28, 1730, William Byrd to John Boyle, Baron Boyle of Broghill, February 12, 1727/1728, and William Byrd to Charles Boyle, Earl of Orrery, July 5, 1726, in Byrd, *Correspondence,* vol. 1, pp. 432, 372, 355.

53 William Fitzhugh to Nicholas Hayward, January 30, 1686/1687, *William Fitzhugh and His Chesapeake World,* p. 205.

54 Green, *Sufferings of William Green,* p. 6.

55 Green, *Sufferings of William Green,* p. 9.

56 Green, *Sufferings of William Green,* p. 11.

57 Kimber, *History of Mr. Anderson,* p. 52.

58 Beattie, *Crime and the Courts,* pp. 540–541; Ekirch, *Bound for America,* pp. 192–193, 209–210.

59 Harrower, *Journal,* p. 130.

60 Beckles, *White Servitude and Black Slavery in Barbados,* p. 5.

61 Beckles, *White Servitude and Black Slavery in Barbados,* p. 5; Galenson, *White Servitude in Colonial America,* p. 10.

62 Quoted in Morgan, *American Slavery, American Freedom,* p. 128.

63 Games, *Migration and the Atlantic World,* p. 89.

64 The legal evolution in Virginia that resulted in "the disposition to regard [the indentured servant] as a chattel and a part of the personal estate of his master" has been traced by Ballagh, *White Servitude in Virginia* (quote from p. 44).

65 Morris, *Government and Labor in Early America,* pp. 487–488; Rozbicki, *Transformation of the English Cultural Ethos,* pp. 100–102; Horn, *Adapting to a New World,* p. 269.

66 Talbot County Court Proceedings, 1662–1674, *Archives of Maryland,* vol. LIV, pp. 360–362.

67 Provincial Court Proceedings, 1664, *Archives of Maryland,* vol. XLIX, p. 308.

68 Provincial Court Proceedings, 1664, *Archives of Maryland,* vol. LXIV, p. 308.

69 Morris, *Government and Labor,* pp. 487–488; Beckles, *White Servitude and Black Slavery,* p. 86; Breen and Innes, *"Myne Owne Ground,"* pp. 62–63; Morgan, *Slavery and Servitude,* p. 21; Billings, "Law of Servants and Slaves."

70 Quoted in Morris, *Government and Labor,* p. 493.

71 Quoted in Wawryzczek, "The Women of Accomack versus Henry Smith," p. 18.

72 Quoted in Wawryzczek, "The Women of Accomack versus Henry Smith," p. 17.

73 Quoted in Wawryzczek, "The Women of Accomack versus Henry Smith," p. 17.

74 Quoted in Deal, *Race and Class in Colonial Virginia,* p. 111.

75 Quoted in Wawryzczek, "The Women of Accomack versus Henry Smith," p. 18.

76 Wawryzczek, "The Women of Accomack versus Henry Smith," p. 20. In addition to Wawryzczek, Deal, *Race and Class in Colonial Virginia,* p. 111, and Morris, *Government and Labor,* pp. 491–496, discuss the legal suits against Smith.

77 Morris, *Government and Labor,* pp. 437, 447, 450, 454–455, 459, 468–469; Rozbicki, *Transformation of the English Cultural Ethos,* p. 117; Smith, *Colonists in Bondage,* p. 271; Ballagh, *White Servitude in the Colony of Virginia,* p. 58.

78 Johnson, *Nova Britannia,* p. 19.

79 Jones, *Present State of Virginia,* p. 129.

80 Hening, *Statutes at Large,* vol. II, p. 509; Cecilius Calvert to Horatio Sharpe, December 23, 1755, *Archives of Maryland,* vol. IV, p. 329.

81 *American Weekly Mercury,* February 14, 1721, quoted in Morgan and Rushton, *Eighteenth-Century Criminal Transportation,* p. 128.

82 Hening, *Statutes at Large,* vol. V, p. 545.

83 Assembly Proceedings, 1694–1728, *Archives of Maryland,* vol. XXXVIII, p. 320.

84 The colonists' animosity toward transported criminals is surveyed by Morgan, "English and American Attitudes."

85 Ekirch, *Bound for America,* pp. 134–135; Morgan and Rushton, *Eighteenth-Century Criminal Transportation,* pp. 58–59.

86 Franklin, *The Pennsylvania Gazette,* April 11, 1751, in *Writings,* p. 358.

87 *Maryland Gazette,* October 12, 1752, quoted in Ekirch, *Bound for America,* p. 152.

88 Eddis, *Letters from America,* pp. 37–38.

89 Cooke, *The Sot-Weed Factor,* p. 12; Shammas, "English-Born and Creole Elite."

90 Bullock, *Virginia Impartially Examined,* p. 14.

91 Child, *New Discourse of Trade,* p. 170.

92 Jones, *Present State of Virginia*, p. 130.

93 "Petition of Sundry Merchants Possessing Estates in America to Lords of Trade and Plantations," quoted in Morris, *Government and Labor*, p. 341.

94 Nicholas Spencer to Lord Culpepper, August 6, 1676, quoted in Morgan, *American Slavery, American Freedom*, p. 236; Cecilius Calvert to Horatio Sharpe, December 23, 1755, *Archives of Maryland*, vol. VI, p. 329.

95 Although some historians have argued that indentured servants had a degree of freedom in shaping their lives, Sharon V. Salinger, in her review of the literature of indentured servitude, concludes, "Servants' choice did not extend beyond the initial decision to become indentured servants. And this too was restricted because servants' options operated within a very narrow plane between continual poverty and servitude" ("Labor, Markets, and Opportunity," pp. 337–338). Richard Dunn reaches similar conclusions: "English servant laborers emigrate to America not because they wanted to but because they had to. Push was more important than pull. The combination of hard times at home and labor demand in the colonies, facilitated by a well-organized servant trade in the chief English port towns, drew thousands of people who knew little or nothing of the Chesapeake or the Caribbean into emigration abroad" ("Servants and Slaves," p. 162).

96 Moraley, *The Infortunate*, pp. 13–14.

97 Moraley, *The Infortunate*, p. 17.

98 Moraley, *The Infortunate*, p. 14.

99 Harrower, *Journal*, p. 3.

100 Harrower, *Journal*, p. 7.

101 Harrower, *Journal*, p. 10.

102 Harrower, *Journal*, p. 11.

103 Harrower, *Journal*, p. 12.

104 Harrower, *Journal*, p. 14.

105 Harrower, *Journal*, p. 15.

106 Harrower, *Journal*, p. 16.

107 Harrower, *Journal*, pp. 16, 17.

108 Harrower, *Journal*, p. 17.

109 Harrower, *Journal*, pp. 17, 19.

110 Alsop, *Character of Maryland*, pp. 19, 87.

111 Harrower, *Journal*, p. 110.

112 Moraley, *The Infortunate*, p. 4.

113 Moraley, *The Infortunate*, p. 4.

114 Moraley, *The Infortunate*, pp. 14, 75.

115 Moraley, *The Infortunate*, p. 7.

116 Moraley, *The Infortunate*, p. 7.

117 Moraley, *The Infortunate*, p. 72.

118 Moraley, *The Infortunate*, p. 72.

119 Klepp and Smith detail Moraley's motives for trying to reintegrate himself into Newcastle society (*The Infortunate*, pp. 113–117).

120 Charles Rodes to Sir John Rodes, November 9, 1693, in *Bases of the Plantation Society*, p. 104.

121 Roberts, "Letters," pp. 124, 128.
122 Ashbridge, *Account of the Life,* p. 147.
123 Horn, *Adapting to a New World,* p. 160.
124 Horn, *Adapting to a New World,* p. 428.
125 Governor Francis Nicholson to the Council of Trade and Plantations, December 2, 1701, *CSP Colonial,* vol. IX, p. 642. There is a large body of scholarship that examines this transition: Isaac, *Transformation of Virginia;* Rozbicki, *Transformation of the English Cultural Ethos;* Walsh, "Servitude and Opportunity"; Carr and Menard, "Immigration and Opportunity"; Burnard, *Creole Gentlemen;* Carr and Walsh, "Changing Lifestyles and Consumer Behavior"; Sweeney, "High-Style Vernacular"; Rozbicki, *The Complete Colonial Gentleman;* Greene, *Pursuits of Happiness,* pp. 81–100; Breen, "Horses and Gentlemen"; Breen, "An Empire of Goods"; Bushman, *The Refinement of America;* Walsh, "Urban Amenities and Rural Sufficiency."
126 See Ekirch, *Bound for America,* pp. 192–193, 209–210.
127 Menard, "From Servants to Slaves," p. 389.
128 Fischer and Kelly, *Bound Away.*
129 Moraley, *The Infortunate,* p. 74.
130 Moraley, *The Infortunate,* p. 74.
131 Moraley, *The Infortunate,* p. 88.
132 Bullock, *Virginia Impartially Examined,* p. 14.
133 Beverley, *History of Virginia,* p. xvii.
134 Alsop, *Character of Maryland,* p. 58.
135 Green, *Sufferings of William Green,* p. 15.
136 Quoted in Kulikoff, *Tobacco and Slaves,* pp. 295–296.
137 Ashbridge, *Account of the Life,* p. 152.
138 Ashbridge, *Account of the Life,* pp. 152–153.
139 Ashbridge, *Account of the Life,* p. 153.
140 Ashbridge, *Some Account of the Life,* p. 153.
141 Hellier, *Prodigal Life and Tragical Death,* p. 111.
142 Hellier, *Prodigal Life and Tragical Death,* p. 112.
143 Hellier, *Prodigal Life and Tragical Death,* p. 112.
144 Hellier, *Prodigal Life and Tragical Death,* p. 113.
145 Hellier, *Prodigal Life and Tragical Death,* p. 113.
146 Hellier, *Prodigal Life and Tragical Death,* p. 117.
147 Annesley, *Unfortunate Young Nobleman,* vol. I, p. 62.
148 Annesley, *Unfortunate Young Nobleman,* vol. I, pp. 62–63.
149 Annesley, *Unfortunate Young Nobleman,* vol. I, pp. 67–68.
150 Annesley, *Unfortunate Young Nobleman,* vol. I, p. 90.
151 Morgan and Rushton, *Eighteenth-Century Criminal Transportation,* p. 11; see also pp. 62–97.
152 Defoe, *The Life, Adventures, and Pyracies, of the Famous Captain Singleton,* p. 19.
153 Wareing, "Violently Taken Away," p. 5.

154 "Petition of sundry merchants possessing estates in America to Lords of Trade and Plantations," quoted in Morris, *Government and Labor*, p. 341.

155 Horn, "Servant Emigration to the Chesapeake," pp. 94, 65.

156 Horn, *Adapting to a New World*, pp. 19–77; Menard, "British Migration to the Chesapeake Colonies"; Galenson, "'Middling People' or 'Common Sort'?"; Souden, "'Rogues, Whores and Vagabonds'?"

157 Ekirch, *Bound for America*, pp. 167–193; Morgan, "Convict Runaways."

158 Ashbridge, *Account of the Life*, pp. 151–152.

159 Harrower, *Journal*, p. 39.

160 Shinagel, *Daniel Defoe and Middle-Class Gentility*.

161 *CSP Colonial*, vol. XXXIII, pp. 22–23.

162 Defoe's defense of George I's treatment of the rebels is canvassed by Novak, *Daniel Defoe*, pp. 515–519. For other ways in which Defoe misrepresented indentured servitude, see O'Brien, "Union Jack, Amnesia and the Law."

163 Earle, *The World of Defoe*, p. 170. Defoe's growing concerns about the danger of social mobility and the decay of social hierarchy are examined in Clark, *Daniel Defoe*, pp. 138–159.

164 Downie, "Introduction" in Defoe, *The Great Law of Subordination Consider'd*, pp. 8–9.

165 Defoe, *The Great Law of Subordination Consider'd*, p. 51.

166 Defoe, *The Great Law of Subordination Consider'd*, p. 97.

167 Defoe, *The Great Law of Subordination Consider'd*, p. 186.

168 Defoe, *The Great Law of Subordination Consider'd*, pp. 106, 51.

CONCLUSION: DEFOE, CANNIBALS, AND COLONIALISM

1 Smith, *Colonists in Bondage*, pp. 96–97; quote from p. 97.

2 Beattie, *Crime and the Courts in England*, p. 475; see also pp. 450–519.

3 Ekirch, *Bound for America*, pp. 3, 111; see also pp. 1–45.

4 Defoe, *A Tour thro' the Whole Island of Great Britain*, vol. III, p. 203.

5 Morgan and Rushton, *Eighteenth-Century Criminal Transportation*, pp. 130–136.

6 Durston, *Moll Flanders*, p. 222.

7 Clark, *Daniel Defoe*, pp. 113–137.

8 Schonhorn, *Defoe's Politics*, pp. 141–164.

9 Moore, "Defoe and the South Sea Company"; Jack, "Defoe's *Roman à Thèse*"; Fishman, "Defoe, Herman Moll, and the Geography of South America"; Markley, "So Inexhaustible a Treasure of Gold."

10 Defoe, *Plan of the English Commerce*, p. 284.

11 Defoe, *Plan of the English Commerce*, p. 284.

12 Defoe, *Plan of the English Commerce*, p. 284.

13 Defoe, *Plan of the English Commerce*, p. 285.

14 Jack, "Defoe's *Roman à Thèse*," p. 335; Novak, *Economics and the Fiction of Daniel Defoe*, p. 141.

15 Aubin, *Madame de Beaumont*, p. 142.

16 Aubin, *Madame de Beaumont,* p. 45.

17 Aubin, *Charlotta Du Pont,* p. 117.

18 Aubin, *Charlotta Du Pont,* p. 118.

19 Aubin, *Charlotta Du Pont,* p. 119.

20 Aubin, *Charlotta Du Pont,* p. 124.

21 Aubin, *Charlotta Du Pont,* pp. 124–125.

22 Aubin, *Charlotta Du Pont,* pp. 94–95.

23 Aubin, *Charlotta Du Pont,* p. 225.

24 Chetwood, *Richard Falconer,* bk. 2, pp. 2, 5.

25 Chetwood, *Richard Falconer,* bk 2, p. 17.

26 Chetwood, *Richard Falconer,* bk. 2, p. 24.

27 Chetwood, *Richard Falconer,* bk. 2, p. 57.

28 Chetwood, *Richard Falconer,* bk. 2, p. 57.

29 Chetwood, *Richard Falconer,* bk 3, p. 44.

30 Chetwood, *Richard Falconer,* bk. 3, p. 140.

31 Chetwood, *Richard Falconer,* bk. 3, p. 160.

32 Rawson, *God, Gulliver, and Genocide,* especially pp. 17–91. The definitive study of the use of cannibalism in the Caribbean to mark the distinction between the European and the savage Other is Hulme, *Colonial Encounters.*

33 Rawlins, *Famous and Wonderful Recovery,* p. 99; Colley, *Captives*; Starr, "Escape from Barbary"; Snader, *Caught between Worlds.*

34 Snader, *Caught between Worlds,* p. 280.

35 Snader, *Caught between Worlds,* p. 280.

36 Snader, *Caught between Worlds,* p. 34.

37 Snader, *Caught between Worlds,* p. 91. These elements in the American narratives are examined by Ebersole, *Captured by Texts,* pp. 1–97; and Vaughan and Clark, *Puritans among the Indians,* pp. 1–28.

38 Snader, *Caught between Worlds,* pp. 62–93.

39 Rowlandson, *Sovereignty and Goodness of God,* pp. 44, 38.

40 Rowlandson, *Sovereignty and Goodness of God,* pp. 37, 35, 34.

41 Rowlandson, *Sovereignty and Goodness of God,* p. 44.

42 Rowlandson, *Sovereignty and Goodness of God,* pp. 57, 49, 44.

43 Rowlandson, *Sovereignty and Goodness of God,* p. 60.

44 Rowlandson, *Sovereignty and Goodness of God,* pp. 74–75.

45 Rowlandson, *Sovereignty and Goodness of God,* p. 68.

46 Rowlandson's *Sovereignty and Goodness of God* and Mather's *A Brief History of the War with the Indians* and the *Continued Account* are in the catalogue of the combined libraries of Phillip Farewell and Defoe, though there is no proof that they were owned (or read) by Defoe (Heidenreich, *The Libraries of Daniel Defoe and Phillips Farewell,* pp. 110, 120).

47 Defoe's sense of the cost of civilization as been astutely analyzed by Flynn, *The Body in Swift and Defoe,* pp. 149–160.

48 Daniel Defoe to Daniel Finch, Earl of Nottingham, January 9, 1702/1703, in Defoe, *Letters,* p. 1.

Bibliography

An Account, Shewing the Progress of the Colony of Georgia, in Peter Force (ed.), *Tracts and Other Papers, Relating Principally to the Origin, Settlement, and Progress of the Colonies in North America,* 4 vols., 1836. Reprint, Gloucester, Mass.: Peter Smith, 1963, vol. 1, no. 5, pp. 1–56.

Addison, Joseph, and Sir Richard Steele, *The Spectator,* edited by Donald F. Bond, 5 vols., Oxford: Clarendon Press, 1965.

Alsop, George, *A Character of the Province of Maryland,* edited by Newton D. Mereness, Freeport, NY: Books for Libraries Press, 1972.

Ames, Susie M., *Studies of the Virginia Eastern Shore in the Seventeenth Century,* 1940. Reprint, New York: Russell & Russell, 1973.

Andersen, Hans H., "The Paradox of Trade and Morality in Defoe," *Modern Philology,* 39 (August 1941): 23–46.

Anderson, Ruth Leila, *Elizabethan Psychology and Shakespeare's Plays,* 1927. Reprint, New York: Russell & Russell, 1966.

Anderson, Terry L., and Robert Paul Thomas, "The Growth of Population and Labor Force in the 17th-Century Chesapeake," *Explorations in Economic History,* 15 (July 1978): 290–312.

Anesko, Michael, "So Discreet a Zeal: Slavery and the Anglican Church in Virginia, 1680–1730," *Virginia Magazine of History and Biography,* 93 (July 1985): 247–278.

Annesley, James, *Memoirs of an Unfortunate Young Nobleman: Return'd from a Thirteen Years Slavery in America,* 3 vols., London, 1743.

Aquila, Richard, *The Iroquois Restoration: Iroquois Diplomacy on the Colonial Frontier, 1701–1754,* Detroit, Mich.: Wayne State University Press, 1983.

Archives of Maryland, edited by William Hand Browne and others, 72 vols., Baltimore, Md.: Maryland Historical Society, 1883–1972.

Armstrong, Katherine A., "'I Was a Kind of an Historian': The Productions of History in Defoe's *Colonel Jack,*" in Alvaro Ribeiro, SJ, and James G. Basker (eds.), *Tradition in Transition: Women Writers, Marginal Texts, and the Eighteenth-Century Canon,* Oxford: Clarendon Press, 1996, pp. 97–110.

Ashbridge, Elizabeth, *Some Account of the Fore Part of the Life of Elizabeth Ashbridge,* in William L. Andrews (eds.), *Journeys in New Worlds,* Madison, Wisc.: University of Wisconsin Press, 1990, pp. 117–180.

Aubin, Penelope, *The Life of Charlotta Du Pont, an English Lady,* London, 1723.

The Life of Madame de Beaumont, a French Lady, London, 1721.

Augustine, *City of God*, edited and translated by Marcus Dods, 2 vols., New York: Hafner, 1948.

Axtell, James, *The Invasion Within: The Contest of Cultures in Colonial North America*, Oxford: Oxford University Press, 1985.

"The Scholastic Philosophy of the Wilderness," *William and Mary Quarterly*, 29 (July 1972): 335–366.

Azim, Firdous, *The Colonial Rise of the Novel*, London: Routledge, 1993.

Ballagh, James Curtis, *White Servitude in the Colony of Virginia: A Study of the System of Indentured Labor in the American Colonies*, 1895. Reprint, New York: B. Franklin, 1969.

Bases of the Plantation Society, edited by Aubrey C. Land, New York: Harper & Row, 1969.

Baxter, Richard, *A Christian Directory; or, Summ of Practical Theology*, London, 1673.

Beattie, J. M., *Crime and the Courts in England, 1660–1800*, Oxford: Clarendon Press, 1986.

Beaver, R. Pierce, "Methods in American Missions to the Indians in the Seventeenth and Eighteenth Centuries: Calvinist Models for Protestant Foreign Missions," *Journal of Presbyterian History*, 47 (June 1969): 124–148.

Beckles, Hilary McD., "The 'Hub of Empire': The Caribbean and Britain in the Seventeenth Century," in William Roger Louis (ed.), *The Oxford History of the British Empire*, 5 vols., Oxford: Oxford University Press, 1998, vol. 1, pp. 218–240.

White Servitude and Black Slavery in Barbados, 1627–1715, Knoxville, Tenn.: University of Tennessee Press, 1989.

Behn, Aphra, *Oroonoko, The Rover and Other Works*, edited by Janet Todd, London: Penguin, 1992.

Bell, Ian A., *Defoe's Fictions*, London: Croom Helm, 1985.

Bennett, J. Henry, Jr., *Bondsmen and Bishops: Slavery and Apprenticeship on the Codrington Plantation of Barbados, 1710–1838*, Berkeley, Calif.: University of California Press, 1950.

Berkeley, George, *The Works of George Berkeley, Bishop of Cloyne*, edited by A. A. Luce and T. E. Jessop, 8 vols., London: Nelson, 1948–1957.

Berkley, Henry J., "Extinct River Towns of the Chesapeake Bay Region," *Maryland Historical Magazine*, 19 (June 1924): 125–134.

Berlin, Ira, *Many Thousands Gone: The First Two Centuries of Slavery in North America*, Cambridge, Mass.: Harvard University Press, 1998.

Berry, John, and Francis Moryson, *A True Narrative of the Rise, Progresse, and Cessation of the Late Rebellion in Virginia,* in Charles M. Andrews (ed.), *Narratives of the Insurrections, 1675–1690*, New York: Charles Scribner's Sons, 1915, pp. 105–141.

Bertelson, David, *The Lazy South*, 1967. Reprint, Westport, Conn.: Greenwood Press, 1980.

Beverley, Robert, *The History and Present State of Virginia*, edited by Louis B. Wright, Chapel Hill, NC: University of North Carolina Press, 1947.

Billings, Warren M., "The Law of Servants and Slaves in Seventeenth-Century Virginia," *Virginia Magazine of History and Biography*, 99 (January 1991): 45–62.

Birdsall, Virginia, *Defoe's Perpetual Seekers: A Study of the Major Fiction*, Lewisburg, Pa.: Bucknell University Press, 1985.

Blair, James, and John Locke, "Virginia at the Close of the Seventeenth Century: An Appraisal by James Blair and John Locke," edited by Michael G. Kammen, *Virginia Magazine*, 74 (April 1966): 141–169.

Blewett, David, *Defoe's Art of Fiction: Robinson Crusoe, Moll Flanders, and Colonel Jack*, Toronto: University of Toronto Press, 1979.

"The Retirement Myth in *Robinson Crusoe*: A Reconsideration," *Studies in the Literary Imagination*, 15 (fall 1982): 37–50.

Bolingbroke, Henry St. John, Viscount, *The Works of Henry St. John, Lord Viscount Bolingbroke*, 5 vols., London, 1754.

Boucher, Philip P., *Cannibal Encounters: Europeans and Island Caribs, 1492–1763*, Baltimore, Md.: Johns Hopkins University Press, 1992.

Boulukos, George, *The Grateful Slave: The Emergence of Race in Eighteenth-Century British and American Culture*, Cambridge: Cambridge University Press, 2008.

Bray, Thomas, *Rev. Thomas Bray: His Life and Selected Works Relating to Maryland*, edited by Bernard C. Steiner, Baltimore, Md.: Maryland Historical Society, 1901.

Breen, T. H., "A Changing Labor Force and Race Relations in Virginia, 1660–1710," *Journal of Social History*, 7 (fall 1973): 3–25.

"An Empire of Goods: The Anglicization of Colonial America, 1690–1776," *Journal of British Studies*, 25 (October 1986): 467–499.

"Horses and Gentlemen: The Cultural Significance of Gambling among the Gentry of Virginia," *William and Mary Quarterly*, 34 (April 1977): 239–257.

Tobacco Culture: The Mentality of the Great Tidewater Planters on the Eve of the Revolution, Princeton, NJ: Princeton University Press, 1985.

Breen, T. H., and Stephen Innes, *"Myne Owne Ground": Race and Freedom on Virginia's Eastern Shore, 1640–1676*, Oxford: Oxford University Press, 1980.

Bridenbaugh, Carl, and Roberta Bridenbaugh, *No Peace beyond the Line: The English in the Caribbean, 1624–1690*, Oxford: Oxford University Press, 1972.

Brown, Kathleen M., *Good Wives, Nasty Wenches, and Anxious Patriarchs: Gender, Race and Power in Colonial Virginia*, Chapel Hill, NC: University of North Carolina Press, 1996.

Bruce, Philip Alexander, *Social Life in Virginia in the Seventeenth Century*, Richmond, Va.: Whittet & Shepperson, 1907.

Bullock, William, *Virginia Impartially Examined*, London, 1649.

Burnard, Trevor G., *Creole Gentlemen: The Maryland Elite, 1691–1776*, London: Routledge, 2002.

Burnet, Gilbert, *Of the Propagation of the Gospel in Foreign Parts: A Sermon Preached ... Feb. 8 1703/4*, London, 1704.

Burns, Alan Cuthbert, Sir, *History of the British West Indies*, London: George Allen & Unwin, 1954.

Burton, Robert, *The Anatomy of Melancholy*, New York: Wiley & Putnam, 1847.

Bushman, Richard L., "American High-Style and Vernacular Cultures," in Jack P. Greene and J. R. Pole (eds.), *Colonial British America: Essays in the New History of the Early Modern Era*, Baltimore, Md.: Johns Hopkins University Press, 1984, pp. 345–383.

The Refinement of America: Persons, Houses, Cities, New York: Knopf, 1992.

Butler, Jon, *Awash in a Sea of Faith: Christianizing the American People*, Cambridge, Mass.: Harvard University Press, 1990.

Butler, Joseph, *A Sermon Preached before the Incorporated Society for the Propagation of the Gospel ... February 16, 1738–9*, London, 1739.

Byrd, William, *The Correspondence of the Three William Byrds of Westover, Virginia, 1684–1776*, edited by Marion Tinling, 2 vols., Charlottesville, Va.: University of Virginia Press, 1977.

History of the Dividing Line, in William K. Boyd (ed.), *Histories of the Dividing Line Betwixt Virginia and North Carolina*, New York: Dover Publications, 1967.

Calam, John, *Parsons and Pedagogues: The S.P.G. Adventure in American Education*, New York: Columbia University Press, 1971.

Calendar of State Papers, Colonial Series, America and West Indies, edited by W. N. Sainsbury and others, 44 vols., London: His Majesty's Stationery Office, 1860–1969.

Camaiora, Luisa Conti, *A Reading of the American Episodes in Defoe's* Moll Flanders, Modena: Del Bianco Editore, 1985.

Canny, Nicholas, "England's New World and Old, 1480s–1630s," in William Roger Louis (ed.), *The Oxford History of the British Empire*, 5 vols., Oxford: Oxford University Press, 1998, vol. 1, pp. 148–169.

"The Ideology of English Colonization: From Ireland to America," *William and Mary Quarterly*, 30 (October 1973): 574–598.

"Origins of Empire: An Introduction," in William Roger Louis (ed.), *The Oxford History of the British Empire*, 5 vols., Oxford: Oxford University Press, 1998, vol. 1, pp. 1–33.

Carr, Lois Green, "Emigration and the Standard of Living: The Eighteenth-Century Chesapeake," in John J. McCusker and Kenneth Morgan (eds.), *The Early Modern Atlantic Economy*, Cambridge: Cambridge University Press, 2000, pp. 319–343.

"'The Metropolis of Maryland': A Comment on Town Development along the Tobacco Coast," *Maryland Historical Magazine*, 69 (summer 1974): 124–145.

Carr, Lois Green, and David William Jordan, *Maryland's Revolution of Government, 1689–1692*, Ithaca, NY: Cornell University Press, 1974.

Carr, Lois Green, and Russell R. Menard, "Immigration and Opportunity: The Freedman in Early Colonial Maryland," in Thad W. Tate and David L. Ammerman (eds.), *The Chesapeake in the Seventeenth Century: Essays on*

Anglo-American Society, Chapel Hill, NC: University of North Carolina Press, 1979, pp. 206–242.

"Wealth and Welfare in Early Maryland: Evidence from St. Mary's County," *William and Mary Quarterly*, 56 (January 1999): 95–120.

Carr, Lois Green, Russell R. Menard, and Lorena S. Walsh, *Robert Cole's World: Agriculture and Society in Early Maryland*, Chapel Hill, NC: University of North Carolina Press, 1991.

Carr, Lois Green, Philip D. Morgan, and Jean B. Russo (eds.), *Colonial Chesapeake Society*, Chapel Hill, NC: University of North Carolina Press, 1988.

Carr, Lois Green, and Lorena S. Walsh, "Changing Lifestyles and Consumer Behavior in the Colonial Chesapeake," in Cary Carson, Ronald Hoffman, and Peter J. Albert (eds.), *Of Consuming Interests: The Style of Life in the Eighteenth Century*, Charlottesville, Va.: University Press of Virginia, 1994, pp. 59–166.

Carroll, Kenneth L., "Maryland Quakers in the Seventeenth Century," *Maryland Historical Magazine*, 47 (December 1952): 297–313.

"Quakerism on the Eastern Shore of Virginia," *Virginia Magazine*, 74 (April 1966): 170–189.

Carson, Cary, Ronald Hoffman, and Peter J. Albert (eds.) *Of Consuming Interests: The Style of Life in the Eighteenth Century*, Charlottesville, Va.: University Press of Virginia, 1994.

Carson, Jane, *Colonial Virginians at Play*, Williamsburg, Va.: Williamsburg Research Studies, 1965.

Chaber, Lois A., "Matriarchal Mirror: Women and Capital in *Moll Flanders*," *PMLA*, 97 (March 1982): 212–226.

Chetwood, William Rufus, *The Voyages, Dangerous Adventures, and Imminent Escapes of Captain Richard Falconer*, London, 1720.

Child, Joshua, Sir, *New Discourse of Trade*, London, 1693.

Chronicles of the First Planters of the Colony of Masachusetts Bay from 1623 to 1639, edited by Alexander Young, Boston, Mass.: Little & Brown, 1846.

Clark, Katherine, *Daniel Defoe: The Whole Frame of Nature, Time and Providence*, Basingstoke: Palgrave Macmillan, 2007.

Clayton, John, *The Reverend John Clayton: A Parson with a Scientific Mind. His Scientific Writings and Other Related Papers*, edited by Edmund Berkeley and Dorothy Smith Berkeley, Charlottesville, Va.: University Press of Virginia, 1965.

"A Letter from Mr. John Clayton ... to the Royal Society, May 12, 1888," in Peter Force (ed.), *Tracts and Other Papers, Relating Principally to the Origin, Settlement, and Progress of the Colonies in North America*, 4 vols., 1836. Reprint, Gloucester, Mass.: Peter Smith, 1963, vol. III, no. 12, pp. 3–45.

Clemens, Paul G. E., *The Atlantic Economy and Colonial Maryland's Eastern Shore*, Ithaca, NY: Cornell University Press, 1980.

"Economy and Society on Maryland's Eastern Shore, 1689–1733," in Aubrey C. Land, Lois Green Carr, and Edward C. Papenfuse (eds.), *Law, Society, and Politics in Early Maryland*, Baltimore, Md.: Johns Hopkins University Press, 1977, pp. 153–170.

"The Settlement and Growth of Maryland's Eastern Shore during the English Restoration," *Maryland Historian*, 5 (fall 1974): 63–78.

Clifford, George E., Jr., "Daniel Defoe and Maryland," *Maryland Historical Magazine*, 52 (December 1957): 307–315.

Cogley, Richard W., *John Eliot's Mission to the Indians before King Philip's War*, Cambridge, Mass.: Harvard University Press, 1999.

Coldham, Peter Wilson, "The 'Spiriting' of London Children to Virginia, 1648–1685," *Virginia Magazine of History and Biography*, 83 (July 1975): 280–287.

Colley, Linda, *Captives*, New York: Pantheon, 2000.

Colonial Captivities, Marches, and Journeys, edited by Isabel M. Calder, Port Washington, NY: Kennikat, 1967.

Cooke, Ebenezer, *The Sot-Weed Factor*, in Bernard Christian Steiner (ed.), *Early Maryland Poetry*, Baltimore, Md.: John Murphy, 1900, pp. 11–31.

Crane, Verner W., *The Southern Frontier, 1670–1732*, 1929. Reprint, Ann Arbor, Mich.: University of Michigan Press, 1959.

Craven, Wesley Frank, *White, Red, and Black: The Seventeenth-Century Virginian*, Charlottesville, Va.: University Press of Virginia, 1971.

Curtis, Laura A., "A Case Study of Defoe's Domestic Conduct Manuals Suggested by *The Family, Sex, and Marriage*," in Roger D. Lund (ed.), *Critical Essays on Daniel Defoe*, New York: G. K. Hall, 1997, pp. 17–30.

Cushman, Robert, *Reasons and Considerations Touching the Lawfulness of Removing out of England*, in Alexander Young (ed.), *Chronicles of the Pilgrim Fathers, from 1602 to 1625*, Boston, Mass., 1844, pp. 239–252.

Danckaerts, Jasper, *Journal of Jasper Danckaerts, 1678–1680*, New York: Charles Scribner's Sons, 1913.

Davis, David Brion, *The Problem of Slavery in Western Culture*, Ithaca, NY: Cornell University Press, 1966.

Deal, J. Douglas, *Race and Class in Colonial Virginia: Indians, Englishmen, and Africans on the Eastern Shore during the Seventeenth Century*, New York: Garland, 1993.

Defoe, Daniel, *The Complete English Tradesman, Volume 1*, edited by John McVeagh. Vol. VII of *Religious and Didactic Writings of Daniel Defoe*, edited by W. R. Owens and P. N. Furbank, London: Pickering & Chatto, 2007.

The Complete English Tradesman, Volume 2, edited by John McVeagh. Vol. VIII of *Religious and Didactic Writings of Daniel Defoe*, edited by W. R. Owens and P. N. Furbank, London: Pickering & Chatto, 2007.

Defoe's Review, edited by A. W. Secord, 22 vols., New York: Columbia University Press, 1938.

The Evident Approach of a War, and Something of the Necessity of It, in Order to Establish Peace, and Preserve Trade, London, 1727.

The Family Instructor, Volume 2, edited by P. N. Furbank. Vol. II of *Religious and Didactic Writings of Daniel Defoe*, edited by W. R. Owen and P. N. Furbank, London: Pickering & Chatto, 2006.

The Farther Adventures of Robinson Crusoe, edited by W. R. Owens. Vol. II of *The Novels of Daniel Defoe*, edited by W. R. Owens and P. N. Furbank, London: Pickering & Chatto, 2008.

The Fortunes and Misfortunes of the Famous Moll Flanders, edited by Liz Bellamy. Vol. VI of *The Novels of Daniel Defoe*, edited by W. R. Owens and P. N. Furbank, London: Pickering & Chatto, 2009.

A General History of Discoveries, edited by P. N. Furbank. Vol. IV of *Writings on Travel, Discovery and History by Daniel Defoe*, edited by W. R. Owens and P. N. Furbank, London: Pickering & Chatto, 2001.

The Great Law of Subordination Consider'd, edited by J. A. Downie. Vol. VI of *Religious and Didactic Writings of Daniel Defoe*, edited by W. R. Owens and P. N. Furbank, London: Pickering & Chatto, 2007.

The History and Remarkable Life of the Truly Honourable Col. Jacque, edited by Maurice Hindle. Vol. VIII of *The Novels of Daniel Defoe*, edited by W. R. Owens and P. N. Furbank, London: Pickering & Chatto, 2009.

Jure Divino, edited by P. N. Furbank. Vol. II of *Satire, Fantasy and Writings on the Supernatural by Daniel Defoe*, edited by W. R. Owens and P. N. Furbank, London: Pickering & Chatto, 2003.

The Letters of Daniel Defoe, edited by George Harris Healey, Oxford: Clarendon Press, 1955.

The Life, Adventures, and Pyracies, of the Famous Captain Singleton, edited by P. N. Furbank. Vol. V of *The Novels of Daniel Defoe*, edited by W. R. Owens and P. N. Furbank, London: Pickering & Chatto, 2008.

The Life and Strange Surprizing Adventures of Robinson Crusoe, edited by W. R. Owens. Vol. I of *The Novels of Daniel Defoe*, edited by W. R. Owens and P. N. Furbank, London: Pickering & Chatto, 2008.

Moll Flanders, edited by G. A. Starr, London: Oxford University Press, 1971.

A New Voyage round the World, edited by John McVeagh. Vol. X of *The Novels of Daniel Defoe*, edited by W. R. Owens and P. N. Furbank, London: Pickering & Chatto, 2009.

A Plan of the English Commerce, edited by John McVeagh. Vol. VII of *Political and Economic Writings of Daniel Defoe*, edited by W. R. Owens and P. N. Furbank, London: Pickering & Chatto, 2000.

The Political History of the Devil, edited by John Mullan. Vol. VI of *Satire, Fantasy and Writings on the Supernatural by Daniel Defoe*, edited by W. R. Owen and P. N. Furbank, London: Pickering & Chatto, 2005.

Religious Courtship, edited by G. A. Starr. Vol. IV of *Religious and Didactic Writings of Daniel Defoe*, edited by W. R. Owens and P. N. Furbank, London: Pickering & Chatto, 2006.

Serious Reflections during the Life and Surprising Adventures of Robinson Crusoe, edited by G. A. Starr. Vol. III of *The Novels of Daniel Defoe*, edited by W. R. Owens and P. N. Furbank, London: Pickering & Chatto, 2008.

A Tour thro' the Whole Island of Great Britain, edited by John McVeagh. Vols. I–III of *Writings on Travel, Discovery and History by Daniel Defoe*, edited by W. R. Owens and P. N. Furbank, London: Pickering & Chatto, 2001.

The True-Born Englishman and Other Poems, edited by W. R. Owens. Vol. I of *Satire, Fantasy and Writings on the Supernatural by Daniel Defoe*, edited by W. R. Owens and P. N. Furbank, London: Pickering & Chatto, 2003.

The Two Great Questions Considered, edited by P. N. Furbank. Vol. v of *Political and Economic Writings of Daniel Defoe*, edited by W. R. Owens and P. N. Furbank, London: Pickering & Chatto, 2000.

Dharwadker, Aparna, "Nation, Race, and the Ideology of Commerce in Defoe," *The Eighteenth Century: Theory and Interpretation*, 39 (spring 1998): 63–84.

Documents Relative to the Colonial History of New York, edited by Edmund B. O'Callaghan and Berthold Fernow, 15 vols., Albany, NY: Weed, Parsons, 1853–1887.

Dollerup, Cay, "Does the Chronology of *Moll Flanders* Tell Us Something about Defoe's Method of Writing?" *English Studies*, 53 (June 1972): 234–235.

Dowdey, Clifford, *The Virginia Dynasties: The Emergence of 'King' Carter and the Golden Age*, Boston, Mass.: Little, Brown, 1969.

Downie, J. A., "Defoe, Imperialism, and Travel Books Reconsidered," in Roger D. Lund (ed.), *Critical Essays on Daniel Defoe*, New York: G. K. Hall, 1997, pp. 78–96.

"*Robinson Crusoe*'s Eighteenth-Century Contexts," in Lieve Spaas and Brian Stimpson (eds.), *Robinson Crusoe: Myths and Metamorphoses*, New York: St. Martin's, 1996, pp. 13–27.

Dunn, Richard S., "Servants and Slaves: The Recruitment and Employment of Labor," in Jack P. Greene and J. R. Pole (eds.), *Colonial British America: Essays in the New History of the Early Modern Era*, Baltimore, Md.: Johns Hopkins University Press, 1984, pp. 157–194.

Sugar and Slaves: The Rise of the Planter Class in the English West Indies, 1624–1713, New York: Norton, 1972.

Durand, of Dauphiné, *A Huguenot Exile in Virginia*, New York: Press of the Pioneers, 1934.

Durston, Gregory, *Moll Flanders: An Analysis of an Eighteenth-Century Criminal Biography*, Chichester: Barry Rose, 1997.

Earle, Carville V., *The Evolution of a Tidewater Settlement System: All Hallow's Parish, Maryland, 1650–1783*, Chicago, Ill.: University of Chicago Press, 1975.

Earle, Peter, *The World of Defoe*, New York: Atheneum, 1977.

Ebersole, Gary L., *Captured by Texts: Puritan to Postmodern Images of Indian Captivity*, Charlottesville, Va.: University Press of Virginia, 1995.

Eddis, William, *Letters from America*, edited by Aubrey C. Land, Cambridge, Mass.: Belknap Press, 1969.

Edmundson, Frank B., and Emerson B. Roberts, "John Edmundson – Large Merchant of Tred Haven Creek," *Maryland Historical Magazine*, 50 (September 1955): 219–233.

Ekirch, A. Roger, *Bound for America: The Transportation of British Convicts to the Colonies, 1718–1775*, Oxford: Clarendon Press, 1987.

Faller, Lincoln B., *Crime and Defoe: A New Kind of Writing*, Cambridge: Cambridge University Press, 1993.

Fischer, David Hackett, and James C. Kelly, *Bound Away: Virginia and the Westward Movement*, Charlottesville, Va.: University of Virginia Press, 2000.

Fishman, Burton J., "Defoe, Herman Moll, and the Geography of South America," *Huntington Library Quarterly*, 36 (May 1973): 227–238.

Fitzhugh, William, *William Fitzhugh and His Chesapeake World, 1676–1701*, edited by Richard Beale Davis, Chapel Hill, NC: University of North Carolina Press, 1963.

Fleetwood, William, *A Sermon Preached before the Society for the Propagation of the Gospel ... the 16th of February 1710/11*, London, 1711.

Flynn, Carol Houlihan, *The Body in Swift and Defoe*, Cambridge: Cambridge University Press, 1990.

Foley, A. M., and Freddie T. Waller, *Elliott's Island: The Land that Time Forgot*, Salisbury, Md.: Dogwood Ridge, 1999.

Force, Peter (ed.), *Tracts and Other Papers, Relating Principally to the Origin, Settlement, and Progress of the Colonies in North America*, 4 vols., 1836. Reprint, Gloucester, Mass.: Peter Smith, 1963.

Franklin, Benjamin, *Benjamin Franklin: Writings*, edited by J. A. Leo Lemay, New York: Library of America, 1987.

Furbank, P. N., and W. R. Owens, *The Canonisation of Daniel Defoe*, New Haven, Conn.: Yale University Press, 1988.

Galenson, David W., "Economic Aspects of the Growth of Slavery in the Seventeenth-Century Chesapeake," in Barbara L. Solow (ed.), *Slavery and the Rise of the Atlantic System*, Cambridge: Cambridge University Press, 1991, pp. 265–292.

"'Middling People' or 'Common Sort'? The Social Origins of Some Early Americans Reexamined," *William and Mary Quarterly*, 35 (July 1978): 499–524.

White Servitude in Colonial America: An Economic Analysis, Cambridge: Cambridge University Press, 1981.

Games, Alison, *Migration and the Origins of the English Atlantic World*, Cambridge, Mass.: Harvard University Press, 1999.

Gibson, Edmund, *Two Letters of the Bishop of London, the First, to the Masters and Mistresses of Families in the English Plantations Abroad; ... The Second, to the Missionaries There*, London, 1727.

Godwyn, Morgan, *The Negro's & Indian's Advocate, Suing for Their Admission into the Church*, London, 1680.

Goodwin, Gerald J., "Christianity, Civilization, and the Savage: The Anglican Mission to the American Indian," *Historical Magazine of the Protestant Episcopal Church*, 42 (June 1973): 93–110.

Graham, Michael, "Meeting House and Chapel: Religion and Community in Seventeenth-Century Maryland," in Lois Green Carr, Philip D. Morgan, and Jean B. Russo (eds.), *Colonial Chesapeake Society*, Chapel Hill, NC: University of North Carolina Press, 1988, pp. 242–274.

Gray, Lewis Cecil, *History of Agriculture in the Southern United States to 1860*, 2 vols., 1933. Reprint, Gloucester, Mass.: Peter Smith, 1958.

Gray, Robert, *A Good Speed to Virginia*, London, 1609.

Green, Martin, *Dreams of Adventure, Deeds of Empire*, New York: Basic Books, 1979.

Green, William, *The Sufferings of William Green: Being a Sorrowful Account, of His Seven Years Transportation*, London, 1774.

Greene, Jack P., *The Intellectual Construction of America: Exceptionalism and Identity from 1492 to 1800*, Chapel Hill, NC: University of North Carolina Press, 1993.

   Pursuits of Happiness: The Social Development of Early Modern British Colonies and the Formation of American Culture, Chapel Hill, NC: University of North Carolina Press, 1988.

Greene, Jack P., and J. R. Pole (eds.), *Colonial British America: Essays in the New History of the Early Modern Era*, Baltimore, Md.: Johns Hopkins University Press, 1984.

Grubb, Farley, "Fatherless and Friendless: Factors Influencing the Flow of English Emigrant Servants," *Journal of Economic History*, 52 (March 1992): 85–108.

Hakluyt, Richard, *The Original Writings and Correspondence of the Two Richard Hakluyts*, edited by E. G. R. Taylor, 2 vols., London: Hakluyt Society, 1935.

Hammond, John, *Leah and Rachel; or, The Two Faithful Sisters Virginia and Mary-land,* in Clayton Colman Hall (ed.), *Narratives of Early Maryland*, New York: Charles Scribner's Sons, 1925, pp. 279–308.

Harrower, John, *The Journal of John Harrower: An Indentured Servant in the Colony of Virginia, 1773–1776*, edited by Edward Miles Riley, New York: Holt, Rinehart & Winston, 1963.

Harvey, E. Ruth, *The Inward Wits: Psychological Theory in the Middle Ages and the Renaissance*, London: Warburg Institute, 1975.

Haskell, Rosemary Anne, "The Antagonistic Structure of the Colonial Experience in Five Novels of Daniel Defoe: A Question of Struggle and Identity," Ph.D. dissertation, University of North Carolina, Chapel Hill, 1985.

Hatfield, April Lee, *Atlantic Virginia: Intercolonial Relations in the Seventeenth Century*, Philadelphia, Pa.: University of Pennsylvania Press, 2004.

Hazard, Ebenezer, "Ebenezer Hazard's Travels through Maryland in 1777," edited by Fred Shelley, *Maryland Historical Magazine*, 46 (March 1951): 44–54.

Heidenreich, Helmut, *The Libraries of Daniel Defoe and Phillips Farewell*, Berlin: Hildebrand, 1970.

Hellier, Thomas, *The Vain Prodigal Life and Tragical Penitent Death of Thomas Hellier,* in "Motive for Murder: A Servant's Life in Virginia," edited by T. H. Breen, James H. Lewis, and Keith Schlesinger, *William and Mary Quarterly*, 40 (January 1983): 106–120.

Hening, William Waller, *Statutes at Large: Being a Collection of All the Laws of Virginia*, 13 vols., Richmond, Va.: Samuel Pleasants, 1809–1823.

Herrick, C. A., *White Servitude in Pennsylvania: Indentured and Redemption Labor in Colony and Commonwealth*, Philadelphia, Pa.: John Joseph McVey, 1926.

Horn, James, "Adapting to a New World: A Comparative Study of Local Society in England and America, 1650–1700," in Lois Green Carr, Philip D. Morgan, and Jean B. Russo (eds.), *Colonial Chesapeake Society*, Chapel Hill, NC: University of North Carolina Press, 1988, pp. 133–175.

Adapting to a New World: English Society in the Seventeenth-Century Chesapeake, Chapel Hill, NC: University of North Carolina Press, 1994.

"British Diaspora: Emigration from Britain, 1680–1815," in William Roger Louis (ed.), *The Oxford History of the British Empire*, 5 vols., Oxford: Oxford University Press, 1998, vol. II, pp. 28–52.

"Moving On in the New World: Migration and Out-Migration in the Seventeenth-Century Chesapeake," in Peter Clark and David Souden (eds.), *Migration and Society in Early Modern England*, Totowa, NJ: Barnes and Noble, 1988, pp. 172–212.

"Servant Emigration to the Chesapeake in the Seventeenth Century," in Thad W. Tate and David L. Ammerman (eds.), *The Chesapeake in the Seventeenth Century: Essays on Anglo-American Society*, Chapel Hill, NC: University of North Carolina Press, 1979, pp. 51–95.

Hubbard, William, *The History of the Indian Wars in New England*, edited by Samuel Drake, 1865. Reprint, New York: Kraus, 1969.

Hulme, Peter, *Colonial Encounters: Europe and the Native Caribbean, 1492–1797*, London: Methuen, 1986.

Hunter, J. Paul, *The Reluctant Pilgrim: Defoe's Emblematic Method and Quest for Form in Robinson Crusoe*, Baltimore, Md.: Johns Hopkins University Press, 1966.

Hutcheson, Francis, *A Short Introduction to Moral Philosophy*, Glasgow, 1753.

Isaac, Rhys, *The Transformation of Virginia, 1740–1790*, Chapel Hill, NC: University of North Carolina Press, 1982.

Jack, Jane H., "*A New Voyage round the World*: Defoe's *Roman à Thèse*," *Huntington Library Quarterly*, 24 (August 1961): 323–336.

Jager, Eric, "The Parrot's Voice: Language and the Self in *Robinson Crusoe*," *Eighteenth-Century Studies*, 21 (spring 1988): 316–333.

Jennings, Francis, *The Ambiguous Iroquois Empire: The Covenant Chain Confederation of Indian Tribes with English Colonies from Its Beginnings to the Lancaster Treaty*, New York: Norton, 1984.

Johnson, C. A., "Two Mistakes of Geography in *Moll Flanders*," *Notes and Queries*, 207 (December 1962): 455.

Johnson, Robert, *Nova Britannia*, in Peter Force (ed.), *Tracts and Other Papers, Relating Principally to the Origin, Settlement, and Progress of the Colonies in North America*, 4 vols., 1836. Reprint, Gloucester, Mass.: Peter Smith, 1963, vol. I, no. 6, pp. 3–28.

Jones, Howard Mumford, "The Colonial Impulse: An Analysis of the 'Promotion' Literature of Colonization," *Proceedings of the American Philosophical Society*, 90 (May 1946): 131–161.

Jones, Revd Hugh, "Maryland in 1699: A Letter from the Reverend Hugh Jones," edited by Michael G. Kammen, *Journal of Southern History*, 29 (August 1963): 362–372.

Jones, Hugh, *The Present State of Virginia, from Whence Is Inferred a Short View of Maryland and North Carolina*, edited by Richard L. Morton, Chapel Hill, NC: University of North Carolina Press, 1956.

Jordan, David W., "Political Stability and the Emergence of a Native Elite in Maryland," in Thad W. Tate and David L. Ammerman (eds.), *The Chesapeake in the Seventeenth Century: Essays on Anglo-American Society*, Chapel Hill, NC: University of North Carolina Press, 1979, pp. 243–273.

Jordan, Winthrop D., *White over Black: American Attitudes toward the Negro, 1550–1812*, Chapel Hill, NC: University of North Carolina Press, 1968.

Kaminknow, Marion, and Jack Kaminknow, *Original Lists of Emigrants in Bondage from London to the American Colonies, 1719–1744*, Baltimore, Md.: Magna Carta, 1967.

Kaplan, Richard Paul, "Daniel Defoe's Views on Slavery and Racial Prejudice," Ph.D. dissertation, New York University, 1970.

Keane, Patrick J., "Slavery and the Slave Trade: Crusoe as Defoe's Representative," in Roger D. Lund (ed.), *Critical Essays on Daniel Defoe*, New York: G. K. Hall, 1997, pp. 97–120.

Kellaway, William, *The New England Company, 1649–1776: Missionary Society to the American Indians*, London: Longmans, Green, 1961.

Kennett, White, *A Sermon Preach'd before the Society for the Propagation of the Gospel ... the 15th of February 1711/12*, London, 1712.

Kimber, Edward, *The History of the Life and Adventures of Mr. Anderson*, 1754. Reprint, New York: Garland, 1975.

Klingberg, Frank J., *Anglican Humanitarianism in Colonial New York*, 1940. Reprint, Freeport, NY: Books for Libraries Press, 1971.

"The Indian Frontier in South Carolina as Seen by the S.P.G. Missionary," *The Journal of Southern History*, 5 (February–November 1939): 479–500.

Knox-Shaw, Peter, "Defoe and the Politics of Representing the African Interior," *Modern Language Review*, 96 (October 2001): 937–951.

Krier, William J., "'A Courtesy which Grants Integrity': A Literal Reading of *Moll Flanders*," *ELH*, 38 (September 1971): 397–410.

Kulikoff, Allan, *Tobacco and Slaves: The Development of Southern Cultures in the Chesapeake, 1680–1800*, Chapel Hill, NC: University of North Carolina Press, 1986.

Kupperman, Karen Ordahl, *Indians and English: Facing Off in Early America*, Ithaca, NY: Cornell University Press, 2000.

Lancaster, R. Kent, "Almost Chattel: The Lives of Indentured Servants at Hampton-Northampton, Baltimore County," *Maryland Historical Magazine*, 94 (fall 1999): 341–363.

Land, Aubrey C., "Economic Base and Social Structure: The Northern Chesapeake in the Eighteenth Century," *Journal of Economic History*, 25 (December 1965): 639–654.

Land, Aubrey C., Lois Green Carr, and Edward C. Papenfuse (eds.), *Law, Society, and Politics in Early Maryland*, Baltimore, Md.: Johns Hopkins University Press, 1977.

Langston, Anthony, "Anthony Langston on Towns, and Corporations; and on the Manufacture of Iron," *William and Mary Quarterly*, 2nd ser., 1 (April 1921): 100–106.

Lawson, John, *A New Voyage to Carolina*, edited by Hugh Talmage Lefler, Chapel Hill, NC: University of North Carolina Press, 1984.

Lefler, Hugh T., "Promotional Literature of the Southern Colonies," *Journal of Southern History*, 33 (February 1967): 3–25.

Le Jau, Francis, *The Carolina Chronicle of Dr. Francis Le Jau, 1706–1717*, edited by Frank J. Klingberg, Berkeley, Calif.: University of California Press, 1956.

Ligon, Richard, *A True & Exact History of the Island of Barbadoes*, London, 1673.

Locke, John, *Some Thoughts Concerning Education*, edited by John W. Yolton and Jean S. Yolton, Oxford: Clarendon Press, 1989.

Louis, William Roger (ed.), *The Oxford History of the British Empire*, 5 vols., Oxford: Oxford University Press, 1998.

Lund, Roger D., *Critical Essays on Daniel Defoe*, New York: G. K. Hall, 1997.

Maddox, James, "On Defoe's *Roxana*," in Roger D. Lund (ed.), *Critical Essays on Daniel Defoe*, New York: G. K. Hall, 1997, pp. 266–284.

Main, Gloria, "Maryland and the Chesapeake Economy, 1670–1720," in Aubrey C. Land, Lois Green Carr, and Edward C. Papenfuse (eds.), *Law, Society, and Politics in Early Maryland*, Baltimore, Md.: Johns Hopkins University Press, 1977, pp. 134–152.

  Tobacco Colony: Life in Early Maryland, Princeton, NJ: Princeton University Press, 1982.

Maltby, William S., *The Black Legend in England: The Development of Anti-Spanish Sentiment, 1558–1660*, Durham, NC: Duke University Press, 1971.

Markley, Robert, "'So Inexhaustible a Treasure of Gold': Defoe, Capitalism, and the Romance of the South Seas," *Eighteenth-Century Life*, 18 (November 1994): 148–167.

Martyn, Benjamin, *An Impartial Inquiry into the State and Utility of the Province of Georgia*, London, 1741.

  Reasons for Establishing the Colony of Georgia, in Trevor R. Reese (ed.), *The Most Delightful Country of the Universe: Promotional Literature of the Colony of Georgia, 1717–1734*, Savannah, Ga.: Beehive Press, 1972, pp. 159–195.

McAllister, James A. (comp.), *Abstracts from the Land Records of Dorchester County, Maryland*, 2 vols., Lewes, Del.: Delmarva Roots, 1960.

McCormac, Eugene Irving, *White Servitude in Maryland, 1634–1820*, Baltimore, Md.: Johns Hopkins University Press, 1904.

McInelly, Brett C., "Expanding Empires, Expanding Selves: Colonialism, the Novel, and Robinson Crusoe," *Studies in the Novel*, 35 (spring 2003): 1–21.

McVeagh, John, "Defoe and Far Travel," in John McVeagh (ed.), *All before Them: Attitudes to Abroad in English Literature, 1660–1780*, Atlantic Highlands, NJ: Ashfield, 1989, pp. 115–126.

Meier, Thomas Keith, *Defoe and the Defense of Commerce*, Victoria, BC: English Literary Studies, University of Victoria, 1987.

Menard, Russell R., "British Migration to the Chesapeake Colonies in the Seventeenth Century," in Lois Green Carr, Philip D. Morgan, and Jean B. Russo (eds.), *Colonial Chesapeake Society*, Chapel Hill, NC: University of North Carolina Press, 1988, pp. 99–132.

"*Economy and Society in Early Colonial Maryland*," Ph.D. dissertation, University of Iowa, 1975.

"Farm Prices of Maryland Tobacco, 1659–1710," *Maryland Historical Magazine*, 68 (spring 1973): 80–85.

"From Servants to Slaves: The Transformation of the Chesapeake Labor System," *Journal of Southern Studies*, 16 (winter 1977): 355–390.

"From Servant to Freeholder: Status Mobility and Property Accumulation in Seventeenth-Century Maryland," *William and Mary Quarterly*, 30 (January 1973): 37–64.

"Immigrants and Their Increase: The Process of Population Growth in Early Colonial Maryland," in Aubrey C. Land, Lois Green Carr, and Edward C. Papenfuse (eds.), *Law, Society, and Politics in Early Maryland*, Baltimore, Md.: Johns Hopkins University Press, 1977, pp. 88–110.

"The Tobacco Industry in the Chesapeake Colonies, 1617–1730: An Interpretation," *Research in Economic History*, 5 (1980): 109–177.

Menard, Russell R., and Lois Green Carr, "The Lords Baltimore and the Colonization of Maryland," in David B. Quinn (ed.), *Early Maryland in a Wider World*, Detroit, Mich.: Wayne State University, 1982, pp. 167–216.

Menard, Russell R., P. M. G. Harris, and Lois Green Carr, "Opportunity and Inequality: The Distribution of Wealth on the Lower Western Shore of Maryland, 1638–1705," *Maryland Historical Magazine*, 69 (summer 1974): 169–184.

Middleton, Arthur, *Tobacco Coast: A Maritime History of Chesapeake Bay in the Colonial World*, Newport News, Va.: Mariners' Museum, 1953.

Moore, John Robert, *Daniel Defoe: Citizen of the Modern World*, Chicago, Ill.: University of Chicago Press, 1958.

"Defoe and the South Sea Company," *Boston Public Library Quarterly*, 5 (October 1953): 175–188.

Moraley, William, *The Infortunate: The Voyage and Adventures of William Moraley, an Indentured Servant*, 2nd edn, edited by Susan E. Klepp and Billy G. Smith, University Park, Pa.: Pennsylvania State University Press, 2005.

Moray, Alexander, "Letters Written by Mr. Moray, a Minister to Sr. R. Moray, from Ware River in Mock-Jack Bay, Virginia, Feb. 1, 1665," *William and Mary Quarterly*, 2nd ser., 2 (July 1922): 157–160.

Morgan, Edmund S., *American Slavery, American Freedom: The Ordeal of Colonial Virginia*, New York: Norton, 1975.

Morgan, Gwenda, and Peter Rushton, *Eighteenth-Century Criminal Transportation: The Formation of the Criminal Atlantic*, New York: Palgrave Macmillan, 2004.

Morgan, Kenneth, "Convict Runaways in Maryland, 1745–1775," *Journal of American Studies*, 23 (August 1989): 253–268.

"English and American Attitudes towards Convict Transportation, 1718–1775," *History*, 72 (October 1987): 416–431.

Slavery and Servitude in Colonial North America: A Short History, New York: New York University Press, 2001.

Morgan, Philip D., *Slave Counterpoint: Black Culture in the Eighteenth-Century Chesapeake and Lowcountry*, Chapel Hill, NC: University of North Carolina Press, 1998.

Morris, Richard B., *Government and Labor in Early America*, New York: Columbia University Press, 1946.

Morriss, Margaret Shove, *Colonial Trade of Maryland, 1689–1715*, Baltimore, Md.: Johns Hopkins University Press, 1914.

Mountgomery, Robert, *A Discourse Concerning the Design'd Establishment of a New Colony*, in Trevor R. Reese (ed.), *The Most Delightful Country of the Universe: Promotional Literature of the Colony of Georgia, 1717–1734*, Savannah, Ga.: Beehive Press, 1972, pp. 3–31.

Mowbray, Calvin W., and Mary I. Mowbray, *The Early Settlers of Dorchester County and Their Lands*, 2 vols., Westminster, Md.: Willow Bend Books, 2000.

Muchel, Francis Louis, "Report of the Journey of Francis Louis Muchel from Berne, Switzerland, to Virginia, October 2, 1701–December 1, 1702," edited and translated by William J. Hinke, *Virginia Magazine of History and Biography*, 24 (April 1916): 113–141.

Nairne, Thomas, *Letter from South Carolina*, in Jack P. Greene (ed.), *Selling a New World: Two Colonial South Carolina Promotional Pamphlets*, Columbia, SC: University of South Carolina Press, 1989, pp. 33–73.

Nelson, John Kendall, "Anglican Missions in America, 1701–1725: A Study of the Society for the Propagation of the Gospel in Foreign Parts," Ph.D. dissertation, Northwestern University, 1962.

Nelson, T. G. A., "Incest in the Early Novel and Related Genres," *Eighteenth-Century Life*, 16 (February 1992): 127–162.

Novak, Maximillian, *Daniel Defoe: Master of Fictions*, Oxford: Oxford University Press, 2001.

   Defoe and the Nature of Man, Oxford: Oxford University Press, 1963.

   Economics and the Fiction of Daniel Defoe, 1962. Reprint, New York: Russell & Russell, 1976.

Oatis, Steven J., *A Colonial Complex: South Carolina's Frontiers in the Era of the Yamasee War, 1680–1730*, Lincoln, Nebr.: University of Nebraska Press, 2004.

Oberg, Michael Leroy, *Dominion and Civility: English Imperialism and Native America, 1585–1685*, Ithaca, NY: Cornell University Press, 2000.

O'Brien, John, "Union Jack, Amnesia and the Law in Daniel Defoe's *Colonel Jack*," *Eighteenth-Century Studies*, 32 (fall 1998): 65–82.

Oglethorpe, James, *A New and Accurate Account of the Provinces of South Carolina and Georgia*, in Trevor R. Reese (ed.), *The Most Delightful Country of the Universe: Promotional Literature of the Colony of Georgia, 1717–1734*, Savannah, Ga.: Beehive Press, 1972, pp. 115–156.

Oldmixon, John, *The British Empire in America*, 2 vols., 1741. Reprint, New York: Augustus M. Kelley, 1969.

Pagden, Anthony, *Lords of All the World: Ideologies of Empire in Spain, Britain, and France, c. 1500–c. 1800*, New Haven, Conn.: Yale University Press, 1995.

Papenfuse, Edward C., and Joseph M. Coale III, *The Hammond-Harwood House Atlas of Historical Maps of Maryland, 1608–1908*, Baltimore, Md.: Johns Hopkins University Press, 1982.

Parent, Anthony S., Jr., *Foul Means: The Formation of a Slave Society in Virginia, 1660–1740*, Chapel Hill, NC: University of North Carolina Press, 2003.

Pascoe, C. F., *Two Hundred Years of the S.P.G.: An Historical Account of the Society for the Propagation of the Gospel in Foreign Parts*, 2 vols., London: Society for the Propagation of the Gospel, 1901.

Patterson, Orlando, *Slavery and Social Death: A Comparative Study*, Cambridge, Mass.: Harvard University Press, 1982.

Pennington, Loren E., "The Amerindian in English Promotional Literature, 1575–1625," in K. R. Andrews, N. P. Canny, and P. E. H. Hair (eds.), *The Westward Enterprise: English Activities in Ireland, the Atlantic, and America, 1480–1650*, Detroit, Mich.: Wayne State University Press, 1979, pp. 175–194.

Perry, William Stevens, *Historical Collections Relating to the American Colonial Church*, 5 vols. Reprint, New York: AMS Press, 1969.

Pocock, J. G. A., "The Classical Theory of Deference," *American Historical Review*, 81 (June 1976): 516–523.

Pollak, Ellen, *Incest and the English Novel, 1684–1814*, Baltimore, Md.: Johns Hopkins University Press, 2003.

Ralegh, Walter, Sir, *The Discoverie of the Large, Rich and Bewtiful Empyre of Guiana*, edited by Neil Whitehead, Manchester: Manchester University Press, 1998.

Ramsey, William L., *The Yamasee War: A Study of Culture, Economy, and Conflict in the Colonial South*, Lincoln, Nebr.: University of Nebraska Press, 2008.

Rawlins, John, *The Famous and Wonderful Recovery of a Ship of Bristol, Called the Exchange, from the Turkish Pirates of Argier*, in Daniel J. Vitkus (ed.), *Piracy, Slavery, and Redemption: Barbary Captivity Narratives from Early Modern England*, New York: Columbia University Press, 2001, pp. 96–120.

Rawson, Claude, *God, Gulliver, and Genocide: Barbarism and the European Imagination, 1492–1945*, Oxford: Oxford University Press, 2001.

Reavis, William A., "The Maryland Gentry and Social Mobility, 1637–1676," *William and Mary Quarterly*, 14 (July 1957): 418–428.

Reese, Trevor R., *The Most Delightful Country of the Universe: Promotional Literature of the Colony of Georgia, 1717–1734*, Savannah, Ga.: Beehive Press, 1972.

Reps, John W., *Tidewater Towns: City Planning in Colonial Virginia and Maryland*, Williamsburg, Va.: Colonial Williamsburg Foundation, 1972.

Revel, James, "The Poor Unhappy Transported Felon's Sorrowful Account of his Fourteen Years Transportation, at Virginia, in America," *Virginia Magazine of History and Biography*, 56 (April 1948): 180–194.

Richetti, John, *Defoe's Narratives: Situations and Structures*, Oxford: Clarendon Press, 1975.

The Life of Daniel Defoe, Oxford: Blackwell, 2005.

Richter, Daniel K., *The Ordeal of the Longhouse: The Peoples of the Iroquois League in the Era of European Colonization*, Chapel Hill, NC: University of North Carolina Press, 1992.

Roach, Joseph, *Cities of the Dead: Circum-Atlantic Performance*, New York: Columbia University Press, 1996.

Roberts, David, "Introduction," in Daniel Defoe, Colonel Jack, Oxford: Oxford University Press, 1989.

Roberts, William, "The Letters of William Roberts of All Hallows Parish, Anne Arundel County, Maryland, 1756–1769," edited by James Horn, *Maryland Historical Magazine*, 74 (June 1979): 117–132.

Rochefort, Charles de, *The History of the Caribby-Islands*, translated by John Davies, London, 1666.

Roundtree, Helen C., and Thomas E. Davidson, *Eastern Shore Indians of Virginia and Maryland*, Charlottesville, Va.: University Press of Virginia 1997.

Rowlandson, Mary, *The Sovereignty and Goodness of God, Together with the Faithfulness of His Promises Displayed*, in Alden T. Vaughan and Edward W. Clark (eds.), *Puritans among the Indians: Accounts of Captivity and Redemption, 1676–1724*, Cambridge: Cambridge University Press, 1981, pp. 29–76.

Rozbicki, Michael J., *The Complete Colonial Gentleman: Cultural Legitimacy in Plantation America*, Charlottesville, Va.: University Press of Virginia, 1998.

Transformation of the English Cultural Ethos in Colonial America: Maryland, 1634–1730, New York: University Press of America, 1988.

Rummell, Katheryn, "Defoe and the Black Legend: The Spanish Stereotype in *A New Voyage round the World*," *Rocky Mountain Review of Language and Literature*, 52 (fall 1998): 13–28.

Rundle, Thomas, *A Sermon ... to Recommend the Charity for Establishing the New Colony of Georgia*, in Trevor R. Reese (ed.), *The Most Delightful Country of the Universe: Promotional Literature of the Colony of Georgia, 1717–1734*, Savannah, Ga.: Beehive Press, 1972, pp. 199–213.

Russo, Jean B., "Self-Sufficiency and Local Exchange: Free Craftsmen in the Rural Chesapeake Economy," in Lois Green Carr, Philip D. Morgan, and Jean B. Russo (eds.), *Colonial Chesapeake Society*, Chapel Hill, NC: University of North Carolina Press, 1988, pp. 389–432.

Rutman, Darrett B., and Anita H. Rutman, "'More True and Perfect Lists': The Reconstruction of Censuses for Middlesex County, Virginia, 1668–1704," *Virginia Magazine of History and Biography*, 88 (January 1980): 37–74.

A Place in Time: Middlesex County, Virginia, 1650–1750, New York: Norton, 1984.

Salinger, Sharon V., "Labor, Markets, and Opportunity: Indentured Servitude in Early America," *Labor History*, 38 (spring–summer 1997): 311–338.

Schlenther, Boyd Stanley, "Religious Faith and Commercial Empire," in William Roger Louis (ed.), *The Oxford History of the British Empire*, 5 vols., Oxford: Oxford University Press, 1998, vol. II, pp. 128–149.

Schonhorn, Manuel, *Defoe's Politics: Parliament, Power, Kingship and* Robinson Crusoe, Cambridge: Cambridge University Press, 1991.

Secker, Thomas, *A Sermon Preached before the Incorporated Society for the Propagation of the Gospel ... February 20, 1740–1*, London, 1741.

Seed, Patricia, *American Pentimento: The Invention of the Indians and the Pursuit of Riches*, Minneapolis, Minn.: University of Minnesota Press, 2001.

Sergeant, John, *A Letter from the Revd Mr. Sergeant of Stockbridge, to Dr. Colman of Boston*, Boston, 1743.

Shammas, Carole, "English-Born and Creole Elite in Turn-of-the-Century Virginia," in Thad W. Tate and David L. Ammerman (eds.), *The Chesapeake in the Seventeenth Century: Essays on Anglo-American Society*, Chapel Hill, NC: University of North Carolina Press, 1979, pp. 274–296.

Sheehan, Bernard W., *Savagism and Civility: Indians and Englishmen in Colonial Virginia*, Cambridge: Cambridge University Press, 1980.

Shields, David S., *Oracles of Empire: Poetry, Politics, and Commerce in British America, 1690–1750*, Chicago, Ill.: University of Chicago Press, 1990.

Shinagel, Michael, *Daniel Defoe and Middle-Class Gentility*, Cambridge, Mass.: Harvard University Press, 1968.

Sill, Geoffrey, *The Cure of the Passions and the Origin of the English Novel*, Cambridge: Cambridge University Press, 2001.

Slotkin, Richard, *Regeneration through Violence: The Mythology of the American Frontier, 1660–1860*, 1973. Reprint, New York: HarperCollins, 1996.

Smith, Abbot Emerson, *Colonists in Bondage: White Servitude and Convict Labor in America, 1607–1776*, Chapel Hill, NC: University of North Carolina Press, 1947.

Snader, Joe, *Caught between Worlds: British Captivity Narratives in Fact and Fiction*, Lexington, Ky.: The University Press of Kentucky, 2000.

Sobel, Mechal, *The World They Made Together: Black and White Values in Eighteenth-Century Virginia*, Princeton, NJ: Princeton University Press, 1987.

Sosin, J. M., *English America and the Restoration Monarchy of Charles II: Transatlantic Politics, Commerce, and Kinship*, Lincoln, Nebr.: University of Nebraska Press, 1980.

Souden, James David, "'Rogues, Whores and Vagabonds'? Indentured Servant Emigrants to North America, and the Case of Mid-Seventeenth-Century Bristol," *Social History*, 3 (January 1978): 23–41.

Spotswood, Alexander, *The Official Letters of Alexander Spotswood*, edited by R. A. Brock, 2 vols., Richmond, Va.: Virginia Historical Society, 1882–1885.

Starr, George A., *Defoe and Casuistry*, Princeton, NJ: Princeton University Press, 1971.

   Defoe and Spiritual Autobiography, Princeton, NJ: Princeton University Press, 1965.

   "Escape from Barbary: A Seventeenth-Century Genre," *Huntington Library Quarterly*, 29 (November 1965): 35–52.

Steele, I. K., *Politics of Colonial Policy: The Board of Trade in Colonial Administration, 1696–1720*, Oxford: Clarendon Press, 1968.

Strachey, William, *The Historie of Travell into Virginia Britania*, edited by Louis B. Wright and Virginia Freund, London: Hakluyt Society, 1953.

A True Reportory of the Wracke, and Redemption of Sir Thomas Gates Knight, in James Horn, *Captain John Smith: Writings with Other Narratives of Roanoke, Jamestown, and the First English Settlement of America,* New York: Library of America, 2007, pp. 979–1037.

Suarez, Michael F., S.J., "The Shortest Way to Heaven? Moll Flanders' Repentance Reconsidered," *1650–1850: Ideas, Aesthetics, and Inquiries in the Modern Era,* 3 (1997): 3–28.

Sutherland, James R., "Some Early Troubles of Daniel Defoe," *Review of English Studies,* 9 (July 1933): 275–290.

Sweeney, Kevin M., "High-Style Vernacular: Life Styles of the Colonial Elite," in Cary Carson, Ronald Hoffman, and Peter J. Albert (eds.), *Of Consuming Interests: The Style of Life in the Eighteenth Century,* Charlottesville, Va.: University Press of Virginia, 1994, pp. 1–58.

Tate, Thad W., *The Negro in Eighteenth-Century Williamsburg,* Charlottesville, Va.: University Press of Virginia, 1972.

Tate, Thad W., and David L. Ammerman, *The Chesapeake in the Seventeenth Century: Essays on Anglo-American Society,* Chapel Hill, NC: University of North Carolina Press, 1979.

Thomas, Gabriel, "An Historical and Geographical Account of Pensilvania and of West-New-Jersey," in Albert Cook Meyers (ed.), *Narratives of Early Pennsylvania, West New Jersey, and Delaware, 1630–1707,* New York: Charles Scribner's Sons, 1912, pp. 307–351.

Thompson, H. P., *Into All Lands: The History of the Society for the Propagation of the Gospel in Foreign Parts, 1701–1950,* London: Society for the Propagation of Christian Knowledge, 1951.

Thomas Bray, London: Society for the Propagation of Christian Knowledge, 1954.

Thompson, James, *Models of Value: Eighteenth-Century Political Economy and the Novel,* Durham, NC: Duke University Press, 1999.

Thorton, A. P., *West-India Policy under the Restoration,* Oxford: Clarendon Press, 1956.

Todorov, Tzvetan, *The Conquest of America: The Question of the Other,* translated by Richard Howard, Norman, Okla.: University of Oklahoma Press, 1999.

Torrence, Clayton, *Old Somerset on the Eastern Shore of Maryland: A Study in Foundations and Founders,* Richmond, Va.: Whittet & Shepperson, 1935.

Tryon, Thomas, *Friendly Advice to the Gentlemen-Planters of the East and West Indies,* London, 1684.

Tynley, Robert, *A Sermon Preached at the Spittle the 17 of Aprill 1609,* London, 1609.

Van Horne, John C. (ed.), *Religious Philanthropy and Colonial Slavery: The American Correspondence of the Associates of Dr. Bray, 1717–1777,* Urbana, Ill.: University of Illinois Press, 1985.

Vaughan, Alden T., and Edward W. Clark (eds.), *Puritans among the Indians: Accounts of Captivity and Redemption, 1676–1724,* Cambridge: Cambridge University Press, 1981.

Vincent, Philip, *A True Relation of the Late Battle Fought in New England*, 1637. Reprint, Norwood, NJ: Walter J. Johnson, 1974.

Virginia's Cure; or, An Advisive Narrative Concerning Virginia, in Peter Force (ed.), *Tracts and Other Papers, Relating Principally to the Origin, Settlement, and Progress of the Colonies in North America*, 4 vols., 1836. Reprint, Gloucester, Mass.: Peter Smith, 1963, vol. III, no. 15, pp. 3–19.

Waddington, Edward, *A Sermon Preached before the Society for the Propagation of the Gospel … Friday the 17th of February*, London, 1721.

Walsh, Lorena S., "Charles County, Maryland, 1658–1705: A Study of Chesapeake Social and Political Structure," Ph.D. dissertation, Michigan State University, 1977.

"Community Networks in the Early Chesapeake," in Lois Green Carr, Philip D. Morgan, and Jean B. Russo (eds.), *Colonial Chesapeake Society*, Chapel Hill, NC: University of North Carolina Press, 1988, pp. 200–241.

"Plantation Management in the Chesapeake, 1620–1820," *Journal of Economic History*, 49 (June 1989): 393–406.

"Servitude and Opportunity in Charles County, Maryland, 1658–1705," in Aubrey C. Land, Lois Green Carr, and Edward C. Papenfuse (eds.), *Law, Society, and Politics in Early Maryland*, Baltimore, Md.: Johns Hopkins University Press, 1977, pp. 111–133.

"Staying Put or Getting Out: Findings for Charles County, Maryland, 1650–1720," *William and Mary Quarterly*, 44 (January 1987): 89–103.

"Urban Amenities and Rural Sufficiency: Living Standards and Consumer Behavior in Colonial Chesapeake, 1643–1777," *Journal of Economic History*, 43 (March 1983): 109–117.

Ward, Ned, *A Trip to Jamaica, with a True Character of the People and Island*, London, 1700.

Wareing, John, "Migration to London and Transatlantic Emigration of Indentured Servants, 1683–1775," *Journal of Historical Geography*, 7 (October 1981): 356–378.

"'Violently Taken Away or Cheatingly Duckoyed': The Illicit Recruitment in London of Indentured Servants for the American Colonies, 1645–1718," *London Journal*, 26, (July 2001): 1–22.

Washburn, Wilcomb E., *The Governor and the Rebel: A History of Bacon's Rebellion in Virginia*, Chapel Hill, NC: University of North Carolina Press, 1957.

Wawryzczek Irmina, "The Women of Accomack versus Henry Smith: Gender, Legal Recourse, and the Social Order in Seventeenth-Century Virginia," *Virginia Magazine of History and Biography*, 105 (winter 1997): 5–26.

Weinbrot, Howard D., *Britannia's Issue: The Rise of British Literature from Dryden to Ossian*, Cambridge: Cambridge University Press, 1993.

Wertenbaker, Thomas J., *The Planters of Colonial Virginia*, New York: Russell & Russell, 1958.

Whitaker, Alexander, *Good Newes from Virginia*, London, 1613.

White, John, *The Planter's Plea*, 1630. Reprint, New York: DaCapo, 1968.

Whitehead, Neil L., *Lords of the Tiger Spirit: A History of the Caribs in Colonial Venezuela and Guyana, 1498–1820*, Dordrecht: Foris, 1988.

Whitelaw, Ralph T., *Virginia's Eastern Shore: A History of Northampton and Accomack Counties*, 2 vols., 1951. Reprint, Gloucester, Mass.: Peter Smith, 1968.

Wilcocks, Joseph, *Sermon Preached before the Incorporated Society for the Propagation of the Gospel in Foreign Parts ... the 18th of February 1725*, London, 1726.

Willis, Richard, *A Sermon Preach'd before the Society for the Propagation of the Gospel ... February the 20th 1701/2*, London, 1702.

Wilson, Daniel W., "Science, Natural Law, and Unwitting Incest in Eighteenth-Century Literature," in O. M. Brack, Jr. (ed.), *Studies in Eighteenth-Century Culture*, vol. XIII, Madison, Wisc.: University of Wisconsin Press, 1984, pp. 249–270.

Wilson, Samuel, *An Account of the Province of Carolina,* in Alexander S. Salley (ed.), *Narratives of Early Carolina, 1650–1705*, New York: Charles Scribner's Sons, 1911, pp. 161–176.

Winslow, Edward, *The Glorious Progress of the Gospel amongst the Indians in New England*, London, 1649.

Winthrop, John, *Life and Letters of John Winthrop*, edited by Robert C. Winthrop, Boston, Mass., 1864.

Wood, Peter H., *Black Majority: Negroes in Colonial South Carolina from 1670 through the Stono Rebellion*, New York: Knopf, 1974.

Woolverton, John Frederick, *Colonial Anglicanism in North America*, Detroit, Mich.: Wayne State University Press, 1984.

Wright, Louis B., *Religion and Empire: The Alliance between Piety and Commerce in English Expansion, 1558–1625*, Chapel Hill, NC: University of North Carolina Press, 1943.

Wyckoff, V. J., "Land Prices in Seventeenth-Century Maryland," *American Economic Review*, 28 (March 1938): 82–88.

Zimmerman, Everett, *Defoe and the Novel*, Berkeley, Calif.: University of California Press, 1975.

Index

Addison, Joseph, 109
Alsop, George, 13, 14, 15, 132, 146, 150
Annesley, James, 133, 151–152
Armstrong, Katherine A., 195
Ashbridge, Elizabeth, 132, 148, 150–151, 153–154
Aubin, Penelope, 152, 163–165, 167, 169, 170
Augustine, Saint, 123

Bacon's Rebellion, 17–18
Ballagh, James Curtis, 199
Banister, Thomas, 52
Baxter, Richard, 77
Beattie, J. M., 159
Beckles, Hilary, 139
Behn, Aphra, 88
Bell, Ian, 127
Berkeley, George, 54, 56, 80
Berkeley, Sir William, 17, 18
Berlin, Ira, 77
Bertelson, David, 194
Best, Thomas, 139
Beverley, Robert, 17, 85, 150
Birdsall, Virginia, 195
Black Legend, 44–45, 58–59
Blair, James, 19, 78
Blewett, David, 102, 192, 194, 195, 196
Bolingbroke, Henry St. John, first Viscount, 123
Boucher, Philip P., 191
Boulukos, George, 195
Bradnox, Thomas, 134
Bray, Thomas, 56, 79, 182
Broderick, Margaret, 137
Bullock, William, 132, 144, 149
Burnet, Gilbert, 56
Burton, Robert, 42
Butler, Joseph, 78
Byrd, William, II, 85, 137

Calvert, Cecilius, second Baron Baltimore, 143, 145

Camaiora, Luisa, 197
Canny, Nicholas, 48
captivity narratives, 76, 170–171, 173
Carr, Lois Green, 20, 23, 132
Chalkley, Thomas, 135
Chetwood, William, 152, 165–167, 170
Child, Sir Joshua, 144
Clark, Katherine, 203
Clayton, John, 136, 137
Clemens, Paul G. E., 182
Cogley, Richard W., 48, 189
Coldham, Peter, 194
Colonel Jack
    chronology of, 183
    credit in, 111–114
    economic success of Jack, 23–24, 27, 185
    gratitude in, 94–95, 97, 102
    "honesty" in, 90, 102, 110
    indentured servitude in, 8–9, 14, 15, 16, 24–25, 30–31, 82–83, 84–85, 86, 90, 127, 131, 155, 157
    Jacobite rebels in, 7, 156, 159
    roles in, 104–108, 110–111, 113–115
    self-transformation of Jack, 30, 82–84, 89, 90–92, 96–97, 101, 104, 110, 114, 124, 156
    setting of, 62, 184
    slaves in, 30, 81, 91, 92, 94–95, 160
    "stupidity" in, 91, 120
    transportation in, 94–96, 158
Cooke, Ebenezer, 144
Cradock, Matthew, 53
Crane, Verner W., 52
Culpeper, Thomas, second Baron Culpeper of Thoresway, 17, 18
Curtis, Laura, 195
Cushman, Robert, 37

Defoe, Daniel
    Anglo-Indian policy and, 56–60
    Black Legend and, 58–59

226